Going for Wisconsin Gold

Karyn Bye at the 1998 Winter Games, Nagano, Japan. COURTESY OF KARYN BYE DIETZ

Debbie McCormick, three-time Olympian.
MICHAEL BURNS JR./USA CURLING

Matt Antoine and Bonnie Blair after the medal ceremony in Sochi, Russia, 2014.
COURTESY OF THE ANTOINE FAMILY

GOING FOR WISCONSIN GOLD

Stories of Our State Olympians

JESSIE GARCIA

WISCONSIN HISTORICAL SOCIETY PRESS

Published by the Wisconsin Historical Society Press
Publishers since 1855

The Wisconsin Historical Society helps people connect to the past by collecting, preserving, and sharing stories. Founded in 1846, the Society is one of the nation's finest historical institutions.

wisconsin**history**.org

Order books by phone toll free: (888) 999-1669
Order books online: shop.wisconsinhistory.org
Join the Wisconsin Historical Society: wisconsinhistory.org/membership

Printed in the United States of America
Cover design by Doug Griffin
Typesetting by Integrated Composition Systems, Spokane, Washington

20 19 18 17 16   1 2 3 4 5

Library of Congress Cataloging-in-Publication Data applied for.

♾ The paper used in this publication meets the minimum requirements of the American National Standard for Information Sciences—Permanence of Paper for Printed Library Materials, ANSI Z39.48–1992.

CONTENTS

Prologue   *vii*
Introduction   *ix*

1 Alvin Kraenzlein   *1*
Track and Field, 1900

2 George Coleman Poage   *11*
Track and Field, 1904

3 Oscar Osthoff   *18*
Weight Lifting, 1904

4 John Brennan   *24*
Track and Field, 1908

5 Carleton Brosius   *27*
Tug-of-War and Fencing, 1920

6 Ralph Metcalfe   *35*
Track and Field, 1932, 1936

7 Lloyd LaBeach and Don Gehrmann   *49*
Track and Field, 1948

8 Buddy Melges   *59*
Sailing, 1964, 1972

9 Connie Carpenter Phinney   *71*
Speedskating, 1972, and Cycling, 1984

10 Eric Heiden   *82*
Speedskating, 1976, 1980

11 Mark Johnson and Bob Suter   *93*
Hockey, 1980

12 Dan Jansen   *108*
Speedskating, 1984, 1988, 1992, 1994

13 Bonnie Blair   127
Speedskating, 1984, 1988, 1992, 1994

14 Mike Peplinski   141
Curling, 1998

15 Ben Sheets   150
Baseball, 2000

16 Karyn Bye   156
Hockey, 1998, 2002

17 Casey FitzRandolph   171
Speedskating, 1998, 2002, 2006

18 Chris Witty   188
Speedskating, 1994, 1998, 2002, 2006,
and Cycling, 2000

19 Paul Hamm   197
Gymnastics, 2000, 2004

20 Garrett Weber-Gale   209
Swimming, 2008

21 Ben Provisor   231
Wrestling, 2012

22 Matt Antoine   235
Skeleton, 2014

Team USA Medal Winners
with Wisconsin Connections   251

Notes on Sources   259
Acknowledgments   271
Index   273

PROLOGUE

U-S-A, U-S-A is a familiar refrain heard in every Olympics, but truly it could be *Wis-con-sin*. Since hurdler Alvin Kraenzlein got his start here in the 1890s, the Badger State has nurtured, trained, or schooled more than 400 athletes in a vast array of sports, and that number continues to rise. In 2014 alone, more than 35 of the 230 United States Olympic athletes had connections to Wisconsin.

The state has a varied landscape that can accommodate serious sports enthusiasts whether they compete on ice, on snow, in the water, or on terra firma. The climate offers a constantly changing array of options as well—from scorching heat to numbing cold—which forces our athletes to be hardy but also flexible in their training. After all, you never know when a Wisconsin snowstorm might change your plans. A typically laid-back Wisconsinite can shake off most weather worries with a shrug and a smile. We tend to bring a Midwestern work ethic to our endeavors, and this can be seen in so many of our top athletes. Wisconsin's Olympians have often been hailed in the press and in public as being among the most humble and down-to-earth people around. We're just plain *nice*, but we know when to work hard and how to achieve our goals. We can bring the sizzle when the world's spotlight is on us, but we do it with class.

Wisconsin has always been a sports state and boasts a thriving youth sports culture where many of our homegrown athletes got their start. Others were drawn by our world-class universities, athletic

Eric Heiden's Olympics pass and skates from the 1980 Winter Games in Lake Placid, New York. WISCONSIN STATE JOURNAL ARCHIVE

facilities, and coaching talent. No matter how an athlete comes to Wisconsin, the state becomes part of his or her Olympic story.

This book introduces you to a sampling of these athletes from a variety of sports, eras, and geographical parts of the state. There were hundreds to choose from, far more than would fit into one volume, and all of them with fascinating stories. Each athlete featured here represents dozens of others. We chose carefully, and with great respect for telling the history of the Olympics along with compelling tales of competition. Even as this book was going to press, we were watching Wisconsin's current slate of Olympic hopefuls with anticipation. As Madison native and Olympic hockey gold medalist Mark Johnson once told the *Milwaukee Journal Sentinel*, "The Olympics is the biggest platform sports provides us. For two weeks the world shuts down and watches, and to have Wisconsin athletes perform on that platform and be so successful, it's pretty neat."

The Wisconsin Historical Society Press wishes to thank the athletes, families, and historians who gave their time, memories, and photographs for this project. On Wisconsin! And Go Team USA! We'll be watching and cheering you on.

INTRODUCTION

Picture this: Olympia, Greece, 776 BCE. Thousands of spectators, all of them men, gather in a stadium with four grassy side slopes to watch a footrace of less than 200 yards. A young cook named Coroebus takes off sprinting with the group, crosses the end point first, and hears the bellowing cheers around him. He is crowned with a wreath made from the branches and leaves of an olive tree.

This was the first recorded moment of the Olympics, and Coroebus's race was its only event. He and his competitors likely wore loincloths, but nudity would later be standard. It wasn't long before the public demanded variety, and more sporting competitions were added, including a four-horse chariot race, longer runs (some with athletes wearing heavy coats of arms), discus, boxing, and wrestling. For many years women were not allowed even to watch—doing so risked execution—but the rules relaxed as the centuries passed. The Games, held during a religious festival honoring the Greek god Zeus, evolved into a carnival atmosphere, with magicians and other entertainers milling about the grounds, and booths and tents as far as the eye could see. The Olympics continued on an every-four-year cycle for over a thousand years.

After the Romans took control of Greece, the sporting event disintegrated quickly, and the Olympics disappeared altogether when Emperor Theodosius of Rome, who opposed what he considered a pagan spectacle, abolished the Games in 394 CE. Thirty years later, the walls of the enclosure were leveled. An earthquake in the next century destroyed whatever might have been left, and the Olympics would not be held again for 1,500 years—until a young Frenchman had the idea of revival.

Baron Pierre de Coubertin had been urged by his parents to enter politics or the military, but he chose education and soon came to the conclusion that sports instilled character in his young male students. He had organized a sports group aimed at getting physical education programs into schools, and he published a monthly sports newspaper. He also worked for the French Ministry of Public Instruction and traveled the world in that capacity. On one such trip he viewed the ruins of ancient

Pierre de Coubertin. BAIN NEWS SERVICE/WIKIMEDIA COMMONS

Olympia, which German archaeologists had unearthed. He became fascinated by stories of the Olympics. He was equally intrigued by the world's
fairs, which brought together people of all cultures and backgrounds.

In 1892 de Coubertin announced a plan to bring back the Olympic
Games as an international sporting event. The Greeks had tried twice
in the 1800s to hold an Olympic-style competition but had failed badly,
with small and mismanaged events. But at just thirty-one years of age,
de Coubertin stepped in with an organized, ambitious proposal. He convened a conference at the Sorbonne University in Paris comprising delegates from many nations. On June 23, 1894, the group voted unanimously
to revive the Olympic Games.

The enthusiastic Frenchman steered the group to establish rules, many of which are still in place today. The group decided to hold the Olympics every four years and at different sites. An International Olympic Committee would oversee the Games. The group also voted to change the original Olympic sporting events to more modern pursuits: gone was racing in a suit of armor; added were gymnastics, cycling, and swimming. De Coubertin, who considered himself a cultured gentleman, pushed to include the arts in the Games, though in this he would not be successful until years later.

Part of de Coubertin's plan was to hold the first modern Olympics in his home country, France, in 1900, to coincide with the already-planned Exposition Universelle, or Paris World's Fair. Doing so, he reasoned, would include both sports and cultural competitions in a single event and would guarantee large crowds. But conference attendees thought six years was too long to wait. The group agreed that Greece would host in 1896, bringing the Games back to where they had started. A Greek philanthropist put up $386,000 to build a stadium in the capital city of Athens.

Between 80,000 and 120,000 people watched the opening ceremony on a cloudy day on April 6, 1896. The Games ran for eleven days and

An artist's depiction of the start of the 100-meter sprint at the 1896 Olympic Games. WIKIMEDIA COMMONS

featured fourteen nations. The small contingent of thirteen American athletes arrived after sixteen days at sea expecting to have a twelve-day rest before competition commenced; instead, they were shocked out of bed the morning after their arrival by a blaring horn announcing the start of the Games. The Americans had overlooked the fact that the Greeks used the Julian calendar, which was eleven days ahead of the Gregorian calendar used in the United States.

Still, an American triple jumper named James Connolly overcame this rude start to win the first Olympic title in the modern age. Winners at the 1896 Games received a medal made of silver, a certificate, and a crown of twisted olive branches, a nod to the victors of thousands of years earlier.

The Athens Games were heralded as a huge success, and Greek authorities wanted the Olympics to remain in their country. Athletes even circulated a petition to that end, but founder de Coubertin insisted they stick with the plan to hold the next Olympic Games in the city that he loved, the city of love: Paris.

—ıı—

As the 1900 Olympics approached, Pierre de Coubertin was scrambling to turn his vision of sports spectacular and World's Fair–style event all in one into reality. But his control of the operation was slipping away. The French government, already overseeing the 1900 Exposition Universelle, had taken over planning the sports events as well. But French officials did not view sports as nearly as important as the cultural and technological exhibits planned for the fair, and authorities even removed the word *Olympics* from the official programs, instead calling the athletic competitions the International Championships.

French organizers decided to spread the athletic endeavors over five months, from May through September. Between the long time span and the lack of promotion of the Games, many athletes said later that they did not even know they were competing in an Olympic Games. Rules were lax, and disorganization reigned. For example, when a Dutch rowing team needed a sudden replacement coxswain, they chose at random a French boy later estimated to be between seven and twelve years old. The boy

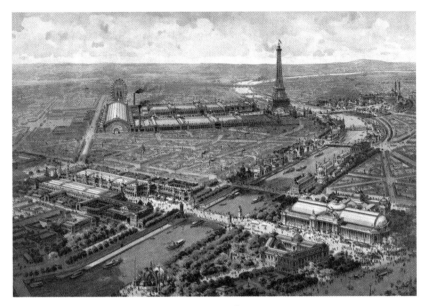

Panoramic view of the 1900 Exposition Universelle in Paris. WIKIMEDIA COMMONS

somehow managed to help his boat to a close win, and he had his picture taken with the victors. But he surely didn't know at the time that he was taking part in the second Olympics, and he disappeared into obscurity.

De Coubertin, meanwhile, had been pushed to serve on a smaller committee and watched helplessly as the Games continued to unravel in the weeks leading up to the track and field events. Unlike the resourceful Greeks, who had found a philanthropist to fund the new stadium in Athens, the French had neglected to arrange proper competition facilities. For track and field events they chose the Racing Club of France, located within the Bois de Boulogne, a large forested park in Paris. Despite its name, the Racing Club was just a grassy picnic area with no hard track surface to run on. De Coubertin scrambled to do what he could, managing to secure a 500-meter oval track that had to be unevenly laid out on top of the lush grass the French refused to pull up. The route wound its way through trees at both the beginning and end. There were other obstacles to contend with as well: long jumpers had to make do with inadequate pits (some were even forced to dig their own landing spots), discus throwers tossed discuses into tree branches that were too close to the action, and hurdlers leaped over barricades the French had constructed partially from bent and broken telephone poles. The competitors—including a Wisconsin athlete named Alvin Kraenzlein—would have to deal with all of it soon enough.

INTERNATIONAL OLYMPIC DAY

National Olympic committees around the world recognize June 23 as International Olympic Day in honor of Pierre de Coubertin's 1894 Paris meeting of international delegates. Milwaukee's Pettit National Ice Center commemorates each June 23 with a special event. For example, in 2014 the Pettit hosted children from a local YMCA camp who rotated among three stations—trying curling, learning about short-track speed-skating, and listening to stories from Olympians. They also got to see a skinsuit worn by speedskating legend Bonnie Blair.

CHAPTER 1

ALVIN KRAENZLEIN

Track and Field, 1900

Alvin Christian Kraenzlein was born in Minneapolis on December 6, 1876, the youngest of four children of German immigrants John Georg Kraenzlein and Maria Augusta Schmidt. Not long after Alvin entered the fold, the family moved to Milwaukee, and John became the proprietor of a malt house in a city known for beer. When Alvin was six, his father bought half of the Red Rock Brewing Company in Fargo, North Dakota, and moved to Fargo with the intention of working there for a few years. But he never returned, abandoning his wife and four children. Young Alvin was forced to look to his brother, Hugo, fourteen years his senior, for guidance.

Despite this early loss, Alvin grew up as most boys do, playing all kinds of games and sports both indoors and out. As he reached his teenage years, Alvin began competitive running and jumping at Milwaukee's East Side High School. He stood out as an athlete and was given permission to practice in the basement of the school.

After graduating from high school, Kraenzlein traveled ninety miles west to the University of Wisconsin–Madison. He enrolled in 1895, studying engineering and joining the track team. He dominated his events, earning a national Amateur Athletic Union (AAU) title in the 220-yard hurdles in 1897. His achievements did not go unnoticed. Mike Murphy, a track coach and trainer at the University of Pennsylvania, began to woo Kraenzlein to transfer to Penn.

Murphy was a small man and was at least partially deaf. His pupils revered him; he was known for his charm and charisma, intelligence,

Alvin Kraenzlein, seen here, and his coach, Mike Murphy, changed track and field with innovations like this crouching technique. FROM THE UNIVERSITY ARCHIVES AND RECORDS CENTER, UNIVERSITY OF PENNSYLVANIA

interest in the world, and uncanny ability to spot talent. In addition to coaching, Murphy was making foundational changes to the sport of track and field. He pioneered the idea of crouching at the starting line before taking off to get more power from the legs, a technique every sprinter uses today. He also developed a method of using liniment or rubbing oil to treat sore muscles, wrote two books on physical fitness, and had revolutionary ideas about looking at an athlete as a whole human being with the need for proper rest and superb nutrition.

Murphy once described Kraenzlein as "the world's best all-around athlete of his time," so it was no wonder he wanted him on his team. He convinced Alvin to say good-bye to his home state and join the Penn team, where Alvin continued to excel, setting the world record for the 120- and 220-yard hurdles and taking the AAU crown in the long jump in 1899. He captured the Intercollegiate Association of Amateur Athletes of America (IC4A) championships in both hurdling events for three straight years and scored a record 18 points at the 1899 meet, where he added a victory in the 100-yard dash and helped lead Penn to the team first-place trophy. In three years, Kraenzlein set nine intercollegiate records.

At Penn Kraenzlein changed his major to dentistry and began tinkering with his hurdling style. The common way of clearing a hurdle at this time was to run up to it, slow down, jump in a modified hopping position with both legs tucked under the buttocks, and then run on to the next hurdle and repeat the cumbersome process. Kraenzlein was the first to master a lead-leg technique. He figured out, perhaps with Coach Murphy's guidance, that extending one leg straight over the hurdle while keeping the other tucked back allowed a runner to glide more naturally over the bar and not waste precious time slowing down. Kraenzlein's polished hurdling method would be adopted worldwide.

Now the twenty-three-year-old Kraenzlein and a group of twelve others from Penn were making plans to attend the 1900 Olympic Games in Paris. Theirs would be one of the largest contingents in track and field. Although it was only the second Olympics in modern history, Coach Murphy—always ahead of his time—must have seen it as an excellent opportunity for his collegiate charges.

Yale, Princeton, Chicago, Georgetown, Michigan, and Syracuse also sent athletes. Enthusiasm for these Games was higher in the United States than it had been for the 1896 Athens affair, but there was still no national unity—no Team USA and no uniforms; athletes simply competed for whatever college or athletic union they belonged to. Thirty-five Americans would take part in track and field, with Murphy a trainer for the entire group. En route to Paris, many of the storied US athletes, most of them national or collegiate champions, took a detour through Britain and cleaned up at the 1900 UK Track and Field Championships. Confidence must have been high as they headed to Paris.

Milwaukee's Kraenzlein perfected the lead-leg style of hurdling. FROM THE UNIVERSITY
ARCHIVES AND RECORDS CENTER, UNIVERSITY OF PENNSYLVANIA

An Olympic Village had not yet been conceived, and upon their arrival
in Paris the athletes were grouped by school for their accommodations.
The Penn contingent was shipped to Versailles, thirty minutes from Paris
today but a much longer journey then.

The American crew's outfits and banter shocked the French. At a time
when the typical Frenchman strolled the streets in a straw hat and light
overcoat, the Americans' frat-boy style was appalling to the home crowd.
The French grumbled that the Americans would throw on a sweater or
even a bathrobe after racing—all except for Kraenzlein, who was later
described as "dressed to the nines, wearing a saucy cloth cap, an Eton collar
and a smart cravat" in the Sports Illustrated book *The Olympics*. It was
equally strange for the US contingent to see how the Europeans dressed.
One reporter from the *San Francisco Chronicle* wrote: "The natty college
costumes of the Americans were a decided contrast to the homemade
attire of some of the best European athletes." Cultural divides were evi-
dent, and cultural practices were lost in translation. When the Americans

used college cheers to root for each other, a European spectator said, "What a band of savages!"

The French and Americans had been in a bit of a feud about scheduling even before the games commenced. France had announced that the sporting events would start on Sunday, July 15. The US group saw this as out of the question for religious reasons—Sunday was the Lord's Day, and the blue laws in effect in some states forbade sporting activities. When the US contingent suggested starting on Saturday, July 14, their hosts politely but firmly pointed out that they had a little something else planned for Saturday: it was Bastille Day, a national holiday akin to the US Fourth of July, and there would be parades and military demonstrations to impress the crowds. The Americans refused to budge, and the French eventually gave in, agreeing to begin sports competitions on Saturday. The US athletes arrived in Europe under the impression that competition would kick off on Saturday and then recess until Monday, with a quiet day of rest and prayer on Sunday.

Kraenzlein would compete in four events: the 110-meter high hurdles, 200-meter hurdles, long jump, and 60-meter dash. His first event was the 110-meter hurdles, scheduled for Saturday. Barely a thousand people watched the entirety of the Saturday competitions, and many of those were said to be affiliated with the United States—either expat Americans or tourists. Almost all Parisians went off to hear the French president review the status of the troops.

A 110-meter distance was unusual for hurdlers competing from the United States or Britain, who normally ran a slightly shorter 120-yard hurdle race. But despite the unusual distance and the ragged, hastily constructed track and hurdles, Alvin Kraenzlein cruised through the qualifying heats. Considering his earlier titles and experience, many felt he had no peer.

In the finals later on Saturday, a Frenchman who was inexperienced with the starting gun (and perhaps one of the only Parisians not enjoying Bastille Day) may have let competitor John McLean of Michigan get away with a false start. Observers said McLean appeared to be a full five yards ahead of Kraenzlein as soon as they took off from the blocks. The 110-meter race is only about a third of the way around a modern track, and Kraenzlein would have less than 15 seconds of running time to make up for the early differential. He still trailed McLean with three hurdles left. But then talent and pure desire took over, and Kraenzlein put on a burst of speed to catch McLean at the eighth of ten hurdles, winning by about three feet. His time was 15.4 seconds, a world record for the 110 meters. McLean took second and fellow American Fred Moloney third.

Instead of medals, the French were handing out objets d'art, including paintings that ranged in value from fifty to two hundred francs. Medals for the gold, silver, and bronze finishers would not be given out until the next Olympics in 1904 in St. Louis. Those objets d'art would be the only prizes McLean and Moloney would collect on the trip, but Kraenzlein was just getting started.

That same day he had qualifying heats for the long jump. The top five jumpers would advance to the final. The heavy favorite to win was Meyer Prinstein of Syracuse University, who had set a world record in an earlier meet with a leap of 24 feet, 7.25 inches (7.51 meters). Prinstein and Kraenzlein had met in track and field events three times in 1900, and their duels were legendary across the athletic world. Between the two of them, they had set six of the last seven world records in three years. Kraenzlein had taken the 1899 world record jump at 7.43 meters only to see Prinstein wrest it back one year later when Kraenzlein was recuperating from malaria. New York sports journalist Malcom Ford described the difference in their styles: "[Prinstein] does not approach the takeoff with as much speed as Alvin Kraenzlein, but he gets higher up in the air and also in better shape. He has an unusually pretty style and impresses one that he always knows what he is doing."

Ireland's Peter O'Connor was also considered one of the best in the world, and the long jump was one of the most highly anticipated competitions in Paris. When O'Connor failed to show up, all eyes turned to Kraenzlein and Prinstein. In the qualifier Prinstein jumped 7.174 meters, setting an Olympic record. Kraenzlein was second at 6.930 meters. Nobody else was over 6.8 meters, and Prinstein held a good lead over Kraenzlein heading into the finals.

Then the French informed everyone that the finals of the long jump and several other events would be held on Sunday. The Americans were incensed. Amos Alonzo Stagg, manager of the University of Chicago team (who would go on to football fame and eventually have the NCAA Division III title game named after him), wrote a letter to the *New York Herald* complaining, "Everybody here feels that it is a most contemptible trick. Not a single American would have sent a team had it not been definitely announced that the games would not be held on a Sunday."

The Americans were in a pinch. Would they compete even though they felt it was sacrilegious? Or would they boycott the Olympics on Sunday? Prinstein's university, Syracuse, was affiliated with the Methodist Church and forbade competing on the Christian Sabbath. Prinstein himself was Jewish, which must have put him in a quandary, as his religious beliefs did not conflict with the Sunday events. The US athletes huddled up. Some were in favor of competing, others violently opposed, and still others uncertain. Nevertheless, at least part of the group reportedly entered into a gentlemen's agreement and said they would show solidarity and refuse to set foot on the track on Sunday. Prinstein went to bed Saturday night believing that Kraenzlein was in on the agreement and would not compete. Whether Kraenzlein had indeed sworn to this pact is unknown. Mike Murphy and the Penn gang did not have the same ardent beliefs as Syracuse. Murphy may have influenced his troops to compete or simply allowed them to make up their own minds, but whatever the reason, Kraenzlein decided to jump.

The day of the final dawned, and Kraenzlein had six unopposed cracks at besting Prinstein's mark of 7.175 meters. Five times he failed. But one of his leaps took him just a centimeter farther than Prinstein: 7.185 meters. It was good enough for first place.

Prinstein was livid. He appealed to the French organizers, who sympathized but would not go so far as to hand him the top spot. The officials conferred and decided that Prinstein should be awarded the second-place trophy based on his marks from qualifying. Pat Leahy of Great Britain was a distant third at 6.950 meters. But Prinstein was still boiling. As Kraenzlein went on to the 60 meters, where he dashed to a third gold in just seven seconds, Prinstein stewed.

By Monday Prinstein had come up with a plan. The day opened blazing hot and would reach 95 degrees Fahrenheit, but Prinstein had but one focus. He sought out Kraenzlein and challenged him to a jump-off to prove the real champion. When Kraenzlein refused, Prinstein charged at him and threw a punch. Other US team members had to physically restrain Prinstein before a fight broke out. After the confrontation, both men collected themselves and ignored the stifling heat well enough to compete again. Prinstein went on to take part in the triple jump, an event that had not been on the original program. Athletes had asked for it, and although the French *Journal des Sports* called it "perfectly boring," officials added it. Prinstein took out all of his frustration on the triple jump track, setting a new Olympic record and winning his first gold, defeating reigning champion James Connolly (the man who had won the first modern Olympic crown four years earlier).

With three golds—in the 110-meter hurdles, the long jump, and the 60-meter dash—there was only one thing left for Kraenzlein: the 200-meter hurdles. The top two hurdlers from each qualifying heat would advance. Both the qualification and final were run on that sweltering Monday.

It was no contest for Kraenzlein. He set a new Olympic record in heat one, blowing away the second-place qualifier, Eugène Choisel of France, by four yards. Norman Pritchard of India and Walter Tewksbury of the United States, who happened to be Kraenzlein's roommate at Penn, qualified in heat two. The four of them would run for first, second, and third. Based on qualifying times, Pritchard seemed to be the only legitimate threat to Kraenzlein.

Still dealing with overwhelming heat plus the shoddy track that was slowing down everyone's times, the four runners took off. Using the lead-leg technique he had by now perfected, Kraenzlein cruised to victory in 25.4 seconds—fast enough for an easy triumph, but still almost two seconds slower than a time he had posted a year earlier on a properly maintained track. Second-place finisher Pritchard crossed five yards behind him, a lifetime in a short track race. Tewksbury crossed in third, and Choisel of France brought up the rear.

The boy who had grown up without his father, trained in the basement of East Side High School, and worked with one of the greatest track coaches of all time was a quadruple champion. Alvin Kraenzlein was the first person to take four individual Olympic golds. He remains the only person to do so in track and field. Thirty-six years later, Jesse Owens would win four times in 1936 in Berlin, but one of those events was a team relay (see chapter 6). Kraenzlein is considered one of the heroes of the 1900 Games.

Yet immediately after his historic win, Kraenzlein announced, "This was my last race. I am through with athletics and shall devote myself to something more serious." After all, he was Dr. Kraenzlein now, having completed his dental degree at Penn a few months earlier. The Paris Olympics continued for several months in ragged fashion, but Kraenzlein's work was done. He returned to the United States and retired from competition.

After the International Championships and the Exposition Universelle wrapped up, Pierre de Coubertin admitted the organizers' shortcomings, saying, "We made a hash of our work." He vowed the Olympics would only get better.

Two years later Kraenzlein married artist Claudine Gilman, whom he had met at the Penn Relays, a track and field event. A year later they had a daughter, Claudine Gilman Kraenzlein. The threesome loved the beach and spent many summer days in Belmar, New Jersey, at The Cedars, a large summer hotel owned by Alvin's in-laws. In 1909 Alvin and Claudine welcomed son Alvin Charles; sadly, he died in 1911.

Ten years after the Paris Games, Mike Murphy, the visionary track coach who helped spur Penn athletes to great success, was in failing health. Some say he caught tuberculosis watching a football game in Ann Arbor, Michigan, on a frigid November evening in 1911. By 1913 he was too weak to attend the collegiate track and field championships. When Penn captured the team title, athletes gathered at his bedside to tell him of the victory. He slipped into unconsciousness and died three days later at home. Alvin Kraenzlein was an honorary pallbearer at his funeral.

Somewhere along the way, Kraenzlein rejected a life of dentistry. Despite his pronouncement that he was devoting himself to more serious pursuits than athletics, he was drawn back to the track and became a coach, work he dove into with a passion. He led teams at the Pennsylvania prep school Mercersburg Academy and the University of Michigan to success. In 1913 he was invited by Kaiser Wilhelm of Germany to coach the German track and field team, which was preparing for the 1916 Olympics, slated to take place on their home turf in Berlin. Kraenzlein signed a five-year contract for a reported $50,000, a handsome sum, and moved his family overseas.

But the time spent in Germany did not last as long as both sides had hoped. War was imminent, and the kaiser warned Alvin to get his family out of the country while he could. The Kraenzleins left Germany not a moment too soon. Alvin returned to coaching at Michigan and went on fishing trips to Canada as often as he could. In 1924, the lure of the Olympics drew Alvin once again, and he accepted a position as Cuba's track coach. Now age forty-eight, he was coaching in Cuba when he began to have heart trouble and was forced to return to the United States for treatment. His rival Meyer Prinstein was having similar health issues. Prinstein passed away of a heart condition in 1925 at the age of forty-six. He was inducted posthumously into the International Jewish Sports Hall of Fame in Commack, New York.

Alvin Kraenzlein developed pneumonia in 1927, then became deathly ill with endocarditis, an inflammation of the inner lining of the heart. He was only fifty-one. He died on January 6, 1928, in Wilkes-Barre, Pennsylvania. At his funeral he was remembered as the best athlete ever to compete for the University of Pennsylvania. His obituary made national news and was featured prominently on the front page of the New York Sun. "Doctor Kraenzlein was one of the greatest track and field athletes ever produced in the United States—or the world," the newspaper crowed. Close to a century later, some still consider him to be in that class of athletic prowess.

More than a hundred years have passed since Alvin Kraenzlein walked the streets of Paris in his "saucy cap" and wowed the sporting world. His grandchildren have donated many of his papers and pictures to the University of Pennsylvania, and Alvin was inducted into the National Track and Field Hall of Fame in 1974 and the US Olympic Hall of Fame in 1984. He remains a powerful Olympic figure, prominently featured in most Olympics history books as the first and only winner of four individual gold medals in track and field.

"Our mother was very proud of her father and loved him very much," recalled granddaughter Susanna Tvede, who was born in Denmark. "It is a shame he died before we were born. He was not on our minds when we were little. . . . We became more aware of our American grandfather as we grew older. My son has his gold watch. We are all proud of him."

CHAPTER 2

GEORGE COLEMAN POAGE

Track and Field, 1904

In 1904 the modern Olympics would come for the first time to the United States. But although Chicago had won the bid to host the Games, St. Louis wanted to move them to coincide with its 1904 World's Fair (more formally called the Louisiana Purchase Exposition). President Teddy Roosevelt, who was honorary president of the US Olympic Committee, sided with St. Louis. Despite the lessons learned in Paris when the 1900 Games were combined with another massive cultural event, the still-young International Olympic Committee agreed to the site switch.

For these "Games of the III Olympiad," sports were once again relegated to sideshow status. After all, it wasn't easy to compete with 1,500 new buildings and modern-marvel rides such as the Magic Whirlpool and Over and Under the Sea at the fair that inspired the song "Meet Me in St. Louis." More than 650 athletes participated, but tensions from the Russo-Japanese War and the difficult journey across the ocean and into the heart of America made it impossible for these Games to truly be an international competition. Eighty-five percent of the athletes represented the United States, resulting in a ridiculous number of medals for Team USA.

World's Fair organizers decided to hold a sporting event every day for the duration of the fair. This led to the Games' unofficial duration of four and a half months, a repeat of Paris. In reality, Olympic events were mixed with other non-Olympic sporting events, including a local YMCA swim competition.

To be sure, the 1904 Games included noteworthy moments. The practice of awarding gold, silver, and bronze medals began, and boxing, dumbbells, freestyle wrestling, and decathlon made their debuts. American gymnast George Eyser won six medals, even though his left leg was made of wood. The marathon, run in brutally hot weather on dusty roads, offered plenty of drama, from an initial winner who in fact faked victory after riding eleven miles in a car, to the actual victor, who needed medical treatment after staggering across the finish line supported by trainers. The exhausted gold medalist had taken rat poison mixed with brandy to stimulate his nervous system. Still other competitors had stopped for apples that turned out to be rotten or were chased nearly a mile off course by aggressive dogs during the miserable race, which included seven hills and only one water break, twelve miles in.

But the most important historical facts of the 1904 Olympics are the remarkable accomplishments of black athletes, who secured medals for the first time. And the very first was a Wisconsin man named George Poage.

George Coleman Poage was born in Hannibal, Missouri, in 1880 to parents James and Anna Poage. When George was four the family moved to La Crosse, Wisconsin, where James Poage found employment as a coachman/horseman for the wealthy Pettibone family. But tragedy soon struck. George's father, older sister, and younger brother died within a year of one another due to illnesses including tuberculosis and diphtheria. Anna took her two surviving children to the affluent household of Lucian and Mary Easton, where Anna managed the household staff and George's sister, Nellie, helped care for Mary and Lucian's six children. The Eastons were both scholarly and generous. In a move unusual for the times, they opened their home, art collection, and library to their housekeeper and her children and encouraged in them a love of learning. George and Nellie are thought to be the second and third black students to enter La Crosse High School (now known as La Crosse Central).

There were only seven boys in George Poage's class, and he could take part in any sport he liked, but track was his love. Poage set a number of sprinting and hurdling records and won a huge number of local meets. He was also known for his fine tenor voice and glee club performances.

George Poage as a child, likely taken shortly after his family moved to La Crosse. MURPHY LIBRARY, UNIVERSITY OF WISCONSIN– LA CROSSE

After graduating second in a class of twenty-five in 1899, his next stop was the University of Wisconsin–Madison, where he majored in history. The Eastons are reported to have offered the Poages financial assistance to ensure his continued education.

Poage became the first black athlete to run for the UW, making the varsity team in 1901 as a sophomore. The *Milwaukee Sentinel* described him after one event as "the most popular athlete of the meet" and said he was "greeted with the most rousing reception of the evening." He also

Poage and the La Crosse High School track team, circa 1899. MURPHY LIBRARY, UNIVERSITY OF WISCONSIN–LA CROSSE

seemed to be shattering race stereotypes. According to the student-run *Daily Cardinal* newspaper, midway through the 1902 season Poage was put in charge of the track team for a time when his coach was called out of town—a highly unusual role for a black man at the time.

Poage was the Big Ten Conference's first African American track champion, winning titles in the 440-yard dash and 220-yard hurdles. He joined the Milwaukee Athletic Club in 1903 as its first nonwhite competitor. He also spoke and read five languages, including ancient Greek and Latin. He went on to postgraduate work while he still had a year of track eligibility, and he became a football trainer for the Badgers to help pay for his classes.

As the 1904 Olympics drew near, African American leaders asked black athletes to boycott the Games in protest of segregated spectator seating and athlete facilities. Despite this, Poage entered four events as a member of the Milwaukee Athletic Club's contingent.

We can only guess what George Poage thought of the spectacle of the World's Fair when he arrived in St. Louis in late August 1904. Most of the track and field events were held at the new Francis Field on the Washington University campus, next to the fairgrounds. Undoubtedly the noise and chaos of the fair spilled over.

In his first event, the 60 meters, George failed to qualify for the finals, beaten by five-foot-five, 130-pound Milwaukee Athletic Club athlete Archibald Hahn, known as the Milwaukee Meteor. Hahn would take the gold in the 60 meters later that day and won two other events, including running an Olympic record time of 21.6 seconds in the 200 meters that stood for twenty-eight years. He had taken up track at age nineteen; a fellow competitor said about him, "He's little, but he certainly can run."

Later that day, Poage was running even with three other Americans on the straightaway of his second event, the 400 meters, when he stumbled. He finished sixth. Poage's Olympics experience was off to a bad start.

On August 31, 1904, the weather was a virtual copy of that of the previous days, clear with a high of 82 degrees and not a drop of rain in the forecast. There were four competitors and no semifinals or qualifications in Poage's next event, the 400-meter hurdles—considered one of the most demanding events in all of track and field. Big Ten Conference hurdling champion Poage took off from the start and whipped around the track. (By this time everyone was using the lead-leg technique developed by Wisconsin hurdler Alvin Kraenzlein.) Harry Hillman of the New York Athletic Club, a twenty-two-year-old bank teller, led from the start and looked to be cruising to a sure victory when he hit the eighth hurdle hard. He briefly lost his balance, and UW athlete Frank Waller caught him at the ninth hurdle. Hillman, who often advised fellow athletes to swallow raw eggs for strength, somehow managed to right himself and won by two yards in world record time. The record part was immediately wiped out for two reasons: Hillman had knocked into the hurdle—a violation at the time—and the hurdles had mistakenly been set at two feet, six inches high instead of the standard three feet. Still, Hillman won the gold, Waller

FRANK WALLER

Wisconsin athlete Frank Waller, the silver medalist who nearly beat New York Yorker Harry Hillman in the 400-meter hurdles, took home two medals in 1904. The Menomonee Falls High School graduate also raced to silver in the 400-meter dash.

After the Olympics, Waller went on to an interesting career in music. He toured with famous singer and actress Lillian Russell as her pianist, studied in Europe, became a voice coach, and served as director of the Milwaukee Philharmonic Orchestra, the National Broadcasting Company in New York, and the WPA Orchestra in Richmond, Virginia.

took silver, and George Poage raced his way to a bronze medal, the first Olympic medal won by a black athlete.

Later that day, African American athlete Joseph Stadler from Cleveland took a silver in the standing high jump, meaning Poage had become the first black medalist by just hours.

George Poage wasn't finished yet. On September 1 he would run the 200-meter hurdles. Hillman was entered again, as was the Eastern Collegiate Athletic Conference champion, E. J. Clapp, but Clapp failed to show up. A commentary on the race reported it this way: "For two hundred yards the race was as pretty as one would want to witness, Hillman and the colored man Poage running together like a team; but when Hillman got ready to distance his opponent he did so, winning the race by two yards in record time."

Hillman was again the victor. Frank Castleman of the Greater New York Irish Athletic Association somehow muscled his way to second, and Poage finished third, winning his second bronze medal and cementing his place in history.

For a man who was brilliant in the classroom and supremely talented on the athletic field, George Poage surprisingly stepped out of the spotlight after his Olympics triumph. He stayed in the St. Louis area, where he spent many years teaching English literature, composition, and Latin at Charles Sumner High School, the first institution for blacks west of the Mississippi River. According to the late Dr. Julia Davis, a former Sumner student who wrote about him in 1959, Poage also oversaw activities that ranged from debates to theater productions and had a knack for connecting with youth. He even organized Sumner's first indoor circus.

In 1913, nine years after Poage shattered the Olympics glass ceiling, a La Crosse newspaper was still celebrating Poage's achievements, calling him "perhaps the greatest athlete that was ever developed in this city." A year later, Poage left teaching for unknown health reasons. He left Missouri never to return and moved to a farm in Minnesota. Some historians have speculated that the land belonged to the Eastons, the family that had nurtured him in his formative years.

Six years later, Poage relocated once again, to Chicago this time, where his mother joined him. He went to work for the US Postal Service, retiring in 1953 at the age of seventy-three. At age eighty-two George Poage was admitted to Cook County Hospital with pneumonia; he died twenty days later. George was buried next to his mother in Chicago's Lincoln Cemetery; as of 2014 his grave remained unmarked. He left no direct descendants.

It was not until 1998, ninety-four years after his historic dual bronze medal wins, that George Poage was inducted into the Wisconsin Athletic Hall of Fame. In 2003 he was added to the University of Wisconsin Athletic Hall of Fame, and in 2013 a park in La Crosse was named in his honor. When children and families play near a statue of Poage in George C. Poage Park, they will learn about the first black medalist in history and know he was once a part of their community. But perhaps it is the caption under Poage's University of Wisconsin yearbook photo, quoting the Greek philosopher Homer, that best embodies this man who made history but who preferred to live a quiet post-Olympics life and lies in a cemetery without a headstone: "Of matchless swiftness, but of silent pace."

CHAPTER 3

OSCAR OSTHOFF

Weight Lifting, 1904

Along with George Poage, seven other athletes with known Wisconsin connections participated in the 1904 Games in St. Louis. Among them was a weight lifter who could just as easily have competed in a number of other events. Oscar Osthoff was that good. He lettered in a whopping four sports at the University of Wisconsin–Madison—track, football, swimming, and gymnastics—and was team captain in all but football, earning ten letters and racking up Big Ten titles in everything from shot put to flying rings. He was three years younger than George Poage, but they competed together as part of the Milwaukee Athletic Club's team.

Osthoff's father, Otto, had been born in Germany in 1840 and came to America in 1867. After running a hotel in Rochester, New York, Otto relocated to Milwaukee and eventually became the manager of Schlitz Park, a beer garden that also featured a concert pavilion, dance hall, bowling alley, and live performers doing all types of circus acts. The *Milwaukee Sentinel* reported that Osthoff owned a pet crow he had trained to call out "open the gates," much to the delight of incoming guests. At night, the park glowed with 250 gaslights as patrons strolled and chatted.

By 1883 Otto had patented his own beer glass, a stout mug with a wide handle, and business was booming. That same year baby Oscar joined the family. But Otto's wife, Paulina, had a nervous breakdown shortly thereafter, and a physician recommended that she convalesce in the tranquil environment of Elkhart Lake, just over an hour north of Milwaukee. It was

Osthoff was a football star at Marquette University before transferring to the University of Wisconsin–Madison. COURTESY OF JOHN AND PATRICK NUGENT

then that Otto hatched a plan to open a summer resort on the banks of the lake. Work began on the resort in 1885.

After his Hotel Muensterland opened, Otto continued to run Schlitz Park in Milwaukee, allowing a manager to handle the day-to-day business in Elkhart Lake. People began referring to the Hotel Muensterland simply as the Osthoff, and the name stuck. Oscar likely spent much of his childhood at the resort, where he had access to a rolling backyard that sloped down to pristine waters for swimming and boating. Guests would frolic on the wide lawn while Oscar and his three siblings chased each other and played. As he grew, Oscar became a bellboy, traveling to the nearby train station to help visitors with their bags and then dragging the trunks and suitcases up and down the stairs to guest rooms. Perhaps that was the root of Osthoff's strength, a physical power that propelled him to Olympic weight lifting.

Oscar was twenty-one when he went to the 1904 Games as part of the Milwaukee Athletic Club team. He would compete in two events. First up was the two-handed lift, where Oscar did not stand much chance for the top spot against mighty Greek competitor Periklis Kakousis, who was also entered in the tug-of-war. In the final standings, Kakousis lifted 111.70 kilograms (246 pounds) for gold, Osthoff 84.37 kilograms (186 pounds) for silver, and Germany's Frank Kungler 79.61 kilograms (175 pounds) for bronze.

Next up for Oscar was the all-around dumbbell competition, a weight-lifting decathlon in which ten different dumbbell movements were presented, with points awarded in each section. First place would net 5 points, second place 3 points, and third 1 point. Nine of the areas were predetermined. The tenth was for optional feats of skill that could earn an athlete up to 25 points based on the judges' opinions of his athletic prowess. Oscar may have felt he had a better shot at gold this time around, as Kakousis was not entered. His biggest competitor was fellow American Fred Winters of the New York Athletic Club.

In section one, lifters had to hold dumbbells over their heads and bring one arm at a time to shoulder height straight out in front of them. Winters took the early edge by hoisting 79½ pounds in his right hand and 57½ in his left to Osthoff's 49¾ for both. Frank Kungler, the German who took bronze in the two-handed lift, was third after the first event.

Section two required curling a dumbbell in one hand. Winters again prevailed, with 110¼ pounds to Osthoff's 73⅞. Section three was for curling in two hands simultaneously. Winter used 78 pounds in his right hand and 57½ in his left. Osthoff countered but could do no more than 74 in the right and 53 in the left. The standings did not change: Winters first, Osthoff second, Kungler third. In section four, Osthoff finally got a win. Competitors tossed a dumbbell up from the ground to the shoulder with one hand, and Osthoff bested Winters 151 pounds to 140½, with Kungler staying in third. But Winters rebounded to take sections five and six, which required more tossing and pushing over the shoulder. In section seven, jerking one dumbbell over the head, Osthoff regained the edge when he pushed 150 pounds to 130 for Winters and Kungler, who tied. The two rivals, Osthoff and Winters, split sections eight and nine, both of which were variations of pushing weights over the shoulder either slowly or hastily. It was now Winters with 38 total points and Osthoff with 33. Only the tenth section remained, and Osthoff would have to wow the judges to leapfrog past Winters. Just the top two competitors advanced to this stage; the bronze went automatically to Germany's Kungler.

As the judges and spectators watched, each athlete readied himself for his showcase moment. Winters put 105¼ pounds on his back and performed six one-armed push-ups. The judges seemed only mildly impressed, giving him 7 points out of the possible 25. Osthoff knew he had to go even further. He opted for a much heavier weight, 177 pounds, loading it all onto his back before lifting himself to create a bridgelike posture six times. The judges conferred and agreed. Osthoff's was the more spectacular showing: 15 points. With 48 total points, the gold was his. Winters settled for silver with 45. Oscar Osthoff had done his family and his state proud, earning two medals. He had made an impressive showing at his first Olympics. It would also be his last.

Returning to Milwaukee, Oscar enrolled at Marquette University. He drifted away from competitive weight lifting in favor of football and played fullback for the blue and gold, where he was so impressive that after one game he came out of the locker room to find coaches from the rival University of Wisconsin–Madison waiting to lure him. Oscar transferred before his sophomore year, and family legend has it that some of his old Marquette teammates were so incensed at what they saw as traitorous behavior, they tried to break his nose the next time the two schools met on the gridiron.

Osthoff thrived in the capital city. He continued playing football and competed in gymnastics in 1907, 1908, and 1909, winning the Big Ten Conference title in flying rings in 1908. He also swam for his first two years in Madison, specializing in diving and short distances, and ran track for two of three, winning the Big Ten shot put title and placing in both broad jump and discus in 1908 as a twenty-five-year-old. He reached the peak of his football career in 1909 when he was named first team All-Western Conference and second team All-American. So instrumental in University of Wisconsin sports was Osthoff that he doubled as secretary of the UW Athletic Association and in that role validated his own document stating that he had won a varsity letter in football in 1907.

After college, Osthoff started a family with his wife, Clara, but when the two divorced he moved west to coach football at Washington State University. Eventually returning to Wisconsin, he became a structural engineer in his hometown of Milwaukee. Osthoff played a role in constructing the Milwaukee County Courthouse and Lincoln Memorial Bridge, worked for the Civilian Conservation Corps and National Parks Service helping to plan and lay out parks during the Depression years, and became an avid conservationist. His three daughters remember their dad teaching them to swim and walking on his hands around the house, much

Osthoff taught his daughters to swim and remained a superb athlete into middle age. COURTESY OF JOHN AND PATRICK NUGENT

to their delight. Oscar remained a superb athlete, and his daughters recall him doing complicated dives from the pier at Oconomowoc Lake more than halfway into his fifth decade.

In his later years Osthoff remarried and moved to Indiana, where he worked as an engineer with the Department of Welfare. In December 1950 Osthoff checked into a hotel in Indianapolis with his second wife, Kay. The story handed down is that sixty-seven-year-old Oscar asked some young lads to carry his and Kay's bags up the stairs. When they turned him down, he hoisted them himself. He had a heart attack, either while hauling the luggage or shortly thereafter. It was a sad twist of fate for a man who spent so many years doing just that sort of work.

Osthoff is recalled as one of the state's best athletes of all time. Tom Larkin, longtime athletic director at the Milwaukee Athletic Club, gave him the highest praise. "The greatest all-around athlete I've ever seen, bar none," he called him in an article on Osthoff's death in 1950. "Name it and he could do it better than anyone else. He had never weighed over 180 but he was strong as a bull, fast as a cat and a terrific competitor. In a letter only a month ago he told me he could still swim 100 yards in about a minute and I believe it. He was that kind of man." The University of Wisconsin recognized Osthoff's tremendous accomplishments in 2004, when he was posthumously inducted into the University of Wisconsin Athletic Hall of Fame.

Although the Osthoff Resort was eventually sold, it retained its founder's name. One of Osthoff's daughters wore his Olympic silver medal on a pendant around her neck for many years. Great-grandson Patrick Nugent now has the document listing football player Osthoff as a varsity letter winner, signed by secretary Osthoff, hanging in his suburban Milwaukee home. Thinking of their father, daughters Barbara and Mary recall that he was proud of his accomplishments, yet he was anything but a show-off.

Oscar didn't get to enjoy the moment when he was inducted into the Hall of Fame, but family members were there to see him memorialized. His grandson John Nugent put it best when he said, "I'm sure proud when I go to Camp Randall and see that plaque."

CHAPTER 4

JOHN BRENNAN

Track and Field, 1908

The International Olympics Committee selected Rome to host the 1908 Games, but the city backed out when it could not get itself ready on time. After the eruption of Mount Vesuvius in Naples in 1906, Italy redirected funds from the Olympics to rebuilding the damaged region, and the IOC quickly changed the venue to London. With only two years to prepare, British officials nevertheless built a stadium and put on a worthy Olympics that included swimming events taking place in a pool instead of open water for the first time. The marathon distance of 26.2 miles (42 km, 195 m) was also established at the 1908 Games, the last .2 miles added so the race could start at Windsor Castle and end precisely below the royal box in the stadium, ensuring the royal family a spectacular view of the finish line. Other firsts at these Games included relay races of 200, 400, and 800 meters; a parade of nations walking into the stadium for the opening ceremony; and an athlete's creed that de Coubertin modified from the words of the Episcopal bishop of Pennsylvania: "The important thing in life is not the triumph, but the fight; the essential thing is not to have won, but to have fought well."

Crossing the Atlantic in a reverse route of a trip he had made a few years earlier was Marquette University student John Brennan, a native of Ireland and a fine track and field athlete. Brennan had won the hop, skip, and jump (later called the triple jump) and finished second in the broad jump (long jump) at the Olympic Trials in Chicago earlier that year. He

The 1908 Games lasted well over six months, making them the longest-running modern Olympics. IMAGE BY ARTHUR STOCKDALE COPE/WIKIMEDIA COMMONS

was the first collegiate athlete from Marquette to make the Olympics, and as an Irishman he hoped to make a statement to the British Empire through his athletic prowess.

Brennan faced his first event, the broad jump, on July 22, 1908. He placed fifth with a distance of 22 feet, 6¼ inches. Three days later was the hop, skip, and jump, in which Brennan was the top American qualifier and a strong favorite to bring home a medal. But he may have ruined his own chances the night before the competition.

It started when fellow Irish American competitor Johnny Hayes won an unexpected gold medal in the marathon. Hayes was trailing South African Charles Hefferon and Italian Dorando Pietri with two miles to go, but Hefferon suddenly tired and faded back. Pietri took the lead and staggered into the stadium for a final burst to the finish line, met by a huge cheer from the massive crowd of 100,000. But Pietri, a five-foot-two-inch pastry chef by trade, was so spent from the previous twenty-six miles that he began running in the wrong direction, away from the royal box. Officials steered him toward the finish line, but Pietri collapsed. Helped to his feet, he staggered a short distance and collapsed again. This happened twice more with officials assisting, including a doctor who told people later he had to massage Pietri to keep his heart beating.

Amid this chaos, Hayes entered the stadium, the Stars and Stripes on his chest. By this time officials were helping Pietri across the finish line. Despite his ragged condition and the clear fact that he had been helped three times in the stadium, Pietri was awarded the gold medal. But the United States cried foul, protesting that no runner could receive outside aid. Olympics officials concurred, handing Hayes the top medal and disqualifying Pietri. The US team was beside itself with joy. An all-night party ensued. And John Brennan was in the middle of it, whooping it up with Hayes and the others.

The hop, skip, and jump was slated for 10 o'clock the next morning. History does not tell us exactly how much sleep Brennan got that night or what kind of shape he was in. It may have been related to the events of that evening or to something else, but John Brennan, a front-runner for the gold, did not medal at all. He never returned to the Olympic stage.

Dorando Pietri became famous for the grit he displayed in those final yards. Queen Alexandra presented him with a gold cup, and Irving Berlin even wrote a song about him, titled "Dorando." Headlines about the race sparked interest in long-distance running and boosted

Unfortunately, John Brennan did not medal at the 1908 Games. DEPARTMENT OF SPECIAL COLLECTIONS AND UNIVERSITY ARCHIVES, MARQUETTE UNIVERSITY LIBRARIES

the spotlight on the Olympics as a whole. It's just too bad John Brennan's event may have been a casualty of the entire affair.

CHAPTER 5

CARLETON BROSIUS

Tug-of-War and Fencing, 1920

The International Olympics Committee awarded the 1916 Games to Berlin with the hope that an Olympics in Germany would help avert World War I. When that failed to happen, the 1916 Games were canceled.

Three years later, the 1920 Games were hastily offered to Antwerp, in recognition of the suffering of Belgium's people during the war. The country had only one year to prepare. Hoping to avoid conflict, the IOC did not invite Germany and allied power nations Austria, Bulgaria, Hungary, and Turkey. Nevertheless, most Belgians were still recovering from the devastation of war and did not have much interest in an international sporting event. Attendance at the new 30,000-seat stadium reached above 10,000 only when children from nearby schools were admitted free of charge toward the end of the Games.

Wisconsin native Carleton Brosius was part of a large 1920 US contingent that also included rower John B. Kelly (who would go on to father movie star Grace Kelly) and swimmer Ethelda Bleibtrey (who was mired in controversy after being charged in New York with swimming nude, when in fact all she had done was remove her stockings.) The entire American squad, 273 men and 14 women, was set to make the ocean crossing together, but those plans began to unravel almost immediately. The United States Olympic Committee (USOC) had not raised the funds for proper transport across the Atlantic and therefore appealed to Congress to use a military ship. The assigned ship, the *Great Northern*, was top of the line

There wasn't much space to practice tug-of-war on the *Princess Matoika*. THE WISCONSIN VETERANS MUSEUM

and fastest in the fleet, but it broke down just before the trip, and the team was reassigned to the *Princess Matoika*.

The twenty-year-old *Matoika* was a disaster for the athletes from the moment they laid eyes on her. The rusted old vessel had just returned from war carrying 1,800 bodies, and hundreds of caskets lined the docks as the US Olympic team was boarding. The ship stank of formaldehyde, and rats scurried about. The sleeping arrangements for men were nothing but hammocks deep in the ship's poorly ventilated underbelly; the tiny contingent of women bunked in upper cabins. A cramped dining hall and food kept at questionable temperatures brought on many complaints. The journey took two weeks, often on rough seas, and there was little space where the athletes could stretch or practice. The only bright spot came from the Hawaiian swimming contingent, who spent most of their time strumming ukuleles on deck, seemingly oblivious to the mess around them.

Even once the athletes were safely on dry land in Belgium, the accommodations were less than ideal. The men were given tiny cots in an overcrowded, aging schoolhouse. The women did not fare much better, sleeping on cornhusk mattresses at a local YWCA. The athletes came close to mutiny, nearly two hundred of them signing a petition threatening to leave the Olympics altogether after Dan Ahearn, a hop, skip, and jumper, was suspended for requesting better living quarters, missing the 10 P.M. curfew at the schoolhouse, and then moving into a hotel. It's not known if Wisconsin's Brosius put his name on the petition, but the high number who did got the USOC's attention. Ahearn was reinstated, and the Games went on.

The 1920 Games saw several firsts, including the first unfurling of the official Olympic flag. The five circles represented the major land masses: Europe, Asia, Africa, Australia, and the Americas. The colors—blue, yellow, black, green, and red—were chosen because at least one of those colors is present on every national flag around the globe. And the Olympic oath was read aloud for the first time, including this line: "We swear that we will take part in the Olympic Games in a spirit of chivalry, for the honor of our country and for the glory of sport."

These Games would also see the first—and last—appearance by Carleton Lyman Brosius, born July 18, 1876, in Milwaukee. Carl was the youngest of four children who grew up tumbling under the tutelage of their father, George, a gymnast and gymnastics instructor at the Milwaukee Turnverein Gymnasium. In fact, George Brosius was the first salaried instructor at the school, which later became the Milwaukee Turners and still operates today.

Carl soaked up the physical activity and thrived not only in gymnastic pursuits but also in sprinting, shot put, and long jumping, yet his true talent and love lay in fencing. Following in the footsteps of his father and grandfather, who had both served in the military, Carl joined the US Navy

Sept 2/20
olympic
stadium

Carleton Brosius at Olympic Stadium in Antwerp, Belgium, in 1920. THE WISCONSIN VETERANS MUSEUM

at age thirteen and later enlisted in the Wisconsin National Guard. His unit was sent to the US–Mexico border in 1916. During much of World War I Carl served as a stateside physical training instructor in Camp Benning, Georgia, and was sent to dozens of bases around the country, promoting a brand of rigorous workouts that included gymnastics, strength, boxing, wrestling, baseball, and basketball. His work was praised by soldiers as well as their superiors, who commented on the marked improvements they saw in the energy and alertness of their men.

As the war ended, the United States looked to military personnel as the primary talent pool for the next Olympic team. Brosius, now forty-four, was ordered to attend a fencing meet in Pennsylvania that would serve as a quasi–Olympics qualifier. He did not make the team outright but was named an alternate. The USOC also liked what Brosius could bring in another sport, the tug-of-war. They made him captain of the team and sent him to the tug-of-war trials in St. Louis in early July to scout for the rest of the squad. From a group of almost three hundred army personnel vying for a spot on the US team, Brosius narrowed his sights on thirteen pullers, including two African American soldiers, Sergeant Joseph Winston and Sergeant William Penn—a progressive move, considering that the army itself was still segregated. The team trained in New York before joining the rest of the US contingent on board the *Matoika*.

As the 1920 fencing competition got under way, Brosius was ready to fill in, but no one was sick, injured, or otherwise indisposed, and he could only watch as his teammates took home a bronze medal in team foil. Fencing was dominated by one man that year: Italian Nedo Nadi, who took home five of six gold medals, including three in team events. His is still

ARLIE SCHARDT

Also competing in the 1920 Games was Arlie Schardt, another Milwaukee native and military man. Schardt graduated from UW–Madison in 1917 and then served as an army lieutenant in France. In 1919 he placed second in the mile at the American Expeditionary Forces championships and was invited to be on the US Olympic team in Antwerp. There he ran the 3,000 meters, which had a format of five competitors per nation racing, with only the first three crossing the line counting for points. On August 22, 1920, the US 3,000-meter team earned a surprisingly easy victory over Great Britain (which took silver) and Sweden (bronze). Three US runners finished in the top six overall, including Schardt, who came in third. Teammates Horace Brown and Ivan Dresser rounded out a strong American trio that gave the US the gold medal. Schardt returned home to coach at South Division High School in Milwaukee.

THE WINTER OLYMPICS AND EDDIE MURPHY

The first Winter Olympics were held in 1924 in Chamonix, France, as a sideshow or "snowy prelude" (as the founder of the modern Olympics, Pierre de Coubertin, called it) to the Summer Olympics in Paris. Before 1924 a few winter activities, such as figure skating, had been tried in conjunction with the Summer Games but had largely failed for obvious weather-related reasons. Plus, many cities did not have proper facilities, and the IOC worried about any country outside of Scandinavia providing capable athletes.

The 1924 Winter Games were at first simply billed as "International Winter Sports Week"; the Winter Games would not be renamed and fully recognized until two years later, when ice and snow sports were deemed worthy of being on the Olympics schedule.

Chamonix saw 294 athletes from sixteen countries compete in only five sports: hockey, figure skating, speedskating, cross-country skiing, and ski jumping. At the conclusion, even de Coubertin had to call the eleven days in 1924 in Chamonix a great success.

It was at the second Winter Games, held in St. Moritz, Switzerland, in 1928, that La Crosse native Edward "Eddie" Murphy became one of Wisconsin's first Olympic speedskaters. At twenty-three, he traveled overseas for the only time in his life and had a respectable but not outstanding showing, finishing fifth in the 1,500 meters, tenth in the 500 meters, and fourteenth in the 5,000 meters. Four years later, at the age of twenty-seven, Murphy competed at the first Winter Games held in the United States, in Lake Placid, New York. His performance improved dramatically, and he crossed the line in the 5,000 meters in second place, but Canada filed a protest, saying Murphy had pushed Canadian skater Harry Smyth during the race. American referee Joseph K. Savage refused to uphold the protest, and the silver medal went to Murphy.

A Norwegian promotional card depicting the US speedskating team in Oslo in 1928; from left: Valentin Bialis, Eddie Murphy, Irving Jaffee, and O'Neil Farrell.
MUNICIPAL ARCHIVES OF TRONDHEIM, NORWAY/WIKIMEDIA COMMONS

The Winter Games stayed on the same yearly cycle as the Summer Games until 1994, when it was decided to separate the two entities to alternate the spotlight every two years. This move would later greatly benefit Bonnie Blair and Dan Jansen (see chapters 12 and 13).

considered one of the greatest Olympic achievements of all time, although Nadi was aided by the absence of fencing power Hungary.

In the tug-of-war, captain Brosius and his thirteen athletes were seeking to end a sixteen-year medal drought for the United States. But success was not meant to be. The US team lost badly in the first round to eventual gold medalist Great Britain. It took the British just 13.4 and 18.8 seconds to yank the Yanks over the line and win 2–0. The US tried to regroup versus the home team, Belgium, but lost again 2–0 and then dropped another match to Italy to finish out of medal contention. Later, the official written report of the 1920 Games erroneously stated that the United States and the Netherlands were scheduled to pull for silver and the US won by forfeit when the Dutch didn't show up; in fact, the Dutch did take silver, but the mistake caused so much confusion that the Belgian Olympic Committee had to clarify with a letter one month later stating: "We cannot be responsible for a typographical error in the program."

Overall, the United States overcame the horrible journey and the subpar living conditions to win the most medals of any country. After the 1920 Games many athletes chose to stay and tour in Europe, including Brosius, who spent more than a month visiting American Occupation Forces and promoting physical fitness.

Back in the United States, Brosius taught briefly in Indiana before returning to Wisconsin for good. He accepted a position at St. John's Military Academy in Delafield, where he shared his passion for physical fitness with the next generation, and he remained affiliated with St. John's for nearly thirty-five years. Brosius opened the Brosius Gymnasium on North Second Street in Milwaukee, and he was an early media pioneer, collaborating with the *Milwaukee Journal* and WTMJ Radio to broadcast a unique show six mornings a week promoting women's physical well-being. He also taught fencing and organized tournaments.

Brosius served in the Officers' Reserve Corps in the 1920s and the Wisconsin National Guard through 1938, leaving with the rank of colonel. He became an adjutant at the Wisconsin Veterans Home at King, a position he held through the beginning of World War II. Brosius and his wife, Frances, decided to stay at King as residents following the war, and he spent part of the last decade of his life organizing a museum at the veterans home; named the Carl L. Brosius Memorial Museum, it is run by the Wisconsin Veterans Museum.

Carl Brosius died September 28, 1956, at the age of eighty. He is buried at Forest Home Cemetery in Milwaukee. Although he didn't obtain an elusive Olympic medal, he left his mark in many other ways.

CHAPTER 6

RALPH METCALFE

Track and Field, 1932, 1936

The 1932 Olympics, held in Los Angeles, marked the first use of an Olympic Village. Thirteen hundred male athletes from thirty-nine nations enjoyed the hastily constructed bungalows, dining rooms, and social hall erected among palm trees in the California sunshine. Women were not allowed; the 121 female athletes stayed in hotels. The village was such a hit that one of the organizers said later, "We damn near had to drive the athletes out to get them to go home after the Games. It was the most grand and pathetic thing you ever saw, those big hulks practically cried. They loved it."

Soaking up the sun in Los Angeles was a bright young African American Marquette University student named Ralph Harold Metcalfe. In 1932 Metcalfe was a college sophomore and America's leading sprinter.

Born in 1910 in Atlanta to seamstress Marie Attaway and stockyard worker Clarence Metcalfe, Ralph moved with his family to the South Side of Chicago and attended Chicago public schools. His high school track coach gave him some advice that stuck with him throughout his track career. "I was told . . . that as a black person I'd have to put daylight between me and my nearest competitor," Metcalfe once said. "I forced myself to train harder so I could put that daylight behind me."

Metcalfe identified Marquette University as a place where he could grow both academically and athletically. Although he lost the first race he ever ran at Marquette—the 40-yard dash—after that he never finished anywhere but first in a Marquette uniform. During his years there he would tie the world records in the 100- and 220-meter dash and win three NCAA championships while competing for Marquette. His teammates bestowed him with the nickname "Rabbit" for his swift feet.

In the summer of 1932, at the age of twenty-two, he took his talents to the Olympic Trials held at Northwestern University in Evanston, Illinois. Metcalfe won in both the 100 and 200 meters, beating rival Eddie Tolan of the University of Michigan, who was a year older and was considered America's best before Metcalfe came along. Both qualified for the Games and were sent to LA as part of the US contingent. Metcalfe was now considered the favorite for gold in both events.

On August 1, 1932, Metcalfe's first competition in the Los Angeles Coliseum was the 100 meters. He was first to cross the line in heat one of the semifinals, putting up a time of 10.6 seconds, with countryman George Simpson of Ohio State coming in at 10.7 and Arthur Jonath of Germany third at 10.71. Metcalfe's rival Tolan reigned in heat two, although film of the race clearly shows Danie Joubert of South Africa and Takayoshi Yoshioka of Japan crossing ahead of Tolan, who appears to finish third. These were the first Olympics to use a photo-finish synchronized with the starting gun, so how Tolan could be declared the winner remains a mystery. In the end, the placement of the three men in this semi did not matter much, as all three advanced to the final.

The crowd, mainly men, packed in near the finish line in their suits and formal hats to watch the fastest men on earth in the final. The race would take only about 10 seconds. It would consist of the three Americans, Metcalfe, Tolan, and Simpson, plus Joubert of South Africa, Yoshioka of Japan (who had the distinction of being the first Asian to make an Olympic final), and Jonath of Germany.

As the gun went off, a wave of spectators rose to their feet and a great cheer went up. Yoshioka dashed out to the early lead. He faded quickly as Tolan caught him about 30 meters in. At 80 meters Metcalfe burst from the middle of the pack to reach Tolan, and the two ran the final 20 meters neck and neck with everybody else a few paces back. They crossed the tape at virtually the same time, although video looked at with the naked eye appears to show Metcalfe with the ever-so-slight edge. It was so close that

From left: George Simpson, Marquette's Ralph Metcalfe, and Eddie Tolan at the Olympic Trials at Northwestern University, 1932. DEPARTMENT OF SPECIAL COLLECTIONS AND UNIVERSITY ARCHIVES, MARQUETTE UNIVERSITY LIBRARIES

the electric timer clocked them both with a finish of 10.38 seconds. Officials were perplexed. It was the closest race in the history of the 100 meters. Judges undertook an exhaustive review. Metcalfe and Tolan waited while race officials studied the photograph of the finish.

One of the men who made the final call stood in front of a film camera and described the decision: "The rule states the official finish line is that white line painted across the track. The rule states that the winner is the runner whose entire torso crosses that line. The official finish line photo will show you that Tolan's entire torso crossed that line while Metcalfe's torso is still behind it. There is nothing else we can do but declare Tolan the winner."

Metcalfe disagreed. "I've never been convinced that I was defeated," he said years later. "I think that it should have been a tie race because the

HELENE MADISON

Modern Olympics founder Pierre de Coubertin was not a fan of female athletic competition. In 1912 he wrote, "I feel that the Olympics must be reserved for men," then went further to reject a proposal that a smaller women's Olympiad be held, calling the idea "impractical, uninteresting, ungainly and, I do not hesitate to add, improper." Furthermore, he said that men should be rewarded by the applause of women.

Although a few scattered women's events were held in earlier years, it wasn't until after de Coubertin's retirement, and against his advice, that one of the big ones—track and field for women—was added to the 1928 Olympics. Even then, there were only five races and plenty of detractors.

The IOC voted to eliminate women's track and field after those 1928 Games and might have succeeded had the United States not stepped in, threatening to boycott the 1932 Games in Los Angeles. The ban was lifted, and women's sports stayed in.

The first Wisconsin woman to compete in the Olympics was a Wisconsin native with the last name of her birth city: swimmer Helene Madison. Although she was born in the Badger State, her family moved to Seattle when she was a child. Dubbed "Queen Helene" by the press, Madison was dominating the water by the age of fifteen (ultimately breaking 117 US and world records). She arrived in LA for the 1932 Olympics at just nineteen years old. The Games themselves were considered wildly successful, with a sprawling new Olympic Village and celebrities such as Clark Gable in attendance. Madison did not disappoint, amassing three gold medals in the 100 freestyle, 400 freestyle, and 4x100 freestyle relay, the latter two in world record times.

While there she crossed paths with Babe Didrikson, widely considered one of the top female athletes of the century. Babe would go on to a stellar golfing career, but in 1932 she won three track and field medals at the age of eighteen—gold in the javelin, gold in the 80-meter hurdles, and silver in the high jump. The only reason the mega athlete missed out on that third gold was because her last high jump was ruled invalid when she dove headfirst over the bar. (In later years this kind of jump, called a

Helene Madison was the first female Olympian from Wisconsin. She was about seventeen in this 1930 photo; two years later she went to the Los Angeles Games, where she won three gold medals. DEPARTMENT OF SPECIAL COLLECTIONS AND UNIVERSITY ARCHIVES, MARQUETTE UNIVERSITY LIBRARIES

western roll, would be permitted.) Babe likely could have swept just about every event, but women were allowed only three track and field entries, as officials continued to fret about their stamina. Didrikson was good at every sport she tried and once was asked if there was anything she didn't play.

"Yeah," she said with a smile. "Dolls."

As talented as she was, she was also cocky. Upon meeting Helene Madison, Babe asked her how fast she could swim the 100-meter freestyle. Madison reported her time, and Babe laughed. "Shucks, lady," she retorted in her Texas drawl. "I can beat that by three seconds just practicin'."

Unfortunately, Madison never got to show her talent on a world stage again. After the 1932 Games, she gave a paid swimming performance at an amusement park and later starred in a film, *The Human Fish,* which was a box office flop. Even these minor gigs were too much for the IOC, who saw her as a professional swimmer at that point and turned her down for the 1936 Games. She wound up working at a hot dog stand in Seattle while her peers competed in Berlin. "Queen Helene" Madison died in 1970 in a basement apartment across from the lake in Washington State where she had first learned to swim. The city of Seattle named two pools after Helene Madison, and she goes down in history for the state of Wisconsin as well.

timers gave me the same time that they awarded to Eddie Tolan. When [Tolan] finished he arched his back."

Despite many spectators believing Metcalfe had won based on what they saw with their own eyes, and despite an exact tie according to the electric timer, that arch gave Tolan the gold medal and Metcalfe the silver. Germany's Jonath took the bronze. Still, Metcalfe, ever the sportsman, put his arm around Tolan on the podium—just two sprinters from the Midwest enjoying their Olympic spoils.

Rabbit Ralph Metcalfe may have thought he had seen his allotment of Olympic unfairness, but his days of controversy were far from over. In the semifinals of the 200 meters two days later, Metcalfe won his heat by $\frac{2}{100}$ of a second, 21.52 to Ohio State's Simpson's 21.54. Germany's Jonath took heat two in 21.51 with Willie Walters of South Africa second and American Tolan third, both of them coming in at 21.7. The final later that same day would be close, of that there was no doubt, but many saw it ultimately coming down again to Metcalfe and Tolan, America's top sprinters. Metcalfe was favored because he was stronger in the event.

In the 200, runners are staggered in their starting spots to account for the curve around the track before hitting the straightaway. After taking off on the starter's gun, Metcalfe appeared to be running a very strong curve. Suddenly, though, as they entered the final straight to the finish, Metcalfe was in third place behind Tolan and George Simpson. This was not what anyone had expected. Had he lost speed or stamina? The medalists finished in that order: Tolan winning gold, Simpson the silver, and Metcalfe the bronze. It wasn't until later that everyone realized what had happened.

Video of the race revealed a horrible mistake. Metcalfe's lane had been measured incorrectly on the stagger and was longer than it should have been. No wonder he fell behind on the curve. It was a testament to his athletic ability that he was able to place third.

Metcalfe and his coaches were offered the chance to protest and rerun the race. They declined. Rerunning the race might push one or more of the Americans out of medal contention, and the coaches decided to put country over individual accolades. Metcalfe left Los Angeles with silver and bronze medals that might have been golds, but he also left with the respect of others and his head held high.

Jesse Owens called Metcalfe, at center, a "locomotive" and said he was the greatest competitor he had ever faced. DEPARTMENT OF SPECIAL COLLECTIONS AND UNIVERSITY ARCHIVES, MARQUETTE UNIVERSITY LIBRARIES

Ralph returned to Milwaukee and continued to compete for Marquette, retaining his status as a world-class sprinter in distances ranging from 40 to 220 meters. A brilliant student, he was inducted into Marquette's elite academic honor society, Alpha Sigma Nu, and was elected president of his senior class. He graduated cum laude in 1936.

That summer the Olympics and politics crashed into each other once again. Berlin had been chosen to be the 1936 host city back in 1931, when it was still a fairly benign location. By 1933, Adolf Hitler was steamrolling his way to power, and many assumed the Games would be canceled. After all, the Nazis were calling the Olympics "an infamous festival dominated by Jews" in propaganda material, and Germany was still smarting from a poor national showing in Los Angeles, where the country won only four gold medals, including one in poetry.

But Hitler saw the value of all eyes turning to Germany, and he poured an unheard-of amount of money, about $30 million (over $508 million today), into building an enormous new stadium, six gymnasiums, a swimming facility, and state-of-the-art timing, photo, and press facilities that would best those in Los Angeles. German officials even had a zeppelin ready to transport newsreel footage out of Germany. These would be the first Games broadcast on television, and the Germans set up twenty-five viewing rooms around Berlin to allow locals to watch free of charge. The Fuhrer ordered construction of an Olympic Village, consisting of attractive cottages that he said would put LA's makeshift bungalows to shame. To reinforce his point about German superiority, Hitler ordered that one of LA's lesser village accommodations be put on display next to his cute brick and stucco cottages so everyone could compare. A cleanup was under way in Berlin as well; all anti-Semitic signs were removed and every house facing an Olympic venue was painted and given flowers for the window boxes. It was a Hitler-masterminded façade, designed to fool the international community and distract them from his anti-Semitic agenda. Little did anyone know the next two Olympics would be canceled due to the genocide of World War II. For now, the show went on. Carl Diem, head of the Berlin games, introduced the torch relay, with a lighted torch making its way from Olympia, Greece, to the opening ceremony—suggesting a link between ancient Greece and Aryan Germany.

Although the world did not yet know the full scope of Hitler's atrocities, he was known to be a tyrant—some thought a madman—and an anti-Semite. Many Americans felt sending an Olympic team to Berlin was tantamount to showing support for Hitler. The USOC president, 1912 decathlon athlete turned Chicago hotel owner Avery Brundage, argued differently. "I don't think we have any business to meddle in this question," he said. "We are a sports group, organized and pledged to promote clean competition and sportsmanship. When we let politics, racial questions, religious or social disputes creep into our actions, we're in for trouble." He continued, "The persecution of minority peoples is as old as history. The customs of other nations are not our business."

General Charles H. Sherrill, a member of both the IOC and USOC, added his ignorant two cents: "It does not concern me one bit the way the Jews in Germany are being treated, any more than lynchings in the South of our own country."

Several black newspapers including the Pittsburgh *Courier-Journal* supported African Americans going to the Olympics. Metcalfe himself told the *Chicago Defender* that he had been to Germany in 1933 on a tour with other blacks and had felt they were treated with respect.

And so the American contingent set sail from New York Harbor on the SS *Manhattan* at noon on July 15. Dressed in straw hats, white pants or skirts, and blue blazers, they waved to the thousands of spectators crowding Pier 60. Among the athletes on board were Metcalfe, age twenty-six, and another athlete destined for infamy, Jesse Owens, twenty-two. (Metcalfe's great rival Eddie Tolan did not compete in any Olympics after 1932.) Owens had burst onto the US track and field scene the year before when he shattered records at Ohio State. In just forty-five minutes at the Big Ten Conference Championships on May 25, 1935, he set three world records and matched another. Now Metcalfe and Owens were friends and Olympic teammates. Little did they know what lay ahead across that vast ocean.

Upon arrival the Americans were greeted with swastikas, German soldiers on patrol, and cries of "Sieg Heil!" (Hail Victory!) ringing out from the crowds.

A record forty-nine nations sent athletes, who endured this spectacle for the sake of sporting competition. Although Hitler was selling his Aryan race to the people of Germany, blacks had not yet been persecuted in the same way as Jews. In time they would be, but for now the air was thick with tension. The US team included ten blacks, and when they entered the 110,000-person stadium for the opening ceremony many spectators whistled—the equivalent to booing in Europe. Athletes representing Nazi-sympathizer countries used the Hitler salute when they passed his box. Hitler himself declared the Games open and then waited for the medals to roll in, confirming Germany as the dominant nation in every aspect. He certainly was not counting on a group of black athletes from American colleges trumping his superior race.

Owens would later credit Ralph Metcalfe with keeping the black athletes on the US team focused in the face of all these distractions and insults in the highly charged atmosphere. "He said we were not there to get involved in the political situation. We were there for one purpose—to represent our country," Owens recalled.

Metcalfe's first event on August 2, 1936, came almost exactly four years to the day after he competed in Los Angeles. He breezed through the opening round and the quarterfinals and then won his semifinal heat in 10.5. Only Jesse Owens posted a better time, in the other heat, with a 10.4. The lone German to advance to the final was six-foot-tall, thirty-one-year-old Erich Borchmeyer with a time of 10.7, ³/10ths of a second slower than Owens, who was nine years his junior. It would be a lifetime for Borchmeyer to make up in the final.

Metcalfe, meanwhile, may have wanted redemption after taking second in the 100 meters in 1932 when he felt he should have at least been awarded a tie. But against Jesse Owens's perfect and seemingly effortless stride, plus a burst of speed at the end, it appeared no one else had a chance. Owens once described his running style this way: "I stick with the field, breathing naturally until 30 yards from the finish. Then I take one big breath, hold it, tense all my abdominal muscles and set sail."

There were no starting blocks in those days. Athletes dug trenches with their toes, then crouched into a starting position and exploded upon the starter's gun. On the day of the final in Berlin, August 3, a light rain was falling with a six-mile-per-hour breeze. The starter, wearing a pale suit with a long white jacket and white shoes to match, held his arm aloft at exactly 4:58 P.M. The ready signal was given in German, and the pistol fired. Hitler leaned forward in his seat to get a better view. Owens was on the farthest inside lane and Metcalfe the farthest outside. From the first step, it looked like Owens had a jump on the rest of the field. One spectator noted, "He seemed to float along the track like water."

Metcalfe had gotten off to a bad start at the gun and was in last place out of the gate, but even in a race that lasted less than 11 seconds he had a knack for closing speed. The sprinters were going about 22 miles per hour. Metcalfe caught up to Owens near the end and almost overtook him, his massively powerful legs providing a different style altogether from Owens's pure grace.

"Ralph and I ran neck and neck," Owens later recalled. "And then, for some unknown reason I cannot yet fathom, I beat Ralph, who was such a magnificent runner."

Metcalfe was a step or two behind his compatriot when they sprinted across the finish line. Owens finished in 10.3 seconds, Metcalfe 10.4, and

Tinus Osendarp of the Netherlands 10.5. Borchmeyer, the thirty-one-year-old German, was a distant fifth in 10.7. The crowd erupted in genuine cheers. Owens gave a grin but nothing else. He would not gain a world record, but he set the world afire nonetheless.

Hitler sat stone-faced through much of the Olympic competition that followed. After the 100 meters, he was nowhere to be seen; some later said he was under the stands shaking hands with two hammer throwers from Germany who had finished first and second. It was no surprise that Hitler was not in sight when Owens went on to win three more golds. "It was all right," Owens told people later. "I didn't go over to Germany to shake hands with Hitler anyway."

Owens did have plenty of nice things to say about Metcalfe, even decades later. "Ralph was my prime competitor in the 30's," he remarked in a 1964 article in the *Decatur Daily News*. "[He] was far and away the greatest competitor I ever encountered. Ralph Metcalfe was a locomotive. If you were ahead of him, you had to worry every second about how fast he was catching up with you. And if you were behind him, you lost."

The long jump was Owens's second medal of the 1932 Games. He also took gold in the 200 meters, in which Metcalfe did not compete. A few days later, Owens and Metcalfe teamed up on the 4x100 relay team, but neither had been on the original roster.

The US coach, Lawson Robertson, had his four-man USA crew set as Foy Draper, Frank Wykoff, Marty Glickman, and Sam Stoller. At the last minute he decided to switch out Glickman (who went on to be a famous New York sportscaster) and Stoller for Owens and Metcalfe. Glickman and Stoller were both Jewish, the only Jews on the US track team. Many thought the coach had bowed to Nazi pressure to remove Jewish people from competition, but Lawson offered a sports-related explanation. "Owens and Metcalfe are our two best sprinters. Our relay team is better with them on it."

In addition, Dean Cromwell, assistant head coach for USA Track and Field, had heard a rumor that the Germans were "hiding" their best sprinters until the 4x100. The United States would have to counter with its absolute best runners, or risk failure. Still, Glickman and Stoller felt slighted, expressed worry that the new foursome did not have enough experience exchanging a baton, and were incensed at the thought that the United States might be trying to avoid the very uncomfortable and real possibility of two American Jews on the winning podium. Stoller later called it "the most humiliating episode in my life." Neither competed in the Olympics in Berlin, and neither forgave Coach Cromwell and the USOC for their decision.

Owens was looking for his fourth gold medal in these games. Metcalfe had the silver he won in the 100, plus the silver and bronze from 1932, and was trying to take home the first gold of his career. The other two legs of the race were Wykoff, the winner of two golds in 1928 and 1932, and Draper, who was seeking his first gold. Even the spurned Glickman had to admit that Metcalfe, his replacement, looked "strong, powerful and confident" in warm-ups.

They were a formidable bunch. In the first-round heats, the American foursome crossed a full second ahead of any other qualifiers. It was their race to lose, with closest competitors Italy, the Netherlands, and Germany seeming to be vying for silver. If the Americans didn't screw up or drop the baton, they could not be denied the gold medal. Owens led off the US team for the first 100 meters, setting a scorchingly fast pace. As he approached runner number two, Metcalfe, both men readied for a handoff that they knew would be tricky due to their lack of practice. The duo accomplished the task, but it was far from perfect. Glickman later called it "only fair." Metcalfe thundered down his 100-meter portion of the race and handed off to Draper. One judge thought he saw Metcalfe step out of the box—the portion of track where the baton exchange must take place—just as he handed it to Draper. Draper would have been unaware of this in the blur of the relay; he sprinted off, giving the baton to the final man, Wykoff, who increased the Americans' already sizable lead. The US cruised to not just a win but a blow-away-the-field performance, setting a new world record at 39.8 and leaving silver medalist Italy in the dust 15 meters and nearly a second and a half behind. Holland thought they had bronze sewn up until anchor leg runner Tinus Osendarp, who had won bronze in the 100 meters behind Owens and Metcalfe, realized he had dropped the baton 30 yards before, disqualifying his team. Thus, Germany squeaked out the bronze. (Osendarp later joined the German SS and spent seven years in prison when the Nazis were defeated.)

The judge who thought he had witnessed Metcalfe foul out of the box walked to the track and studied the spike marks, trying to determine if his eyes had deceived him. He couldn't be sure, so he had no choice but to let it go. Officials later determined that the exchange took place just barely in the box, and history was made by a few millimeters. The world record time of 39.8 set by Owens, Metcalfe, Draper, and Wykoff would stand for twenty years.

The US track and field team won twelve gold medals in the 1936 Games, more than all other nations combined. Of that number, the four black athletes on the roster accounted for six of the individual golds and the relay.

Metcalfe returned to the United States and had a long and fulfilling post-Olympics career. He earned his bachelor of philosophy degree from Marquette University and a master's in physical education from the University of Southern California in 1939. He taught political science and coached track at Xavier University in New Orleans, working with five future national track and field champions. He served in World War II as an army first lieutenant and received the Legion of Merit award for program planning as director of physical training.

After the war, Metcalfe returned to his childhood home of Chicago, where Governor Adlai Stevenson appointed him Illinois athletic commissioner in 1949. Metcalfe married Madalynne Fay Young, and they had one child, Ralph Jr. Ralph and Jesse Owens remained such good friends that they played golf together three times a week for twenty-two years.

In 1955 Metcalfe ran for office to help the neighborhoods where he grew up. He became an alderman and was eventually the first black president pro tempore of the Chicago City Council. In 1970 he was elected to the US House of Representatives for the First District. Metcalfe was cofounder of the Congressional Black Caucus and introduced a Congressional resolution that established February as Black History Month. He was founder of the Ralph H. Metcalfe Youth Foundation for amateur athletes, was inducted into the US Track and Field Hall of Fame, and was a member of the President's Commission on Olympic Sports. He mentored young men who would later become the first two black mayors of Chicago, the first black president of the Cook County Board of Commissioners, and the first black chief justice of the Illinois Supreme Court.

On October 10, 1978, Metcalfe suffered a fatal heart attack at the age of sixty-eight just one month before near-certain reelection to a fifth term in Congress. Yet his legacy lives on. In 1991 the Ralph H. Metcalfe Federal Building was christened in Chicago. Marquette University established the Metcalfe Scholarship, which awards tuition and financial support to two minority students each year, and the Metcalfe Chair, which provides funds for visiting educators to teach African American studies. Ralph H. Metcalfe Community Academy in Chicago and Ralph H. Metcalfe School in Milwaukee were named for him.

Ralph Metcalfe broke or tied every sprinting record in the world, thirteen in all, over his lifetime. In his heyday in the 1930s, he was considered "the world's fastest human." But considering all his accomplishments, a comment from *Los Angeles Times* sportswriter Braven Dyer after the 1932 Games seems especially powerful: "There may be better sprinters in the world, but I doubt it. There may be better sportsmen in the world, but I doubt it."

CHAPTER 7

LLOYD LABEACH AND DON GEHRMANN

Track and Field, 1948

The Olympic Games saw a twelve-year hiatus during World War II and its aftermath. Olympic competition returned in 1948, when the Winter Games were hailed as the Games of Renewal. The Games opened in January of that year in St. Moritz, Switzerland, a neutral country untouched by the war. The Summer Games went to London.

It would be that city's second time hosting, but the world had changed considerably since Marquette University's John Brennan competed in the 1908 London Games. Critical supplies were lacking thanks to wartime rationing, and the city still bore scars from heavy bombing. Yet London rose to the Olympics challenge, putting on a well-executed Games. No athletes from Germany, Japan, or the USSR competed, however. The first two were still shunned by the international community and were not allowed to compete; the Soviet Union had not been to an Olympics since 1917 and continued its self-imposed isolation. Some nations, including Puerto Rico, Venezuela, Lebanon, and Syria, took part for the first time.

Two very different University of Wisconsin athletes competed in the Summer Games. Lloyd LaBeach and Don Gehrmann could not have been less alike in their upbringings or experiences. About the only thing that bound them was the cardinal and white they both wore in college. They even competed for different countries in the Olympics.

LaBeach's parents were Jamaican but had relocated to Panama so his father could work in construction on the Panama Canal. Lloyd was born there, but when he was still a small boy the family returned to Jamaica. It was there that LaBeach began to find success as a runner. At Kingston's Tutorial College he captained the track team and set several Jamaican records. The University of Wisconsin took notice and offered LaBeach an athletic scholarship. Veteran coach Tom Jones, who steered hundreds of UW athletes from 1913 to 1948, lavished praise on the newcomer, saying he was "destined to become one of the Badger all-time greats and possibly one of the nation's top performers." Far from home and studying agriculture, LaBeach lived up to his coach's prediction, setting records in the 100-yard dash, 220-yard dash, and broad jump. Nicknamed "the Jamaican Flash," he was responsible for 17 of the UW's 18¾ points at the 1946 National Collegiate Athletic Association (NCAA) Championships, and the yearbook editors called him "perhaps the greatest track star ever to perform in Cardinal toggery."

In 1946 LaBeach felt the impact of his skin color during a meet in San Antonio, Texas. African American leaders urged black athletes to boycott the meet because Texas was still segregated. LaBeach and others chose to participate but were told they would be housed in accommodations separate from white athletes. The situation turned in the black athletes' favor, however, as a wealthy African American publisher named Valmo Bellinger not only paid their room and board but found them extravagant lodging with plentiful dining. LaBeach went on to finish second in the 200.

Lloyd's time in Madison did not last. He hit a rough patch academically and was declared ineligible. He dropped out and headed west for the warmer climate of southern California, where he began training with UCLA track and field coach Elvin Drake while taking classes through UCLA's extension school.

As the 1948 Olympics approached, LaBeach broke the world record for the 200-meter run. He decided to represent his native country, Panama, in the Games, and in May 1948 he headed to London with Coach Drake as Panama's only athlete in the Games. *Time* magazine dubbed him "Panama's one-man Olympic team." Tom Jones was there too, capping his illustrious UW coaching career by acting as an assistant for the US Olympic track team.

LaBeach would have two chances to medal: the 100 and 200 meters. Qualifying rounds for the 100 took place on July 30. Twelve heats were

Lloyd LaBeach was the second African American Badger to medal, after George Poage. COURTESY OF THE UW–MADISON ARCHIVES

held, with the top two runners from each advancing. LaBeach won heat three by a full half-second to easily move to the quarterfinals later that day. This time, the top three from each heat would advance. LaBeach barely edged out the second-place finisher, but it was enough to secure a spot in the semifinals.

The next day was bright and sunny, and spectators sat in shirtsleeves and hats, some fanning themselves, all watching with great anticipation as the fastest men on the planet assembled at Empire Stadium in Wembley. The race would take just over 10 seconds. There were only two heats in the semis, six competitors in each. The top three athletes from each heat, six total, would make the final. LaBeach was in heat two with two runners from Great Britain and one each from the United States, Australia, and Cuba. LaBeach took second in the heat, one-tenth of a second behind Mel Patton of the United States, who was considered an overwhelming favorite. Both must have known it would be a tight final, with all of the finalists qualifying at between 10.4 and 10.7 seconds.

Later that day the six competitors crouched for the final, their feet in the starting blocks. (This was the first Olympics to use blocks for sprint races.) The group consisted of three competitors from the United States, two from Great Britain, and LaBeach, in lane four.

Then England's McDonald Bailey false-started, causing all of the athletes to return to their starting spots. Tension rippled through both the crowd and the athletes. The six resettled in their crouches, muscles taut. The gun went off and all six men took off at top speed, their arms and legs a blur of movement as they hurtled forward.

Just over 10 seconds later, the group crossed the line, but the finish was too close to call. The oldest competitor in the group, thirty-year-old American Barney Ewell, threw his arms up in joy just after crossing, clearly thinking he had won. Mel Patton, the favorite, went to congratulate Ewell. But both soon learned the truth: Harrison Dillard of the United States had matched the Olympic record of 10.3 seconds and won the gold. The photo finish sorted out who had taken second and third. Ewell won the silver with a time of 10.4. Third place went to the lone athlete from Panama, "the Jamaican Flash," the former Badger, Lloyd LaBeach, at 10.6. Alastair McCorquodale of Great Britain finished fourth, prerace favorite Patton fifth, and false-starter Bailey sixth. LaBeach's medal was historic for the UW, making him the first African American Badger to medal since George Poage in 1904. But LaBeach wasn't done yet.

The heats for the 200 meters were held August 2, and once again LaBeach had little trouble advancing. In a similar pattern to the 100 meters, he cruised through the first round, scraped to the top spot in the quarterfinals, and finished second in the semifinals, vaulting him to the finals with five others, two of them familiar names from the 100: Patton and Ewell. One of the world's top sprinters, Nikolay Karakulov of the USSR, was not in the field at all due to his country's not taking part.

Silver medalist Ewell took off fast and led at the curve, but Patton, trying to make up for his fifth-place finish, pushed ahead at the beginning of the stretch run and kept his edge all the way across the finish line. LaBeach crossed in third. Patton finally got his elusive victory.

If LaBeach's two bronze medals were special for the UW, they were monstrous for Panama. In fact, fifty years would pass before the tiny country won another medal. The medals made LaBeach a superstar in Panama, where he was honored with awards, parades, and banquets. LaBeach returned to the California sun, eventually becoming a US citizen and working in the dairy industry in both Jamaica and California. He died after a stroke in 1999 and was posthumously elected to the Central American and Caribbean Athletics Confederation Hall of Fame.

—ıɪ⊢

The day after Lloyd LaBeach wrapped up his second bronze medal, Don Gehrmann was getting ready for his one and only event in the 1948 Games, the 1,500 meters. Gehrmann, a Milwaukee south-sider who grew up on 27th and Harrison Streets, had an unusual training experience at Pulaski High School that he later credited with helping him on indoor tracks. Runners at Pulaski practiced in the basement. Not only was it a small space, it had four concrete pillars smack in the middle that supported the rest of the building, and it was crowded with bikes left by students when they got to school.

"I learned to run in that bicycle room," Gehrmann told the *Milwaukee Journal Sentinel* in a 2012 interview. "Making those sharp turns on a slippery floor around those cement posts. That's why I think I was so good at indoor meets."

Gehrmann was twenty and coming off his sophomore year at the UW when he went to London with coach Jones, who called him "potentially the greatest runner the world has ever known." Don had won the 1,500 meters in the Olympic Trials in Evanston, Illinois, and was considered the United States' best hope in the 1948 Games. Two top milers during the World War II years, both from Sweden, had been deemed ineligible for accepting expense money. Still, the Swedish team included other excellent runners, and they hoped to sweep the podium.

Don Gehrmann excelled at the University of Wisconsin but called his one
Olympic event "the worst race I ever ran." © 2015 JOURNAL SENTINEL, INC.,
REPRODUCED WITH PERMISSION

There was only one qualifying round before the finals. The top three
from four heats would advance to a twelve-man final. Gehrmann finished
third in heat one at 3:54.8, not bad for the heat but a full three seconds
slower than the fastest qualifier, Gosta Bergkvist of Sweden.

The day of the final, August 6, a cold rain pelted down. Gehrmann was
the only athlete from the United States who had made the finals.

The group took off from the starting line. Belgium's Marcel Hansenne
set a ridiculous pace, running the first lap in less than a minute and opening a wide lead, but he couldn't sustain it and lost steam quickly. Henry
Eriksson took the helm at the 1,000-meter mark with Swedish country-

man Lennart Strand on his heels. Meanwhile, Gehrmann was struggling. The rain had turned the track to mud. This was not his weather. He excelled on the hard surface of indoor facilities. Had the sun shone that day, as it had for Lloyd LaBeach a day earlier, things might have ended differently.

"Whenever we had a muddy track, I was very much handicapped," Gehrmann recalled for the *Journal Sentinel*. "The track was completely under water. And the last turn, I stepped on the curb and fell down and picked myself up again. And then I was too late for the sprint because these guys are the best in the world."

By now the runners were splattered with dirt and mud, their hair plastered to their foreheads in soaked strands. Ignoring the weather, they pushed on. The Swedes did take gold and silver, and Wim Slijkhuis of the Netherlands won the bronze. There is some dispute over places seven through twelve, with Gehrmann being credited as seventh, eighth, or tenth in various accounts. Regardless, it was not the outcome Gehrmann had hoped for.

"Probably the worst race I ever ran," he told the *Journal Sentinel*.

Gehrmann would go on to be nicknamed "Mr. Mile of Wisconsin" after prevailing in four straight Big Ten outdoor meets. He also took home three NCAA titles, won the coveted Wanamaker Mile in Madison Square Garden his junior and senior years, and swept Amateur Athletic Union titles in the 1,000 in 1952–53. He left his mark on the UW with a record twelve conference titles and was named the greatest miler of the Big Ten's first fifty years and a member of the one-hundred-year anniversary Big Ten team.

In 1952 he considered giving the Olympics another run, but he did not have the money to travel to the trials in Los Angeles. When the *Milwaukee Sentinel* quoted him saying that he couldn't afford the three hundred dollars in expenses, Milwaukeeans opened their wallets, donating a whopping $3,500 to Gehrmann. But the trials ended in disappointment. He entered the 800 meters because he felt he wasn't properly conditioned for the 1,500, but he finished eighth, which meant no trip to the Olympics. He retired from competitive running a year later.

Don married Lori, his high school sweetheart from Pulaski, and together they raised five children. He had several careers, including teach-

Gehrmann at home in Pardeeville in 2012, displaying some of the medals he won at UW–Madison. GARY D'AMATO PHOTO, 7/24/2012, © 2015 JOURNAL SENTINEL, INC., REPRODUCED WITH PERMISSION

ing and coaching at Wauwatosa East High School. He may not have won that elusive Olympic medal, but along with the rest of the athletes of the 1948 Summer Games, Gehrmann helped restore faith in humanity after so much of it had been lost in the war.

MILWAUKEE BUCKS IN THE OLYMPICS

Basketball was invented in 1891 and was allowed as a demonstration sport at the Olympic Games thirteen years later in St. Louis. It wasn't until 1936 that it became a full-fledged official Olympic sport. That year in Berlin, competitors used outdoor tennis courts as their arena, and medals were presented by basketball's creator himself, James Naismith. The United States took home the very first gold and has dominated the hoop ever since.

By 1948 competition was moved to the more weather-friendly indoor hardwood, and in 1960 in Rome the first two players in a long line of Olympians with connections to the Milwaukee Bucks took part. They were twenty-one-year-old Oscar Robertson (nicknamed "the Big O"), a cocaptain and also Olympic co–leading scorer, and twenty-three-year-old Bob Boozer.

That 1960 team, known as the original "Dream Team," is considered one of the greatest groups of amateur basketball talents ever assembled. They won their nine games by an average margin of more than 42 points and ran away with the gold. The team was later inducted into the Naismith Memorial Basketball Hall of Fame. The 1960 Olympics were held in Rome, Italy, and were broadcast on television live in Europe and tape-delayed in America, making history by bringing basketball to millions of living rooms.

Ten years after that historic title, both Robertson and Boozer joined the Bucks and in the 1970–71 season helped the team to its first and only championship. Over the next forty-four years, nineteen other Milwaukee Bucks players would take part in nine different Olympic basketball tournaments, fourteen of them donning the Team USA red, white, and blue jersey and five playing for their home countries. Following is a list of Milwaukee Bucks players who played in one or more Olympics.

Player	Olympics	Country	Years w/Bucks
Bob Boozer	1960	USA	1970–1971
Oscar Robertson	1960	USA	1970–1974
Quinn Buckner	1976	USA	1976–1982
Adrian Dantley	1976	USA	1990–1991
Phil Ford	1976	USA	1982–1983
Ernie Grunfeld	1976	USA	1977–1979 (later coached the Bucks)
Scott May	1976	USA	1981–1982
Alvin Robertson	1984	USA	1989–1993
Jeff Grayer	1988	USA	1988–1992
Danny Manning	1988	USA	1999–2000
J. R. Reid	1988	USA	1999–2000
Toni Kukoc	1988, 1992, 1996	CRO	2002–2006
Gary Payton	1996, 2000	USA	2002–2003
Ray Allen	2000	USA	1996–2003
Vin Baker	2000	USA	1993–1997
Richard Jefferson	2004	USA	2008–2009
Andrew Bogut	2004, 2008	AUS	2005–2012
Carlos Delfino	2004, 2008, 2012	ARG	2009–2012, 2013–present
Yi Jianlian	2004, 2008, 2012	CHN	2007–2008
Michael Redd	2008	USA	2000–2011
Roko Ukic	2008	CRO	2009–2010

Every player on this list who competed for Team USA won a gold medal except Grayer, Manning, and Reid in 1988 and Jefferson in 2004. Those teams left their respective Olympic sites with bronze. Delfino's Argentina squad was the gold medalist in 2004, and he added a bronze in 2008. Kukoc and Croatia won silver in 1992. Bogut, Jianlian, and Ukic did not medal.

CHAPTER 8

BUDDY MELGES

Sailing, 1964, 1972

Zenda, Wisconsin, is a tiny spot. An unincorporated community with a population of one hundred, it sits seven miles south of Lake Geneva. For years Zenda was famous for just one thing: an eight-pound meteorite that fell from the sky and landed in Bert and Lillian Palmer's farm field in 1955.

Buddy Melges was twenty-five years old when this momentous event occurred. Little did anyone know that Melges would soon surpass the space rock as Zenda's most famous import. In fact, he was destined to be called "the Wizard of Zenda."

Buddy was born Harry Melges Jr. in 1930 in Elkhorn, Wisconsin. He grew up on Delavan and Geneva Lakes, and he still remembers a sunny June day when he was five years old and his father, Harry Sr., brought home a small cedar-planked dinghy. Harry Sr. gave the kindergartner some simple instructions before pushing him off from shore alone. Buddy traveled in a more or less straight line for a bit, then turned and came back to shore, where his dad was waiting. The youngster liked the feel of the boat and surged with confidence.

His sail, however, was badly in need of repair from mice inhabiting the cloth over the winter. Buddy used one of his mother's sheets to do the mending and then tacked up a sign on a tree offering ten-cent rides across the lake. He had a plan for all of those dimes: he was going to replace the patched-up sail material with something brand-new from Joy Brothers, a well-known sailmaker in Milwaukee. The advertising did the trick, and Buddy entered first grade that fall with a summer full of yachting behind him and a crisp, fresh sail on his tiny rig.

Buddy's father, a boatbuilder and racer, taught his son all he knew about sailing, then quizzed him on every aspect, asking why the boy chose to turn this way or his rationale for moving the sail an inch that way, and thus instilling in Buddy a lifetime of sailing knowledge. Harry Sr. was stern and didn't like second place. After dinner he would turn the salt and pepper shakers into buoys and the spoons and knives into boats as he demonstrated his techniques. The repetition and rigid teaching style sometimes brought Buddy to tears while his mother, often standing nearby doing dishes, admonished Harry Sr. for being so harsh.

"Buddy's got to learn," was his father's response. "He can't be making the same mistakes over and over."

Like many father-and-son pairs of the era, Harry and Buddy spent as much time as they could outdoors, often going fishing and bird hunting together. Even Wisconsin's brutally cold winters didn't keep them from racing iceboats across frozen Geneva Lake. In fact, Wisconsin's changing seasons wound up being a big help to Buddy. "Growing up on the lakes and sailing scow-type boats taught me how to fool Mother Nature, where offshore sailors use instruments in [their] attempts," he explained years later. "In other words, [I was] reading the wind on the water and making the adjustments 'quicklier' [a term friends affectionately call a 'Buddy-ism'] than the competition."

Melges was eleven years old in the summer of 1941 and had just sailed in his first junior race when America entered World War II, putting a serious damper on the young man's plans for more water adventures. Junior and senior competition came to a halt as sailors were sent off to Europe or relocated stateside to make wartime supplies. Harry Sr. saw his boatbuilding business grind to a stop, so he found work as the field manager of the Val-Lo-Will chicken farm. Those were hard years for everyone, the Melgeses included, but as soon as the war ended Harry Sr. went back into the business he loved, setting up Melges Boat Works in the tiny hamlet of Zenda. At first he produced mostly flat-bottomed boats suitable only for fishing, but the sailor had imagination and a plan. He and Buddy spent a year designing and building their first sailboat, which they named *Widgeon* after the mallard-type duck, a nod to their love of hunting waterfowl.

They tested their new vessel the night before a regatta, sneaking down to the lake under cover of darkness and sliding her into the placid water. Satisfied she would do the trick, they went back to bed dreaming of the next day's race. And *Widgeon* did more than perform—she soared. Sixteen-year-old Buddy won his first regatta and went on to take ten more top finishes that season, easily capturing the Lake Geneva Sailing Championship.

Buddy's career was launched, but his father still doled out plenty of advice. In one race, as Buddy struggled to get off the line correctly, an exasperated Harry Sr. finally said, "All right, kid, that's enough. Tomorrow I get on the boat with you." With his dad at his side the next day, Buddy sprinted from the start and won the race. Buddy recalled in his 1983 book *Sailing Smart* that this taught him that his father really did know what he was doing.

When Buddy was twenty-two, international conflict once again interrupted his sailing dreams. He went to serve in the Korean War with the army and would not touch a boat for two years. When he returned to Zenda, he found his father's boat business booming, and he quickly went to work driving all over the Midwest for deliveries and service calls. On occasion he threw in a tactical suggestion or two for the boat's skipper while he was there.

Buddy Melges was a student of Mother Nature and carefully examined both wind and rain. "There's a lot of science in sailing that a lot of people don't really analyze," he said. "I did it by feel. If a sail shape looked good to me, then that made me a happy camper. You talk about sailing by the seat of your pants, I thought I sailed by the seat of my stomach. If it didn't feel good in my stomach I would make some changes to make it feel good. Sensitizing yourself to the motion of the boat is so critical." He also used his sense of smell and the tickle of breeze on his bare arms to pick up subtle shifts in wind velocity or direction.

Just before departing for Korea, Buddy had met Gloria Wenzel, another successful sailor, at a regatta in Chicago. Buddy and a friend were carrying in their sails when she caught his eye. He turned to his chum and said, "See that girl up there? I'm going to marry her." It wasn't long before Buddy's prediction came true. After Buddy returned from Korea, he and Gloria were married, the start of a lifelong partnership. He also picked up where he had left off in sailing competitions and soon was winning races around the state, from Madison's Lake Mendota to Green Lake.

Buddy's sailing career saw one more hiatus, this one self-imposed. When Buddy was about thirty, a fellow sailor, someone Melges considered a friend, protested Melges's taking part in the Inland Lakes

Buddy Melges on a boat delivery in 1960.
PHOTO BY GUS LARSON, PROPERTY OF NEENAH NODAWAY YACHT CLUB

races due to the fact that he made boats and sails for a living. This experience, said the friend, gave Buddy an unfair advantage. Melges argued that some tennis players crafted rackets and some golfers clubs. The friend took the matter to sailing's upper echelons, and Buddy was so disgusted by the accusation that he quit for a year. After the dispute was thrown out, Buddy returned to the circuit with a vengeance, storming his way to three consecutive Mallory Cup titles—the men's North American championship.

With the 1964 Olympics three years away and slated for Tokyo, Japan, the first time they would be held in Asia, Buddy learned that the US sailing team needed a strong sailor in the Flying Dutchman boat class. These small, fast vessels had crewmen who, according to a 1964 *Sports Illustrated* article, "must swing outboard like circus performers on a trapeze to give them stability." Melges dove into training on the Flying Dutchman rig.

In 1963, a spell of unusual Wisconsin weather gave him a huge advantage. That winter Lake Geneva—which previously had always frozen over—did not ice up on its west end. This allowed Melges and his crewman, Bill Bentsen, the chance to work in water all winter, even if it was 10 degrees outside. They donned rubber suits and boots and braved the elements each day, learning, as Buddy later described it, "how to beat, how to reach, and how to go downwind in a Flying Dutchman."

At the Olympic Trials held in Atlantic Highlands, New Jersey, that July, Melges and Bentsen were heralded by *Sports Illustrated* as "brilliant." All of their subzero work had paid off. They won the trials and that fall headed to Tokyo for their first Olympics. Buddy's father, who was not a fan of the Flying Dutchman class of boats, did not travel to Tokyo, but Gloria was there at Buddy's side. The sailing events took place over the span of nine days in October in Sagami Bay off Enoshima Island. Melges and Bentsen were entered in the Flying Dutchman mixed two-person heavyweight dinghy with a boat they named *Widgeon* in honor of Harry and Buddy's original. Twenty-one teams would compete for the three podium spots. Points would be awarded on a descending scale from first (1,423 points) to last (101 points). Every team would participate in seven races and was allowed to throw out its worst results.

In the opening race, *Widgeon* got off to a mediocre start. Melges and Bentsen could steer her to no better than a tenth-place finish. They finished six minutes behind leader Italy but still earned 423 points and sat in the middle of the pack. In race two, *Widgeon* zoomed home in second place, three minutes behind new pacesetter Great Britain. For this, Melges and Bentsen earned 1,122 points and vaulted from tenth to fourth place overall.

Race three was the worst of the bunch. The Wisconsin duo capsized three times in 35-knot winds, and *Widgeon*'s rudder broke. Unable to finish, the pair threw out the race, and *Widgeon* dropped to seventh.

The two men stayed up most of the night repairing the boat. After three hours of sleep they awoke groggily the next morning knowing they needed a good race to stay in the hunt. They were beaten off the line by a strong Denmark team, but Buddy and Bill found a well of stamina to finish in second place. Another second-place mark the next day in race five earned them 1,122 points. The United States was now in third place behind Great Britain and New Zealand. If they could just hold on for two more events, a medal would be theirs.

Each race was a different distance, and race six was one of the longest, lasting just under an hour. It was an incredibly close battle, with less than a minute separating the top three finishers. *Widgeon* came in third. Catching the top two countries in the standings was now mathematically impossible, but they would have a bronze medal if they could hold off hard-charging Denmark and its boat, *Miss Denmark 1964*. The Americans held an 800-point edge going into the last race.

Race seven was a speed race and could be done in about 10 or 15 minutes. Denmark would need a top-four finish to gain the 800 points needed to catch Team USA, plus *Widgeon* would have to simply fail.

Miss Denmark 1964 came across in 14 minutes, 29 seconds. That was only good enough for seventh place and 578 points. Although Melges and Bentsen were tenth, 22 seconds behind Denmark, they were able to fend off the Danes for the coveted bronze. Thirty-four-year-old Buddy had his first Olympic medal.

WISCONSIN ROWERS IN THE OLYMPICS

Wisconsin is blessed with many lakes and rivers, and athletes from the state have competed in a variety of water sports. One of the most consistent areas of excellence is in rowing. The state can boast at least one Olympic rower in every Summer Olympics year from 1968 to 2012.

Rowers require incredible strength and energy in addition to remarkable determination. It turns out that Wisconsin's weather is another factor in their success. In an article with *Row2k* magazine, University of Wisconsin men's crew coach Chris Clark cited the cold weather as a big advantage: "For those that are not from cold weather rowing climates, there is no conception of how cold-water rowing helps promote speed. Why? In the spring, you are frozen to the bone every stroke. The only chance you've got at warmth is rowing as hard as you can all the time."

There is no doubt that the University of Wisconsin's oldest sport, which began in 1874, is consistently ranked among the nation's elite.

Summer or winter, warm or cold, University of Wisconsin rowers hit the
water for practice. Here the 1913–1914 team poses on a pier on Lake Mendota.
COURTESY OF THE UW—MADISON ARCHIVES

Year	Athlete	Medal
1920	Alden "Zeke" Sanborn	gold
1968	Larry Hough	silver
	Stewart MacDonald *	
1972	Larry Hough	
	Stewart MacDonald *	
	Tim Mickelson *	silver
1976	Bob Espeseth *	
	Carie Graves *	bronze
	Neil Halleen *	
	Peggy McCarthy *	bronze
	Jackie Zoch *	bronze

Year	Athlete	Medal
1980**	Chris Cruz *	
	Bob Espeseth *	
	Carie Graves *	
	Peggy McCarthy *	
	Daniel Sayner	
1984	Bob Espeseth *	bronze
	Carie Graves *	gold
	Kris Thorsness *	gold
	Chari Towne *	
1988	Cindy Eckert *	
	Bob Espeseth *	
	Sarah Gengler *	
	Mara Keggi *	
	Dave Krmpotich *	silver
	Kim Santiago *	
	Kris Thorsness *	
1992	Mark Berkner *	
	Cindy Eckert *	silver
	Yasmin Farooq *	
	Carol Feeney *	silver
	Sarah Gengler *	
	Tracy Rude	
	Chris Sahs	
	Kim Santiago *	
1996	Yasmin Farooq *	
	Melissa Iverson *	
	Eric Mueller *	silver

Year	Athlete	Medal
2000	Chris Ahrens	
	Torrey Folk *	
	Sarah Garner	bronze
	Eric Mueller *	
2004	Chris Ahrens	gold
	Benjamin Holbrook	
	Beau Hoopman *	gold (WR)
	Matt Smith *	
2008	Beau Hoopman *	bronze
	Micah Boyd *	bronze
	Megan Kalmoe	
2012	Kristin Hedstrom *	
	Grant James *	
	Ross James *	
	Megan Kalmoe	bronze

* Rowed for UW–Madison
** US boycott of Olympic Games
WR = world record

Buddy considered a run for the next Mexico Olympic Games in 1968, but he became disillusioned with the Flying Dutchman class when he saw other sailors using shady, even illegal techniques in international competitions. According to Buddy, they were sculling their boats with a larger rudder—which was effective in light winds but also against the rules. So it wasn't until 1972 that he rekindled his Olympic dream. This time Buddy and Bentsen teamed up with a third partner, Bill Allen, in a three-man boat in the Soling class. The US Olympic Trials were to be held in San Francisco Bay in June 1972 and would consist of seven races. The trio wanted to be the most prepared team in the competition, and they knew where to start. The Army Corps of Engineers maintained a scale model of the bay in their offices in Sausalito, and the three sailors visited and studied it. Later they sat at the water's edge, watching the tide roll in and out and making notes.

They thought they were more than ready, but in the first race Melges had to maneuver a tight turn with another boat and promptly forgot most of what he believed he had committed to memory. At one point they found themselves shockingly in eighteenth place. Somehow they managed a late surge and finished fifth. The second race presented a major obstacle: their mast broke. But they showed remarkable skill in fixing it during a race and also managed to recall their recent studies of the water and tides to win the trials. They were going to Munich.

These Games would be remembered for the horror inflicted when Palestinian terrorists broke into the Olympic Village on September 5 and killed nine Israeli athletes. Buddy and his sailing compatriots were 541 miles away, in the seaside village of Kiel, for the sailing events, where Buddy was chosen as the US flag bearer in a separate opening ceremony. Hearing the news of what had happened in Munich rattled the sailors, but it actually had little impact on the sailing competition other than the withdrawal of the Israeli team. The International Olympic Committee suspended the Games for twenty-four hours, but the sailors were already scheduled to take September 6 and 7 off.

Melges was now forty-two and an experienced helmsman. He, Bentsen, and Allen complemented each other well. In the Soling class scoring system, the team with the *lowest* number of points wins. The winners of each of the six races would earn zero points, with the numbers increasing for finishers further from the top spot.

Other than a fourth-place finish in one race, which they threw out, the US team was in the top three in all six competitions. Buddy and his crew steered their boat, *United States*, to a gold medal, blowing away the rest of the field with 16.7 points. Sweden took second with 53.7 and Canada third with 68.1.

The three Americans stood on the podium in red pants, white blazers, and red, white, and blue striped ties and felt their pride swell. Across the ocean, an entire state celebrated with Buddy, particularly those who re-

"The Wizard of Zenda," seen here with wife Gloria, learned sailing techniques from his father and later shared his knowledge with Wisconsin youth. COURTESY OF BUDDY AND GLORIA MELGES

sided in lake country and in Zenda, where now the brightest thing to have come out of their galaxy was the laid-back Wisconsin sailor. He remains the only US sailor to win Olympic gold.

Melges went on to bring home titles in more than ninety major national and international sailing championships, including the World Star Championships and the America's Cup alongside Bill Koch, making Buddy the first sailor to have won both an Olympic gold and an America's Cup. He was named Yachtsman of the Year three times and One-Design Sailor of the Year twice. As if that wasn't enough, he took first place in the International Skeeter (ice boat) Association Championship a record seven times. At the age of eighty, Melges was still beating everyone in the A-Scow Inland Yachting Association Championship held on Geneva Lake.

Buddy was inducted into the Wisconsin Athletic Hall of Fame in 2007. There is a bronze statue of him in Zenda, and Lake Geneva commissioned a life-sized painting depicting Melges at the helm of a sailboat after the America's Cup victory. The Geneva Lake Museum devoted a section to Buddy, chock full of artifacts, and at the Buddy Melges Sailing Center at the docks, visitors might see Buddy himself, now in his eighties, teaching children to sail and telling anyone who will listen that kids need to be out in nature. Buddy has said that he wants to be on the water until he has to be carried off the boat and that he loves sailing so much because it's something you can do "from eight to eighty."

Buddy and Gloria stayed in Wisconsin and raised three children, Laura, Harry III, and Hans. Their kids grew up as avid sailors and hunters. Buddy's grandson, Harry IV, was already an accomplished sailor by age thirteen and in 2014 was training in the junior Olympic ski program.

When a Lake Geneva newspaper reporter asked Buddy if he ever considered moving out of Wisconsin, the internationally known athlete wondered aloud why he would, then went on to cite his reasons for staying put: four seasons, good ice, ducks to hunt, and waters to sail. He summed it up with just a few words:

"It's a helluva life."

The Wizard of Zenda, much like the Wizard of Oz, knew all along that there's no place like home.

CHAPTER 9

CONNIE CARPENTER PHINNEY

Speedskating, 1972, and Cycling, 1984

C onnie Carpenter grew up in Madison, a city that, like so many others around Wisconsin, flooded playgrounds, baseball diamonds, and other open spaces in winter to create public skating rinks. Connie was born in 1957 and lived on the city's east side, just across from one such elementary school rink. In the 1960s, there was not much incentive to stay inside—the television had only a few channels—and Carpenter's parents shooed her and her three brothers outside every night after dinner, even on the long, cold evenings when the sun set early. The rink lights came on at 7 P.M., and the kids often skated for two hours before bed.

Connie, who thought of herself as a shy, awkward tomboy, loved to be physically active along with her siblings and father, who played every sport hard. At first she tried to get serious about pursuits deemed more appropriate for girls, but none of them were the right fit: gymnastics (she thought she was too tall), swimming (she didn't like to do laps), and figure skating (she felt too rigid and slow) all fell by the wayside.

But she took quickly to speedskating. Half of the neighborhood playground rink was reserved for hockey, and the other half, easily the size of a soccer field, was a giant sheet of fresh ice available for free skating. Girls were not given the option to play hockey, and if Connie ventured to the hockey side to knock the puck around with her dad and brothers, she would be sent back when the action got too intense.

On the free-skate side of the rink, the neighborhood kids played an endless cycle of games—a tag-style race the kids called pom-pom and an elaborate version of capture the flag. Connie soon discovered she was one of the fastest skaters in any age group. She loved the feeling of this sport on blades. "If you have never skated under lights on a dark night, you may not know the acute sensation of speed that accompanies the lessening of peripheral vision," she later wrote. "That, combined with skills honed from hours on the ice, allowed me to be elusive when chased or cunning when I was the hunter, gave me a sense of power beyond my age."

The city of Madison hosted annual skating championships. Young athletes who qualified at a neighborhood rink moved on to the finals, held at Vilas Park, and winners were rewarded with their pictures in the paper. Connie quickly began trouncing the competition and won every year from kindergarten through sixth grade. Each win was followed by a phone call from the Madison Speedskating Club, asking Connie's parents to sign her up for the team. But the Carpenters were already swamped, juggling youth hockey with their three boys. In addition, Connie's mother, Darcy, was battling multiple sclerosis while raising four children. Darcy and Charlie didn't feel they could add the time commitment it would take to shuttle Connie three miles across town to practice and back. So they politely declined year after year, and Connie continued with free skating.

In sixth grade, Connie went to a local open race hosted by the Madison Speedskating Club. She wore her everyday clothes—corduroy pants and a baggy sweater—while more seasoned youth athletes lined up in their fancy skating tights. And she was one of the best. In one race, a one-and-a-half-lap event, she had once again pulled out to a huge lead when she heard a bell. It signified the final lap, but Connie, not having been given any formal instruction on speedskating, thought the event was over and stood up out of her crouched racing position mid-stride. As she watched in baffled silence, the rest of the field zipped past her, gunning for the finish line. Connie spent the rest of the afternoon crying in the family station wagon. That day, her parents decided it was time to sign up for the club.

"In an instant, my life changed, and for the first time, I belonged. It was my first sports team. Sport gave me a sense of community and a purpose that had structure: a season filled with meets. I was hooked on the lifestyle: packing into someone's family car to go to a race because my parents were consumed by hockey. Speedskating was a family sport, and I believe that is why girls have always had equal opportunity," Connie explained.

Adding to the sport's attraction was the fact that the club's practices took place on the other side of town, far from the minutiae of junior high school. She felt she could be one person during the day at school and don a new persona in the fifteen minutes it took to get to practice. Soon she decided to train year-round, skating all winter and then riding her trusty fluorescent-orange Peugeot bicycle to the University Arboretum or a grassy park on the UW campus called Picnic Point to run on the hidden trails in the woods during the summer.

Connie intrinsically knew at an early age that she would go fast because her mother could not. "When you have a parent with a disease, I think it gets inside of you and it changes you very subliminally," Connie once told the *New York Times*. "My mother would look at me and say, 'I don't know how you do all of these extraordinary things.' And I would think, how could I do these things? Me? My gosh, you are the one who is extraordinary."

Three years after joining the Madison Speedskating Club, Connie Carpenter made her first Olympic team at the shockingly young age of fourteen. She was just a freshman at Madison East High School when she headed off with Team USA to Sapporo, Japan, for the 1972 Winter Olympic Games. She remains in the history books as one of the youngest American Olympians ever. But because the top-ranked girl on the team, Anne Henning, was only sixteen, Connie didn't feel out of place. She also felt empowered by her coach, Finn Halvorsen, who had been brought over from Norway to steer the US team. Halvorsen took Carpenter under his wing, teaching her the proper way to train and sparking in her a lifelong curiosity about exercise physiology that would later lead her to seek a graduate degree in the topic.

Connie was scheduled for just one event in Sapporo, the 1,500 meters. She was the youngest competitor in the field of thirty-one skaters by two full years, and some of the women in the race were more than twice her age, yet Connie finished a very impressive seventh. Twenty-year-old Dianne Holum, who trained in Milwaukee, took the gold. And Connie wasn't

Women made great strides in Olympic speedskating in the 1960s and 1970s. In this photo taken in 1976 in Innsbruck, Austria, Nancy Swider Sr. (center) stands with four other members of the US team. From left: Beth Heiden of Madison, Wisconsin; Peggy Crowe of St. Louis; Swider; Cindy Seikkula of Minneapolis; and Lori Monk of Madison. AP PHOTO

A MOTHER-DAUGHTER STORY

How many mother and daughter duos have competed in the Olympics? Nancy Swider-Peltz Sr. and Jr. are a unique speedskating pair from the Chicago area who trained at Milwaukee's Pettit Center. Nancy Sr. went to four Olympics, in 1976, 1980, 1984, and 1988. Her daughter, Nancy Jr., competed in the 2010 Games in Vancouver and just barely missed a medal, finishing fourth in the women's team pursuit with Pettit-trained athletes Jilleanne Rookard of Wyandotte, Michigan, and Catherine Raney-Norman, a native of Elm Grove, Wisconsin.

Nancy Sr. had used a creative technique to motivate her kids, Nancy Jr. and Jeffrey. She had the tiles in the family shower inscribed with great quotes such as, "Far better is it to dare mighty things, to win glorious triumphs, even though checkered by failure, than to rank with those poor spirits who neither enjoy much nor suffer much because they live in the gray twilight that knows neither victory nor defeat" (Teddy Roosevelt). Her kids took these themes to heart every single time they took a shower.

the only teen making her mark in Sapporo; Anne Henning won gold in the 500 and bronze in the 1,000. The new guard had arrived.

After her notable Olympic showing, Connie returned to Madison and the routines of training and high school. She graduated from Madison East in 1975 and that same year began cycling during the off-season with fellow speedskater Sheila Young. "Apart from our sporting choices, we could not have been more different," Connie recalled. "I was long and lanky, she was short and muscular. In 1975, I spent many hours riding the track with her. Take the bike away, and the speed skating position is quite similar—the active muscle groups are more or less the same."

To Connie, the cycling community felt more active and engaged than the speedskaters, and she was excited about this new pursuit. At the same time, she remained one of America's top speedskaters, winning the US national overall outdoor title prior to the 1976 Winter Olympic Games in Innsbruck, Austria. She should have been a shoo-in for a medal, until an injury altered her path.

"I had been dealing with chronic tendonitis in my ankle during an era when access to physical therapy was limited and orthotic inserts were virtually unknown," Connie explained. "Coming out of a turn in one of my final workouts prior to the Olympic trials, [a tendon] snapped. Technically it was more of a micro-tear, but it felt like a snap and in an instant I was hobbled."

It felt like the end of the world. She was eighteen, left out of the Olympics during her peak, and now without a plan for her future. She felt lost and lonely. Then, in marched fate in the form of her older brother, Chuck. He was home from college for Christmas break and dragged Connie on an adventure trip with some buddies. To her amazement, her injured tendon could do things she had never dreamed of. "My ankle, which didn't move side to side very well, could quite easily move up and down," she said. "I could cross-country ski, and I could ride a bike."

She never looked back, shedding skating's frozen training grounds for the warmer climates and open roads of cycling. As a student at the University of Wisconsin–Madison in the mid-1970s, she fell into a fun-loving bicycle racing community, and by the end of her first season on a bike she was winning national titles, beating previous champion Miji Reoch in the individual pursuit and road race by slim margins. Sheila Young, who had gotten Connie started in cycling, had exclusive-access passes to the 1976 Summer Olympics in Montreal and invited Connie to join her. Watching the track cycling events from the infield confirmed her love of her new sport. She now thought of herself solely as a bike racer.

Miji Reoch became a mentor and a friend, teaching Connie everything she knew about cycling. "[Miji] didn't start riding and then racing until her mid-twenties while supporting her husband as he went through law school," Connie said. "Most of what I learned in the early years of racing was channeled through her."

Of all the lessons Miji passed on to Connie, one stands out most. "She taught me how to dig deep and race aggressively, primarily in men's races," Connie said. "In the late 1970s, most women's races were run simultaneously with the master's men, the junior men, or a lower category men's field to save time. If there was a women's-only event, it quite typically was a short race—sometimes as short as five miles, maybe ten. Fortunately, I could race in the women's race and then a few hours later race in the elite men's field, a pattern I continued through most of my career."

No longer dependent on Mother Nature to cool her track, Connie began bike racing as often as five times a week, sometimes in Kenosha, Wisconsin, or Northbrook, Illinois, other times in intense mash-up races at an abandoned military base outside of Madison. Those races in particular honed her corner and breakaway skills.

It wasn't long before she felt a change of venue was needed, to someplace warm. Connie left the UW and moved to the vibrant cycling community of Berkeley, California. Her boyfriend at the time was also a bike racer, and the two of them threw a mattress on the floor of a studio apartment and soaked up their vagabond lifestyle in Berkeley.

"The urban roads were a stark comparison to the country roads of Wisconsin," Connie remembered. "To get out of town, we'd 'tunnel up' or 'spruce out'—depending on the route—giving me access to climbs that did not exist in Wisconsin." She was accepted to the University of California–Berkeley and resumed her college studies in 1979. She also joined the crew team, making a varsity team that finished second at collegiate nationals and won the Collegiate 4 at the NCAAs in 1980. She began taking part in a bike race in Boulder, Colorado, called the Red Zinger, sponsored by Celestial Seasonings, the maker of Red Zinger tea (the event would later be called the Coors Classic). The race began to attract international competitors, and Connie found herself competing against increasingly formidable foes, including the feisty Keetie van Oosten-Hage from the Netherlands.

During this time Connie convinced a few of her Madison friends, including speedskaters Beth Heiden and Sarah Docter, to try cycling. Both did, and both were successful. Beth won the 1980 UCI Road World Championships in Sallanches, France, one of the toughest road courses in the world; she later turned to cross-country skiing, taking home a collegiate national title at the University of Vermont. A generation of athletes including Connie, Beth, and Sarah were starting to change the way people thought about women's sports.

"We were a generation somewhat unconfined by convention, floating between two different schools of thought," Connie said. "The generation before us quit sport early—if they pursued sport at all—to start a family. Once the landmark Title IX passed into law [in 1972], universities across the country were required to include more gender equality in all collegiate sports. It did not happen all at once, but quite suddenly the call to sports for women was widespread."

In 1980 Connie took the year off from cycling to finish college and row crew. She also started dating another bike racer, Davis Phinney; one of the first things he mentioned to Connie was that he didn't see that she had lived up to her potential in cycling. She realized he was right. After graduating from Berkeley in 1981 and learning that women's cycling would be included on the Olympic program for the first time at the 1984 Los Angeles Games, she was more motivated than ever. She had three years to prepare for the 79-kilometer race, the only women's event on the Olympic cycling docket.

Connie and Davis loaded up their old VW Rabbit and started hitting every race in California, crashing in cheap motels or friends' spare bedrooms. Sponsors were suddenly excited about women's Olympic cycling, and Connie and some other women were able to form a sponsored team. They were still scraping by, but they loved the sport and the camaraderie. One teammate, Sue Novara-Reber, had been a sprinter and shared her sprinting techniques with the group. "The luxury of having an in-house master cannot be overstated," Connie explained. "Working with a sprinter of her caliber week in and week out made me quicker and boosted my confidence."

Connie focused all of her energy on the upcoming 1984 Los Angeles Olympics. She and Davis got married, but he soon went off to train in Europe while she remained in the States. In this age before email or cell phones, they would often go weeks on end without talking. She missed him and also missed his feedback and opinions as a trusted training partner.

In January 1984 Connie saw the women's Olympic course in person in the urban enclave of Mission Viejo. On that day she decided to devote almost 80 percent of her time until the Olympic Trials training with a category 1 (top of the line) men's team. This would afford her a more aggressive style of training and more quality time on the bike. She focused on the bike handling and tactics required for shorter, faster races and pushed herself to stay near her limit of exertion.

Meanwhile, hype over the women's cycling team and the new Olympic event had exploded. The team had to hire a full-time publicist when they found themselves turning down as many interviews as they accepted. The height of the publicity blitz was a photo shoot in Death Valley with mega-star photographer Annie Leibovitz behind the lens. The photo ran in the January 1984 issue of *Vanity Fair* magazine.

Connie Carpenter Phinney made her second Olympics a full twelve years after her first, a rare feat. She would be part of the inaugural road-race team for women, and she couldn't have been prouder. But Los Angeles would be an entirely different experience from her first Olympics in Sapporo, Japan. This was a massive undertaking in one of America's largest cities. Connie's husband, Davis, was entered in two events, and the couple felt the pressure from a press corps that was wringing out the "husband and wife cyclist duo" story for every drop they could get. The Phinneys were hounded with interview requests when all they wanted to do was train.

On July 29, 1984, forty-five women cyclists convened at the starting line in Mission Viejo for the 79-kilometer race (just under 50 miles). It would take more than two hours, and most of the race would be shown on national

TV. Together these women were making history. Many eyes were on France's Jeannie Longo, who would go on to be considered the greatest female cyclist ever, but Connie and fellow American Rebecca Twigg were also under intense scrutiny. Twigg was known for being a model and for having skipped four years of high school due to her high IQ, and she had been under the press's relentless spotlight too. In fact, the media had made this into a personal battle between twenty-seven-year-old Connie, "the veteran," and twenty-one-year-old Rebecca, "the newcomer." They were intense rivals, but Connie also respected Rebecca's talents and feared her as a competitor.

The race played out exactly as Connie had expected. A small group of strong women—including Connie, France's Longo, and Twigg, as well as Italian rider Maria Canins and West Germany's Sandra Schumacher—rode away from the rest of the pack midway through. Less than a kilometer from the finish, the cyclists poured it on for a final sprint. Twigg then shot off from the pack and appeared to have a gold medal in hand, but she made a slight tactical mistake: she started too early, drifting a little to her right. Connie caught up, and they were dead even with 50 meters to go. As they neared the finish line, still neck and neck and with the roar of the American crowd all around them, Connie pulled out a trick she had learned from Davis. She pulled up on the handlebars and threw her bike forward about a foot. It would be a photo finish, but the evidence was clear: Connie Carpenter Phinney had won a gold medal by only inches. Twigg won the silver and Schumacher the bronze.

"Looking back at 1984, I wish I could have enjoyed that experience more," she reflected in 2015. "But there was simply too much pressure to win, and at the time winning was the only thing that mattered. It was clearly the most intense time in my life, but I was able to keep my focus, and when it was over I knew immediately that I would not race my bike again. It was especially meaningful with the Olympics at home in the USA and because Davis was also competing. Yet it was also bittersweet because he didn't win and was so disappointed."

Connie had prevailed in dramatic fashion in the first Olympic women's bike race. She had simultaneously decided it would be her last. Davis did not take gold but won a bronze medal that year in the 100-kilometer team time trial and finished fifth in the individual road race. Today Davis

Phinney remains the leader in total race victories by an American with more than 300, and he is one of only three Americans (along with Lance Armstrong and Greg LeMond) to win multiple stages of the Tour de France.

The Phinneys settled in to Davis's hometown of Boulder and started Carpenter/ Phinney Bike Camps in 1986. Davis did television commentary for bike racing. The couple had two children,

Connie Carpenter Phinney won gold in the inaugural women's Olympic bike race in Los Angeles in 1984. AP PHOTO/STF

Taylor in 1990 and Kelsey in 1993. Life seemed just about perfect. Then, in 2000, Davis, nicknamed "Thor" by his teammates for his physical power, was diagnosed with young-onset Parkinson's disease. The progressive neurological disorder slowly robbed him of many of his favorite activities. "There's a lot of sadness to see your best friend go through something like this," Connie said. "It would be foolish to think that I didn't lose something too. It isn't fair. It was devastating. I don't think anything prepares you for the news that you basically aren't going to get any better."

Connie and Davis run the Davis Phinney Foundation, which assists people living with Parkinson's. Davis gives motivational talks to Parkinson's groups and wrote a memoir, *The Happiness of Pursuit*, detailing his journey through cycling and Parkinson's. And their children are a source of endless joy. Kelsey became a competitive Nordic skier with plans to be a doctor specializing in neurology to help people like her father. Taylor carved out his own Olympic legacy, going to two Olympics in cycling. In 2008, at the age of eighteen, he finished seventh in the men's 4,000-meter individual pursuit, and four years later he just missed a medal, coming in fourth in both the individual road race and the individual time trial. Collectively, they're still known as America's First Family of Cycling.

Taylor Phinney draws inspiration from his dad. "I remember him being very playful and fit all the time," he reflected in 2008 to the *New York Times*. "So it's hard for us to see him struggle the way he does. I know sometimes he wishes he could pull me up some hill, drop me at the end and sprint away, but there are little things he does for himself where he finds happiness. It makes me feel good for him to see my results, because I enjoy making him a little happier than he would be every day."

Added Davis: "I could easily slip into a very, very dark place with everything I've lost, so I have to focus on the pinpricks of light to stay positive. But with Taylor, that's easier. I just look at what he's been doing and I'm instantly connected to a magnificent source of energy."

Connie manages her son's business, advocates for women's cycling, and paints. She has been inducted into the US Bicycling Hall of Fame, International Sports Hall of Fame, Colorado Sports Hall of Fame, Wisconsin Athletic Hall of Fame, and US Olympic Hall of Fame, among others.

She has known pain and hardship but has also become the person she was meant to be: an athlete forever etched in history, a mother, a wife, and someone who has left an indelible mark on the world. An old saying goes, "Well-behaved women rarely make history." Connie Carpenter Phinney was not going to fit into the mold so many just a generation before her accepted. She loved sports, and she helped to permanently change the landscape for US women's athletics. But despite her own fame, Connie says there is one thing she never tires of hearing: "'Are you Taylor Phinney's mom?' or 'Are you Kelsey Phinney's mom?' That's the best thing you could say to me."

In 2014, Connie Carpenter Phinney returned to LA and rode the Olympic course for the first time in thirty years, this time just for fun. She was stunned at how difficult some of the hills were. Afterward, she said in an interview with the LA84 Foundation, "It's been a fast 30 years. The '84 Olympics will live forever in my heart as a real defining moment in my life but I don't hang my hat on just being an Olympian or just being an Olympic gold medalist. I'm really proudest of being a really good person. I contribute to my community and I contribute especially to my family. . . . There's a lot to be really proud of."

CHAPTER 10

ERIC HEIDEN

Speedskating, 1976, 1980

Has there ever been an athlete more grounded than Eric Heiden? While the down-to-earth superstar from Madison was busy wowing spectators with his unparalleled skill, he learned at a young age that sports can take you only so far and that hype is just that. "People ask me to give speeches," Heiden lamented a few months after winning five gold medals. "But I'm only twenty-one years old. What can I tell anybody?"

Heiden's humble journey began with a pair of skates, his grandfather, and Lake Mendota. Eric Arthur Heiden was two years old on the 1960 day when his grandfather took him out to the ice to try skates for the first time. Heiden's father, Jack, was an orthopedic surgeon and former fencing champion. His mother, Nancy, reigned as Wisconsin's senior tennis champion. Both were also cyclists. Eric had one sibling, Beth, a year younger. The Heidens spent many years just enjoying skating as a family pastime and would all race each other around the frozen lake. Eric and Beth joined the neighborhood pickup games and tried more formal training with both figure skating and hockey clubs.

Eric dreamed of being a professional hockey player for a time but felt his hand-eye coordination was not superb. He would always be quick to chase down an errant puck, though. And both Eric and Beth loved speed. Hockey and figure skating failed to satisfy that desire, and as teens the brother and sister began to focus on speedskating. Beth later told the *Los Angeles Times* the sport might not have been her best choice due to her

Eric Heiden is fifteen months older than his sister, Beth. The two tried figure skating and hockey before settling on speedskating. WISCONSIN STATE JOURNAL ARCHIVE

petite stature: five foot two and 106 pounds. "At my size skating outdoors was tough," she said in a 2002 interview. "Cutting through the wind made things harder for me."

Asked once by a *Washington Post* reporter what he liked about speedskating, Eric said, "It's fun to get dizzy. You can go fast. It's not like you have to rely on something technical. It's only you. If you goof up, you have no one to blame but yourself."

Both Heidens began to win, taking national and international titles as teens. School remained a priority, a mantra handed down from their parents, and they picked up cycling from their dad. Dr. Heiden knew it was a good way for the kids to cross-train their legs for speedskating, and he encouraged them to take part in other sports. Eric played soccer and ran with the high school cross-country team.

Seventy-five miles east of the Heidens' home was the Wisconsin Olympic Oval, an outdoor rink in West Allis, Wisconsin. Built in the late 1960s, it was the first refrigerated 400-meter rink in North America. It could be kept frozen for up to six months of the year, and it quickly became a hub for speedskaters, pulling athletes from all over the Midwest. The Heidens began to travel there almost daily, attending high school in the morning, doing homework in the car, and skating until exhaustion at night. At the oval they hooked up with Dianne Holum, a four-time Olympic medalist (silver and bronze in 1968 and gold and silver in 1972) who was only in her early twenties but looking to kick-start a coaching career. (For more on Holum, see page 130.) Dianne became a friend, mentor, big-sister-type protector, and indispensable source of knowledge. She added to the Heidens' routine weight lifting, more running, and specially designed exercises aimed at helping a skater's crouched position. Eric's legs became so big that he had to buy size 38 pants even though he had a 32-inch waist.

By the time Eric was seventeen and Beth sixteen, they were already members of Team USA for the 1976 Games in Innsbruck, Austria. While they didn't make it to the podium in 1976, each gave a hint of what was to come four years later. Eric finished seventh in the 1,500 and nineteenth in the 5,000, and Beth was eleventh in the 3,000.

Four years later, leading up to the 1980 Winter Games, the siblings were on a major roll. Beth won four gold medals and the all-around title at the 1979 World Championships. Eric was a three-peat winner on the men's side of the same championships—becoming the first American to win the title in 1977 and then repeating the feat in 1978 and 1979. Both were looked upon as major medal contenders at the 1980 Games, held in Lake Placid, New York, a small town with big Olympic problems. As Lake Placid prepared for the Games, traffic jams were out of control, especially after a bus system broke down. People were stranded in the cold waiting for transportation to and from venues. Left without a ride after the opening ceremonies, Heiden and two figure skaters flagged down a passing bus only to be told the van was reserved for the Lake Placid Olympic Organizing Committee. Many good things were about to happen in Lake Placid for Team USA, but the execution of these Games from a logistical standpoint was not one of them. Heiden shook it all off for a mind-boggling showing that remains one of sport's all-time great performances.

Consider the enormity of it: Heiden took first place in every speed-skating event offered, from the shortest distance (the 500-meter sprint) to the longest (the grueling 10,000 meters). He broke five Olympic records and one world record in the process and became the first athlete in Summer or Winter Games to bring home five individual gold medals. Heiden won more golds in one Olympics than the entire US *team* had done in any Winter Games since 1932. His accomplishments have never been repeated—and they never will be, because athletes today specialize in either the shorter or longer distance events.

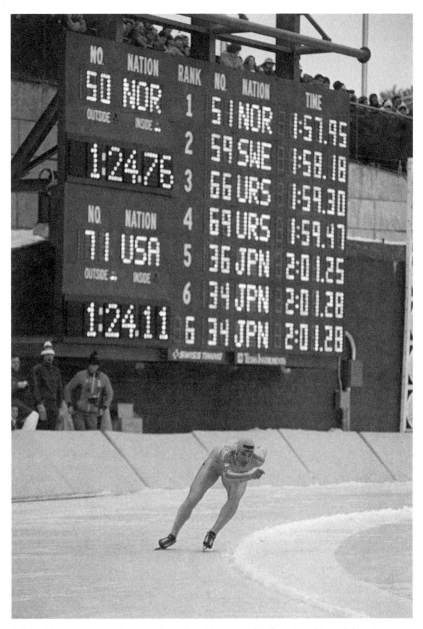

Eric Heiden races past the scoreboard on his way to his fourth gold medal in the 1,500 meters in Lake Placid, New York, February 21, 1980. He went to see his friends Mark Johnson and Bob Suter compete in the Miracle on Ice hockey game the next night.
AP PHOTO

"What Heiden is doing is comparable to a guy winning everything from the 400 meters to the 10,000 meters in track," marveled US marathon runner Bill Rodgers. "My God! It is doing the impossible!"

The coach of the Norwegian speedskating team summed up the wishes of all of Heiden's rivals when he said: "We just hope he retires."

Heiden was the only one who was unimpressed. He began calling the media blitz around him "the Big Whoopee" and admitted it was all "kind of a drag," adding, "I liked it better when I was a nobody." He told people he was happy the US hockey team's "Miracle on Ice" victory over Russia in that same Olympics upstaged him, as it saved him a lot of media hassles. In fact, Heiden was in the stands to watch the US beat Russia. He had already won four of five medals and took a night off to see friends Mark Johnson and Bob Suter, fellow Madisonians, compete for a spot in the finals. After the game, Eric was so excited that he had a hard time falling asleep.

The next morning he woke up an hour and a half late and hurried to the track with a few pieces of bread in his hands for breakfast. Despite this less-than-nutritious meal, Heiden shattered the world record in his most arduous event, the 10,000, besting the world mark by more than six seconds. Immediately after destroying the rest of the planet on ice, he told the *Washington Post* on February 23, 1980: "[The five golds] will probably sit where the rest of them are—in my mom's dresser, collecting dust. Gold, silver and bronze isn't special. It's giving 100 percent and knowing you've

MILWAUKEE-TRAINED SPEEDSKATERS

"It must be the cheese," NBC broadcaster Bob Costas joked, speculating on why so many speedskaters have come from Wisconsin.

Nearly every Olympic speedskater has spent time in Milwaukee, whether for a few days for competition or for a lifetime of training, because of the city's exceptional training facilities and coaching talent. Those who have spent a significant amount of time in Wisconsin are listed below.

Skater	Discipline	Olympics	Gold	Silver	Bronze
Wayne LeBombard	long track	1964, 1968			
Dianne Holum	long track	1968, 1972	1	2	1
Connie Carpenter	long track	1972			
Anne Henning	long track	1972	1		1
Kay Lunda	long track	1972			
Sheila Young	long track	1972, 1976	1	1	1
Leah Poulos	long track	1972, 1976, 1980		3	
Peggy Crowe	long track	1976			
Lori Monk	long track	1976			
Cindy Seikkula	long track	1976			
Beth Heiden	long track	1976, 1980			1
Eric Heiden	long track	1976, 1980	5		
Kim Kostron	long track	1976, 1980			
Peter Mueller	long track	1976, 1980	1		
Dan Immerfall	long track	1976, 1980, 1984			1
Michael Woods	long track	1976, 1980, 1984			
Nancy Swider-Peltz	long track	1976, 1980, 1984, 1988			
Sarah Docter	long track	1980			
Thomas Plant	long track	1980			
Michael Plant	long track	1980			
Kent Thometz	long track	1980			
Erik Henriksen	long track	1980, 1984, 1988			
Mary Docter	long track	1980, 1984, 1988, 1992			
Mark Huck	long track	1984			
Connie Paraskevin	long track	1984			
Lydia Stephans	long track	1984			
Jane Goldman	long track	1984, 1988			
Nick Thometz	long track	1984, 1988, 1992			
Bonnie Blair	long track	1984, 1988, 1992, 1994	5		1

Skater	Discipline	Olympics	Gold	Silver	Bronze
Dan Jansen	long track	1984, 1988, 1992, 1994	1		
Becky Mane Sanfelippo	long track	1988			
Mark Greenwald	long track	1988, 1992			
Jeff Klaiber	long track	1988, 1992			
Marty Pierce	long track	1988, 1992			
David Cruikshank	long track	1988, 1992, 1994, 1998			
Eric Flaim	long track/ short track	1988, 1992, 1994, 1998		2	
Darcie Dohnal	short track	1992		1	
David Besteman	long track	1992, 1994			
Michelle Kline	long track	1992, 1994			
Nathaniel Mills	long track	1992, 1994			
Brian Wanek	long track	1992, 1994			
Angela Zuckerman	long track	1992, 1994			
Chantal Bailey	long track	1994			
Christine Scheels	long track	1994			
Tony Goskowicz	short track	1994, 1998			
David Tamburrino	long track	1994, 1998			
KC Boutiette	long track	1994, 1998, 2002, 2006			
Christine Witty	long track	1994, 1998, 2002, 2006	1	1	1
Cory Carpenter	long track	1998			
Moira D'Andrea	long track	1998			
Kirstin Holum	long track	1998			
Julie Goskowicz	short track	1998, 2002			
Becky Sundstrom	long track	1998, 2002			
Jondon Trevena	long track	1998, 2002			
Marc Pelchat	long track	1998, 2002			

Skater	Discipline	Olympics	Gold	Silver	Bronze
Casey FitzRandolph	long track	1998, 2002, 2006	1		
Derek Parra	long track	1998, 2002, 2006	1	1	
Amy Sannes	long track	1998, 2002, 2006			
Catherine Raney-Norman	long track	1998, 2002, 2006, 2010			
Jennifer Rodriguez	long track	1998, 2002, 2006, 2010			2
Kip Carpenter	long track	2002, 2006			1
Joey Cheek	long track	2002, 2006	1	1	1
Elli Ochowicz	long track	2002, 2006, 2010			
Nick Pearson	long track	2002, 2010			
Margaret Crowley	long track	2006			
Charles Leveille	long track/ short track	2006			
Shani Davis	long track	2006, 2010, 2014	2	2	
Tucker Fredricks	long track	2006, 2010, 2014			
Maria Lamb	long track	2006, 2010, 2014			
Ryan Bedford	long track/ short track	2010			
Trevor Marsicano	long track	2010		1	
Nancy Swider-Peltz Jr.	long track	2010			
Alyson Dudek	short track	2010, 2014			1
Alyson Dudek	long track	2010, 2014		1	
Jonathan Kuck	long track	2010, 2014		1	
Jilleanne Rookard	long track	2010, 2014			
Mitchell Whitmore	long track	2010, 2014			
Emery Lehman	long track	2014			
Jessica Smith	short track	2014			
Sugar Todd	long track	2014			
TOTAL			21	17	12
			Gold	Silver	Bronze

done the best you can." He had thought he could realistically win one or two medals, not five, and certainly not all gold.

Eric wasn't the only talented Heiden. Beth might have done just as well at the Olympics that year if not for a lingering ankle injury. She fought through it, competing in four events but winning a medal in only one of them—a bronze in her best event, the 3,000 meters. Still, Eric and Beth accounted for half of the medals won by Team USA in speedskating in 1980.

There is little doubt that Eric Heiden could have returned to the Olympics four years later and added to his medal collection. He was young, in prime shape, and the terror of the skating world. But he had other plans. "I don't like to see athletes hanging onto their past," he stated. "You've got to move on."

Eric Heiden retired from skating after 1980 and turned down all but three offers to be involved in TV shows or films. The few commercials he did were for sportswear, toothpaste, and bicycles. He tried cycling and, to the surprise of no one, became an instant star, qualifying to be an alternate on the 1980 Summer Olympic cycling team; the United States boycotted

THE 1980 BOYCOTT

Eric Heiden did not approve of President Jimmy Carter's plan to boycott the 1980 Summer Olympics due to Soviet troops invading Afghanistan. At a White House reception on February 25, 1980, Heiden told reporters, "I hope we don't boycott. The winter athletes in general just don't feel that a boycott is the right thing."

His words meant little in the end. Carter ordered the United States to withhold all athletes from the 1980 Games in Moscow and threatened to revoke the passport of any US athlete found traveling to the USSR. It was a harsh approach, especially when compared to that of allies such as Great Britain and Australia, who allowed their athletes to choose. Sixty-seven nations eventually followed Carter's lead and pulled out, leaving just eighty competing, the lowest number since 1956.

Eric Heiden and the rest of the 1980 Olympians returned to a huge welcome-home ceremony at Camp Randall Stadium and appeared on the cover of the *Wisconsin State Journal*. WISCONSIN STATE JOURNAL ARCHIVE

the Moscow Games, and he never got the chance. Heiden won a professional cycling championship in 1985 and rode in the 1986 Tour de France. But his true passion lay elsewhere.

"Ever since I was a little kid, I wanted to be a doctor. You can only use that athletic talent when you're young," he said. In 1991, Eric Heiden graduated from Stanford Medical School at the age of thirty-three and followed in his dad's footsteps to become an orthopedic surgeon. He specialized in sports medicine and was the team orthopedist for US Speedskating in several Olympics. He also occasionally lent his speedskating knowledge to analyzing the sport on television.

Beth Heiden's athletic career was just getting started after her Olympic experience. She won a US cycling championship and became the first women's NCAA cross-country skiing champion at the University of Vermont. She holds an undergraduate degree in math and a master's of science in civil engineering. She and her husband, Russell Reid, a former college wrestler, have three children. In 2013 their daughter, Joanne Reid, came full circle for her mother, winning an NCAA freestyle cross-country skiing title for the University of Colorado.

Eric Heiden belongs to the National Speedskating Hall of Fame, the US Olympic Hall of Fame, the Wisconsin Athletic Hall of Fame, and the US Bicycling Hall of Fame. He and his wife, fellow orthopedic surgeon Karen Drews, settled in Utah and have two children. Eric co-wrote the book *Faster, Better, Stronger: Two Doctors Who Train World-Class Athletes Reveal the Tricks of the Trade for the Rest of Us*.

Looking back, Eric can't quite believe what he accomplished as a twenty-one-year-old in 1980. "I still wonder sometimes how I did it—I really do," Heiden told a newspaper in 2010. "Being in medicine and understanding physiology, it's rare for someone to compete at all those distances. But my coach [Dianne Holum] summed it up: I was a good 1,000-meter skater who had the ability to skate at 10,000. It was unusual to have that combination."

Today ice skaters in the Madison suburb of Shorewood Hills can take a break in the Heiden Haus, a warming house that Eric and Beth created to nurture and encourage future generations.

CHAPTER 11

MARK JOHNSON AND BOB SUTER

Hockey, 1980

"**D**o you believe in miracles? . . . *Yes!*"
Al Michaels's call of the game still sends shivers down many a spine. Ask anyone to name the greatest moment in sports history, and it's a good bet they'll say the 1980 Miracle on Ice in Lake Placid.

Mark Johnson and Bob Suter were both twenty-two-year-olds out of the University of Wisconsin that magical winter. They were smaller guys—Suter five foot nine and Johnson five foot ten—but they were spark plugs. Johnson was the top hockey forward in the country and Suter a hard-nosed defenseman who still holds the UW record for penalties (177) and penalty minutes (377). Both were raised in Madison and started off playing on outdoor rinks right in the heart of neighborhoods often surrounded by industrial buildings. "You hoped that the wind was blowing in the direction of the paper mill because the odor was just unbearable," Johnson recalled in 2015 for the *New York Daily News*. "No referees, no parents, just a sheet of ice, the stars."

Speedskater Eric Heiden, who occasionally joined in the neighborhood skating, told the *Daily News* about Johnson, "I remember the guy was just a super gifted hockey player. We all kind of looked up to him, jealous of the skills that he had, even as a young kid."

Suter attended Madison East High School, where he won a state tournament in 1975, and Johnson went to James Madison Memorial. When Mark was a senior at Memorial, his father, Bob, coached at the University of Wisconsin and steered the 1976 Olympic team. At first Bob Johnson added Mark to the pre-Olympics roster, and the teenager might have been good enough to make the final squad, but father cut son over Sunday dinner for two reasons: the pressure would have been too great on a high school kid, and Bob didn't want anyone to think he was giving his own offspring preferential treatment. Instead of playing in the 1976 Olympics, Mark remembers the family home becoming the headquarters for Team USA's gear. "If something got delivered, sweatsuits, equipment, it went right into our garage," he told the *Daily News*.

Bob Johnson's team finished fifth at those Games in Innsbruck, Austria, while watching the Soviet Union take a whopping fourth consecutive gold medal. That's how powerful the Soviets were. The United States had taken gold in 1960, but that was a generation earlier, and the Soviet Union had become a fully entrenched hockey behemoth since then. By 1980 the USSR would have 1,202 Olympic-size speedskating rinks; the United States had two.

In 1977 Mark Johnson led Wisconsin to a national title as a freshman and became the first Badger to earn the Western Collegiate Hockey Association Rookie of the Year award. He had a highly decorated career at the UW, becoming the school's all-time leading scorer with 256 points, including a school-record 125 goals, in just three seasons.

Johnson and Suter were selected for the US Olympic team by new coach Herb Brooks, who had just guided the University of Minnesota to a national championship, the third under his tutelage. Brooks's motivation was personal: as a player he had been the last man cut from that 1960 team that went on to win America's first and only hockey gold. Now, he had a chance to compete and win a medal in a different way.

Brooks decided to stick to what he knew and select college and young players over experienced veterans. He chose them from around the country—mainly Minnesota and Boston University, but Wisconsin as well. Brooks created a three-hundred-question psychological exam to aid in his selection of players. When one player refused to take it, Brooks said, "Okay, fine, you just took it. You told me everything I need to know."

"How'd I do?" asked the player.

"You flunked."

The player took the test the next day.

There was an interesting dynamic at work for Mark Johnson. His father, Bob, and Brooks were bitter rivals from neighboring states, and Mark wondered if Brooks might cut him for that reason. But Brooks knew talent when he saw it, and he told Johnson during their six-month warm-up to the Olympics that he was counting on him to be a leader as well as a player. It was only then that Johnson realized he had made the team.

Known for his "Herb-isms," Brooks was a master of motivating with words. Some of his sayings included: "The name on the front is a hell of a lot more important than the one on the back," "Look the tiger in his eye, then spit in it," and "Hard work beats talent when talent doesn't work hard." He wanted his players to emulate international hockey, including the wide-open passing style called "the weave." Brooks pushed the team in a mentally and physically exhausting training program so that they would not be outskated or tired in the third period. Wind sprints up and down the ice to the point of near collapse became known as "Herbies," and the players did them often, even long after a game one night when everyone else had gone home and the maintenance crew had turned off the lights. The US played a grueling 61 games in a pre-Olympic schedule against teams ranging from college to foreign and professional. They came out of it with a 42-16-3 record and the ability to skate long stretches against anybody.

His players were well aware of the talent they would be up against in the 1980 Winter Games in Lake Placid. Known as the Big Red Machine, the Soviet Union was a monster, some of their players a full ten years older than the US players. Some considered it the best hockey team ever assembled. Since their loss in the 1960 Olympics, the Soviets had been sequestering their athletes, shielding them from the public eye and creating a veil of secrecy around them. The players seemed almost robotic, showing little emotion and barely celebrating after scoring goals.

No one expected much out of Team USA; the ragtag college kids weren't even considered long shots for the National Hockey League in their own country. The Americans had to scrounge around for sponsor money just to pay for equipment, food, and housing. Along with rising stars Johnson and Suter, the US team boasted a line nicknamed "the Coneheads" after the *Saturday Night Live* sketch. The threesome—Mark Pavelich, John Harrington, and William "Buzz" Schneider—all came from Minnesota's

Iron Range and played a unique style all their own. Team captain Mike Eruzione said he once tried to play on their line and had no idea what they were doing. As for Suter, his teammates called him "Woody" for his resiliency, after the wood duck, which has a way of popping up in any type of water conditions. Eruzione also called him "Bam Bam" after the Flintstones character because he was a master of banging people around.

A few weeks before the Olympics, the US and USSR met for an exhibition at New York's Madison Square Garden. At the opening faceoff, Mark Johnson and a teammate exchanged a look that silently conveyed the same thought: "What the hell are we doing here?" Actually, Johnson may have been less intimidated than anyone else on the US team thanks to a hockey game his father had created. Years earlier, Bob Johnson had red jerseys sewn up with the names of Russian players on the backs. He would gather a group of local players together to play what he called "the Russian game." Years of seeing last names like Mikhailov on jerseys took away some of the intimidation factor for Mark.

Still, the Soviets made a statement, crushing the United States 10–3 in the exhibition. It was men against boys, the Soviets toying with the youngsters. Afterward, Brooks decided it was time to get real with his team. Forget the gold medal. Clearly that would be the Soviet Union's for a fifth consecutive time. But maybe they could bring home silver. Yet even that seemed a pipe dream. The US was the most inexperienced team in the Olympics and was seeded seventh out of twelve teams in Lake Placid. The Soviets did not think America would be a serious threat for a medal, and neither did sportswriters. Dave Anderson of the *New York Times* wrote, "Unless the ice melts, or unless the United States team or another team performs a miracle, as did the American squad in 1960, the Russians are expected to easily win the Olympic gold medal for the sixth time in the last seven tournaments."

As the 1980 Games drew near, the American public was hungry for good news. Households were fretting about inflation. Dozens of Americans were being held hostage in Iran. The Cold War was heating up following the Soviet invasion of Afghanistan, leaving many to wonder if the United States would boycott the upcoming Summer Games in Moscow. The country was still recovering from Vietnam and Watergate. Some said

You didn't mess with Bob Suter. The Madison native, nicknamed "Woody" for his resiliency and "Bam Bam" for his hard hits, set the UW record for penalties. COURTESY OF THE UW–MADISON ARCHIVES, #11068-R

Mark Johnson feared he might be cut from Team USA, but he went on to be the top goal scorer at the 1980 Games in Lake Placid. COURTESY OF THE UW–MADISON ARCHIVES, #S05689

American self-esteem was at an all-time low. No one could have thought that this collection of young hockey players would provide the country a much-needed jolt of excitement and patriotism.

The IOC instituted a new hockey format in 1980, dividing teams into two round-robin pools called red and blue for the preliminary round. The United States was in the blue pool with Sweden, Czechoslovakia, Norway, Romania, and West Germany. Czechoslovakia and Sweden were favored. Only the top two teams from each pool would advance to the medal round, meaning there was very little margin for error.

Competition would mainly take place in the Olympic Center. Team USA kicked things off on February 12 against the Swedes. The arena was only half full; most of the four thousand in attendance likely thought they would see Sweden dominate, and indeed, the Swedes took a 1–0 lead at 11:04 of the first period. In the second period, the US delivered the first of many late heroics. With just 28 seconds left, Dave Silk scored to tie it up, with an assist to both Johnson and Mike Ramsey. It stayed 1–1 until the third. Things did not look good when Sweden pushed ahead again on a goal that made it 2–1 at the 4:45 mark. In the final minute of the game the score remained the same. Brooks decided to pull his goalie, Jim Craig, and the extra man did the trick. Bill Baker scored with just 27 seconds on the clock to give the US a surprising 2–2 tie. They hadn't beaten the Swedes since 1960.

The next game really got them going. Knotted with highly touted Czechoslovakia 2–2 after the first period, the US suddenly poured it on. Perhaps a late skirmish added to the fuel: Johnson was checked hard by a Czech player, and Brooks started screaming at the Czech, threatening to jam a hockey stick down his throat. The US went on to a 7–3 win, utilizing seven different goal scorers, that gave the young squad a ton of confidence.

They went on to crush Norway 5–1 and Romania 7–2 before facing West Germany in the final game of the pool. This was the team that had knocked the US out of a bronze medal and eventually into fifth place in the last Olympics, and the US was thinking payback. But the tough West Germans

MILWAUKEE ADMIRALS IN THE OLYMPICS

William "Buzz" Schneider was a teammate of Mark Johnson and Bob Suter on the Miracle on Ice team in 1980. Ken Berry and Bob Dupuis were competitors on Team Canada. All three also played on the Milwaukee Admirals minor league hockey club. The Admirals have sent more than thirty Olympians to the international stage, playing for the United States and many of their own countries. The following is a complete list through the 2014 Winter Games.

Player	Olympics	Country
Stu Irving	1972	USA
William "Buzz" Schneider	1976/1980	USA
Ken Berry	1980/1988	Canada
Bob Dupuis	1980	Canada
Robin Bartel	1984	Canada
Paul Guay	1984	USA
Bob Mason	1984	USA

Player	Olympics	Country
Ken Yaremchuk	1988	Canada
Claude Vilgrain	1988	Canada
Jim Johannson	1988/1992	USA
Guy Dupuis	1988	France
Mikhail Shtalenkov	1992/1998	USSR
Fabian Joseph	1992/1994	Canada
Adrien Plavsic	1992	Canada
Brad Werenka	1994	Canada
Corey Hirsch	1994	Canada
Brett Hauer	1994	USA
Ville Peltonen	1994/1998/2006/2010	Finland
Kimmo Timonen	1998/2002/2006/2010/2014	Finland
Andreas Johansson	1998	Sweden
Aleksandr Galchenyuk	1998	Belarus
Tom Searle	1998/2002	Austria
Richard Lintner	2002	Slovakia
Peter Smrek	2002	Slovakia
Oliver Setzinger	2002/2014	Austria
Janne Niskula	2010	Finland
Ryan Suter	2010/2014	USA
Shea Weber	2010/2014	Canada
Patric Hornqvist	2010	Sweden
Tomas Vokoun	2006/2010	Czech Republic
Martin Erat	2006/2010/2014	Czech Republic
Aleksandr Radulov	2010/2014	Russia
Dan Hamhuis	2014	Canada
Antti Pihlstrom	2014	Finland
Roman Josi	2014	Switzerland
Simon Moser	2014	Switzerland
Peter Olvecky	2014	Slovakia

led 2–0 in the first period. It took everything the US had to rally back. Somehow they pulled out a 4–2 win to finish 4–0–1 in pool play and advance to the medal round. Johnson had contributed two goals and five assists by this point. Suter, known for his defensive toughness, spent some time in the penalty box. The Coneheads and the rest of the team also did their part to get them this far.

The US was feeling good coming out of pool play, but one glance at the standings provided a dose of reality. The Soviet Union had won all of their pool games by a combined score of 51–11, including 16–0 over Japan and 17–4 against the Netherlands. They had even pounced on traditional hockey power Canada, 6–4. The Canadians failed to even make the medal round.

For the semifinals, slated to start on February 22, there were only four teams left: the Soviet Union, the United States, Finland, and Czechoslovakia. It would be the upstart US versus the battled-tested Soviets in one semi, Finland versus Czechoslovakia in the other. At the same time, political tensions were running high, with President Jimmy Carter slamming the Soviet Union for the invasion of Afghanistan and calling the country a threat to global peace. The stage was set for a showdown that had implications far beyond hockey. Telegrams poured in supporting the players, including one that said, "Beat those Commie bastards."

The fact that this was playing out on home ice made crowd support for Team USA soar. Some players later said they felt the hair on the backs of their necks stand up as they walked into the Olympic arena to see the oversized US flags waving and the crowd dressed in patriotic hats and shirts, screaming U-S-A. The world's best goaltender, Vladislav Tretiak, was in net for his country. If the US was going to win, they would have to penetrate the impenetrable. Brooks, ever the master at getting inside the minds of young hockey players, wanted to break the image of these guys as superheroes. He pointed out to the team that one Russian player, Boris Mikhailov, resembled Stan Laurel of old-time comic duo Laurel and Hardy. "You can beat Stan Laurel, can't you?" Brooks asked.

Then he sat them down for a pep talk, telling them, "You were born to be a player. You were meant to be here. This moment is yours."

It was a tight game the whole way.

"When you are an underdog, all you are looking to do is keep the game close so you will have a chance to win it in the end," Johnson said later. That was their focus—just keep it within reach.

The Soviets jumped out to a 2–1 lead in the first period, but Johnson brought the US back. With just one second to go he split two defenders to drive to the net for a rebound goal and made it 2–2. That goal completely changed the momentum of the game. When they came back from the break for period two, the Soviet coach, Victor Tikhanov, had benched his all-star goalie for backup Vladimir Myshkin, much to the surprise of the Americans. Perhaps the youngsters were scaring them after all. But the Big Red Machine did not back down. The Soviets scored the only goal of the second period, regaining the edge at 3–2. Players in those distinctive red and white uniforms sent a flurry of pucks Jim Craig's way, and the Soviets outshot Team USA 30–10 after two periods.

Now there were only 20 minutes left for America to tie it up, or it would be a loss and no chance for the gold medal. Oddly, although they trailed, US players had gained some confidence from the fact that, despite having been badly outshot, they were down by only one goal. The general feeling was that the score could easily have been 5–2, 6–2, or 7–2 instead of 3–2.

Seven minutes in, the Soviet Union committed a penalty and the US was on a power play. Once again, Johnson was the hero. The Madisonian scored his second goal on a somewhat broken play for the equalizer. The puck got away from a Soviet defender, and Johnson snagged it, scoring from just a few feet out. Brooks pumped his arms in the air, fans went bananas in the stands, and the players swarmed Johnson in the corner of the ice, slapping his back and helmet. The noise in the arena was deafening. There was a buzz now, a feeling that anything could happen, and the players were as juiced as they had ever been in their lives. Brooks had been keeping his skaters on short shifts to maintain fresh legs, and less than two minutes later team captain Mike Eruzione bounded onto the ice with the energy of a puppy. Mark Pavelich fired a perfect pass toward Eruzione at the top of the circle, and Eruzione wound up for a wrist shot that went through a screen, past Myshkin, and in. It would become known as "the shot heard round the world."

4–3, USA on top.

But there were still ten minutes on the clock. The Soviets went into a bit of a panic and started firing like crazy on Craig. One shot hit the pipe; another was smothered by a defenseman. In hockey they say you "stand on your head" if you make some great saves, and that's exactly what Craig did. Time seemed to move at a glacial pace as Team USA fought off shot after shot. Then, at last, they were into the final minute. The crowd was in an absolute fervor. The players could barely feel the skates on their feet.

Al Michaels helped viewers watch the clock:

"Twenty-eight seconds . . . the crowd going insane . . . eleven seconds . . . you've got ten seconds, the countdown going on right now, Morrow up to Silk, five seconds left in the game. Do you believe in miracles? *Yes!*"

Simultaneously, on the radio, the call went like this: "Ten seconds to play . . . if they can clear it here . . . four, three, two, one—it is over! The US has beaten Russia!"

The crowd drowned out everything else at that point, and for TV viewers Michaels wisely let the pictures tell the story. The bench immediately emptied of US players, red, white, and blue uniforms swarming like ants, arms raised and heads thrown back, all surging toward Craig to celebrate. They mobbed him and each other to the left of the net, hugs and tears flowing freely, while the Soviets, leaning on their sticks, looked on in stunned silence, their faces masks. Coach Brooks slapped a few hands, but he was also quick to remind everybody that these were the semifinals. The team still had another game to play.

Brooks may have felt he had to show restraint, but around the country it was a different story. Although the game was not televised live (it was taped to be shown that evening), many were listening on the radio, and many more tuned in later to watch the televised version. It became a defining moment, an "I remember where I was when . . ." in American history. People sobbed with pent-up emotion. Jimmy Carter later told the team that it was one of his proudest moments as president.

On the ice in Lake Placid, Brooks would have none of it. Champagne was sent to the locker room, but no one touched it. Brooks screamed at the team not to get too cocky and even told them that they had just gotten lucky. He wanted his guys to feel some fire in their bellies again before the gold medal match with Finland, winner of the other semi, but he couldn't tell them that. He just had to be hard.

Yet there was no denying the swell of patriotism, even for the players. Various accounts say they sang "God Bless America" either in the locker room or on the bus ride back to the media center, one guy starting it and the others joining in, forgetting the words, singing, "From the mountains to the valleys . . . na-na-na-na-na-na-na" but swaying with emotion nonetheless. Brooks is said to have locked himself in the bathroom to vent his emotions in private. "Finally I snuck out in the hall," he recalled, "and the state troopers were all standing there crying."

The next day at practice, Brooks was back to showing no mercy—putting the group through an exhausting workout and shouting that he was not their friend and they had yet to prove anything. The whole country may have been celebrating—the *Boston Globe* ran a humongous front-page headline reading "WE WON!"—but Brooks knew they hadn't won a thing except the minds and hearts of fellow Americans. In fact, because of the round-robin structure, the US would finish in third place if they lost to Finland in the final, set to take place on Sunday, February 24.

This time the game would be shown live on TV, albeit on a Sunday morning at 10 A.M. central time. But the entire nation had hockey fever and had gotten caught up in the "Little Engine That Could" story that was USA hockey that year. Back in Madison, hardly anyone left the house; grocery stores and streets were completely empty.

By the second period, Team USA was down 1–0 and once again needed a comeback. Steve Christoff fired a wrist shot that evened the score, but Finland also scored, going into the third period up 2–1. During the intermission Brooks took one last motivational tool out of his box, telling the young players that if they let this moment slip away, they would regret it for the rest of their lives and take it to their graves. Inspired, the US scored less than three minutes into the period, a goal from Phil Verchota. Now the score was tied again, but the Americans were on fire. Just three minutes later, Mark Johnson passed to Rob McClanahan for the go-ahead goal at 3–2.

The US team mobs goalie Jim Craig immediately after the clock hit zero in the 4–3 win against the Soviets. AP PHOTO

"I was working the corner, and I saw Robbie about six feet in front," Johnson said afterward. "I was lucky to get it to him."

Minutes after that, Johnson did even more, adding a shorthanded, backhanded insurance goal to up the score to 4–2.

Now it was up to the goalie Craig again, and he rose to the task, deflecting all shots in the final countdown as Michaels bellowed, "Nobody in their right mind would have believed this" with about a minute left; "Who were they a week and a half ago? We know them all now!" with 23 seconds on the clock; "It's bedlam in here!" with 6 seconds to go; and "This impossible dream has come true!" as the second hand struck zero. Once again the players swarmed Craig, who still wore his goalie's mask. Moments later, a fan jumped the glass and handed Craig a giant American flag, which he draped around his shoulders.

On the bench, Brooks shook hands with his assistants, both relief and joy on his face. In the press conference afterward, Brooks said simply, "I love this hockey team. All I can say is that the good Lord works in strange ways."

Mark Johnson added, "We can't believe what just happened. I don't know how to describe it. I'm just here in awe. It took all of us and we all did it together."

The streets of Lake Placid had become a makeshift pep rally, with people shoulder to shoulder outside the arena soaking it all up in a light snow, flags waving. Team USA had just won the gold medal, toppling one powerhouse after another. It was so big *Life* magazine would call it "the Sports Achievement of the Decade," and *Sports Illustrated* named the entire team Sportsmen of the Year for 1980. The Miracle on Ice is still considered by many the greatest upset in the history of sports.

"It was a sliver of the Cold War played out on a sheet of ice," noted ABC announcer Michaels. "Here you have a bunch of fresh-faced college kids taking on the big, bad Soviet bear."

"It was more than a hockey game, it was us against them, it was freedom versus Communism," Eruzione said many years later. And center Neal Broten said, "If we played that team ten times we would lose all ten games. On one night the stars were aligned or something."

After the national anthem played, team captain Eruzione was brought up to the podium alone, to accept a gold medal on behalf of the rest of the group. But Eruzione motioned for the others to join him, and they all crowded up on the top step, the winner's perch, together. Their hands reached in one mass toward the sky with fingers in the "number one" position. Mark Johnson, who led the team in Olympic scoring, was so good teammates had nicknamed him "Magic Johnson," after the basketball star. The next day the team was flown to the White House to meet President Carter, and on the bus ride from the airport they saw more stunning examples of patriotism and pride. People were lined up twenty deep for miles just to wave and cheer as they passed.

The USSR team's homecoming was markedly different. One Soviet player told BBC Radio that their journey home was torturous. Relations between the United States and the Soviet Union had disintegrated to the point that the Soviets couldn't fly direct, so they took buses to Canada and flew home from there. It was a long and pensive journey as the athletes wondered if they would be punished upon their return. "We figured we probably wouldn't be sent to Siberia labor camps, but on the other hand, nobody had any idea on how they'd greet us or what the loss would mean for our coaches," Alexei Kasatonov told the BBC. As it turned out, they simply had to answer the same question for the next four years until they won another gold: "Why did you lose?"

The members of Team USA had no such doubts about their standing in the hearts of their fellow Americans. And few places could compete with Wisconsin in terms of a warm welcome home. More than thirty thousand people packed Camp Randall in March 1980 to greet the contingent of fifteen Wisconsin Olympians, which along with hockey players Mark Johnson and Bob Suter included speedskaters Eric Heiden, Beth Heiden, Mary Docter, Sarah Docter, Dan Immerfall, Leah Mueller, Peter Mueller, Mike Plant, Tom Plant, and Mike Woods; ski jumper Reed Zuehlke; and speedskating coaches Dianne Holum and Peter Schotting.

Years later, Mark Johnson was on an NHL team with two Soviet players from that 1980 game. He asked one of them why their coach had pulled top goalie Tretiak after the first period right after Johnson's goal in the semifinal game. The response came in two words delivered in a thick accent: "Coach crazy."

Johnson played eleven seasons in the NHL, most notably with Pittsburgh and Minnesota, but then home beckoned. He returned to Madison, first as a high school coach and then as an assistant to the UW men's program and, starting in 2002, head women's hockey coach. He became the winningest coach in UW women's hockey history. Johnson returned to the Olympic stage in 2010, coaching the United States women's hockey team to a silver medal in Vancouver.

Mark's father, Bob Johnson, died of cancer in 1991. His famous saying, "It's a great day for hockey," still hangs on a sign in the UW's Kohl Center and at ice rinks around the state.

The glow of victory lasted for decades; indeed, it might never fade. Jim Craig was still receiving letters from fans at the rate of six hundred per year a full twelve years later. At the 2002 Winter Olympics in Salt Lake City, just five months after the tragedy of 9/11, the entire Miracle on Ice team was given the honor of lighting the opening flame at the Games. It was a deeply patriotic moment. As of the 2014 Winter Games, the United States has not won another gold in men's hockey.

Tragically, Herb Brooks was killed in a one-car accident in Minnesota in 2003, a loss felt deeply within the hockey community. At his funeral, players lined both sides of the walkway leading from the church to the waiting hearse and held hockey sticks in the air as a sign of respect and love as his casket passed. The team's journey to gold was chronicled in at least two movies, including a major Hollywood blockbuster, *Miracle*, immortalizing the team and providing a new generation insight into what happened in Lake Placid.

Bob Suter had a brief stint in professional hockey, playing for Minnesota's farm club, but he focused on the sporting goods store he opened in Madison, Gold Medal Sports, coached youth hockey, and raised a family. His brother, Gary, played hockey in two Olympics, winning silver in 2002. And Bob's son Ryan became a standout for the Nashville Predators and Minnesota Wild and played in the 2010 and 2014 Olympics, also taking home silver in 2010.

Bob Suter was the first player from the Miracle on Ice to pass away, dying in 2014 of a heart attack. But he left a huge legacy. "With respect to all of my teammates, I don't think anybody has done more for the game of hockey in terms of the youth level, high school level, the community level than Bobby Suter," Mike Eruzione stated on Team USA's website after Suter's death.

It's still hard to quantify the impact of those events of February 1980. The Miracle on Ice changed America, shifting the public's attention to something positive, something to be proud of. And it changed hockey as well. After those remarkable games, the NHL began drafting more Americans, believing that they could be as good as or better than international players. Perhaps most significant, watching replays of those final seconds against the Soviet Union still brings grownups to tears. How many things stand the test of time to do that?

CHAPTER 12

Dan Jansen

Speedskating, 1984, 1988, 1992, 1994

He became one of the most famous Olympians ever, but if you'd like to know how or why Dan Jansen got into speedskating, you have to look past the obvious: athletic genes (his dad, Harry, was a basketball player and so good at football that he once was asked to try out for the Los Angeles Rams), the family's proximity to a world-class ice rink (they lived in West Allis near the Wisconsin Olympic Oval, one of America's only outdoor speedskating ovals), or even the influence of his eight siblings, who always motivated him. The real reason is that Dan's parents, Harry and Geraldine, needed four-year-old Dan to be occupied.

As Dan explains it, "It was literally and honestly so they didn't have to get a babysitter for me. That was the truth. [My siblings] were already skating, and they said, 'Just take him along.'"

Little Dan followed behind his brothers and sisters—Mary, Janet, Jim, Diane, Dick, Joanne, Jane, and Mike—in everything they did, and he relished being part of a big family. "It was just fun," he remembered. "Always sports. About half my siblings were very athletic and half not as much. We always seemed to be out in the back playing basketball or baseball."

In winter, the Jansen kids skated, competing in indoor short track races at Wilson Park in Milwaukee and outdoor long track events at the Olympic Oval in West Allis. But Dan was not an instant success story. "I was decent, but I wasn't even the best in my age group in my club," he recalled. "We had one other kid that would beat me, but my brothers and

Dan, Mike, and Jane Jansen were always very close. This photo was taken at their West Allis home before a skating meet. COURTESY OF DAN JANSEN

sisters would always encourage me when I got down and say, 'One day you'll beat him.'"

At age eleven, Dan suffered his first major competition disappointment. He had a poor showing at the National Pack Style Longtrack Championships in Minnesota and then cried for the better part of the 300-mile ride home. "When we arrived home, my dad took me aside and said, 'Dan, there's more to life than skating around in circles.'"

It was the first in a long line of lessons about perspective handed down from Harry Jansen to his youngest son. But Dan's father would have to admit he loved the sport too. He became a volunteer speedskating timer and soaked up the family atmosphere that prevails around skating, so much so that athletes from surrounding states, such as Bonnie Blair, would often stay at the Jansens' home.

After his sophomore year at West Allis Central High School, Dan was torn between speedskating and football. The seasons conflicted, and he was forced to choose. It was a grueling decision for a young athlete. He was good at football and liked it, plus it was more popular than speedskating. But then something unfolded on his TV screen in the winter of 1980 that clinched his decision. "Honestly, I think it was because of Eric Heiden," he said many years later. "I was fourteen and saw him do what he did. I knew then that I wanted to go to the Olympics. I didn't have any medal dreams yet, but I thought the Olympics were everything at that point because of watching him—and not just watching, but [the idea of] literally being able to train right beside him [at the outdoor oval]."

The sporty Jansen family had always enjoyed watching the Olympics together, and Dan still recalls being seven years old and watching young phenom speedskater Anne Henning win two medals in the 1972 Winter Games in Japan. In 1976 Dan stayed glued to the television for the duration of both the Summer and Winter Games. He was fully devoted to speedskating after admiring Eric Heiden, and he never looked back.

In 1981 Dan made his inaugural Junior World Team at the age of sixteen and was sent to Davos, Switzerland, for his first international meet. He skated the 500, which would become his specialty. His winning time is etched in his memory, and he can recite it in an instant: 38.24.

"They announce on the [loudspeaker] that this is a junior world record," he recalled, "and I had no idea there even was a junior world record, so I started to have a clue that I could be pretty good. It was kind of motivating."

There was a drawback to being on the junior circuit, though. At that time, all juniors had to skate a variety of distances instead of focusing on one. Dan knew he was a sprinter, built to soar in the 500 and with the 1,000 as a second choice, but he was forced to compete in the 500, 1,500, 3,000, and 5,000 in every competition. His legs would be so tired by the end of these long events they felt like they could fall off. He couldn't wait to graduate from juniors.

He had fallen in love with speedskating on his own, never feeling pushed by Harry or Geraldine, never forced to skate or train when he didn't want to. He understood that he had to devote time and energy to the craft if he wanted to be good at it. Harry Jansen was a dedicated sports parent, though. A West Allis police officer who worked a variety of shifts, he still made time to sharpen the kids' skates no matter the hour or how long a day he had just endured. He would sit on the basement floor scraping away at pair after pair of skates while his children slumbered overhead. He and Geraldine also drove the kids all over the state for meets—Waupaca, Oconomowoc, Madison, and up to St. Paul, Minnesota, more often than one could keep track of. As Dan recalls it, they were the best kind of supportive: "They did everything for the kids."

Harry even became a leader for the US team, managing hotel bills and other details, which gave him the opportunity to travel to Europe with Dan, sometimes for six weeks at a stretch. This gave teenage Dan mixed emotions. "At certain times I'd be like, nobody else's dad is here! But by the end it was great. He fit right in and played cards with us, and I could tell he loved it so much being there." When Dan set his first world record in Davos, Switzerland, Harry was there. Dan looked across the track and saw his father give a bellow and throw his mittens up in the air in jubilation when Dan's time was posted. Sharing that experience with his father would become more important as time went on.

As his high school years drew to a close, Dan focused on the 1984 Games. The Olympic Trials were held in his old stomping ground, at the oval in West Allis. Dan felt extremely nervous with his whole family there to cheer him on. The dream he had set his sights on four years earlier as he watched Eric Heiden win gold was in the balance, but it could tilt either way.

Dan's brother, Mike, twenty months Dan's senior, competed in these same Olympic Trials, just missing a spot on Team USA. It would be the first of two Games, 1984 and 1988, where Mike came within a tenth of a second of making the roster. Dan won the trials in the 500 and also made it in the 1,000, but his heart was heavy. "That was hard for me when Mike didn't make it. To skate the Olympics with him would have been the best," he said.

Dan would be the only Jansen competing. The 1984 Winter Olympics were held in Sarajevo in what was then Yugoslavia, making them the first Winter Games in a Communist state. The brutal war that would engulf the city was still eight years away. It wasn't financially feasible for the whole gang of Jansens to fly to Yugoslavia, but Mike, Harry, and Geraldine were in the stands. Dan hadn't known Mike would be making the trip until he looked up into the bleachers a few days before his race and saw him there. He knew how much Mike wanted to be competing himself, and having him there as a fan meant so much to eighteen-year-old Dan.

He held his expectations for himself in check. He was just happy to be there and thought that a top-ten finish would be great. After all, this was his first Olympic experience. And Dan did well, finishing fourth in the 500 and sixteenth in the 1,000. He felt satisfied about his overall performance— that is, until he returned home to mountains of people saying "Oh, it's too bad you didn't win a medal." It would be a lesson for Dan in how medal-obsessed outsiders can be. They didn't realize or appreciate how good fourth place was for an inaugural Olympian. In fact, both the press and public painted the entire 1984 US team as a failure for not bringing home any medals. It was Dan's first real experience with the media, and it was hard not to take it personally.

But Dan knew this was only the start of his Olympic journey, if he could stay healthy and motivated. He kept competing and winning, and everything was running smoothly. In 1986 he was at the top of the World Cup rankings in both the 500 and 1,000. Then when he was twenty-one and training for the 1988 games in Calgary, Canada, he started feeling fatigued. He had to lie down after a 500-meter race. His power was zapped, and he couldn't figure out why. Finally he was diagnosed with mononucleosis, something he had apparently been walking around with for three months.

As he began to recover from the mono, the family received much more devastating news. While Dan was home to watch a race at the West Allis oval, his brother Jim told him that their sister Jane had leukemia. "Jim's my oldest brother and he's really straightforward," Dan explained. "He said, 'You usually die from leukemia.' I was floored." Dan had been training with his good friend Bonnie Blair that day, and she was at the house. "I went into my bedroom and cried on Bonnie's shoulder a little bit," Dan remembered.

Jane was only twenty-six years old, married, and had just given birth to her third daughter. The leukemia was discovered during a routine blood test when her platelets were low after the birth. The family was stunned. Doctors hoped that because she had no symptoms that they had caught it early, and Jane started chemotherapy right away. Soon it was obvious that she was not improving, and doctors decided a bone marrow transplant was the best course of action. Jane was sent to a leukemia-specialty hospital in Seattle, and the whole family was tested to see who might be a donor match. Dan and his sister Joanne were the only two, both perfect matches, but the family decided that Joanne would be the donor because Dan was coming off mono and was training for the Olympics. Dan was cleared to donate platelets, however, and he flew to Seattle numerous times, spending a week or more each visit as they drew blood from his arm and put it into Jane. The time spent with his sister made Dan feel like he was helping to improve her chances of life. Dan turned twenty-two that June—a relatively young age to be trying to save one's sister and facing issues of mortality. He felt his priorities shift and started to question how important the Olympics really were. From that time forward, Dan never felt that winning a medal was a life-or-death proposition.

Dan regained his own strength and breezed through the Olympic Trials again, getting set to travel to Calgary for the Games. The World Championships were held in Milwaukee a few weeks before the Olympics, and Dan skated brilliantly. He took his World Championship gold medal to show to Jane, who had been transferred to West Allis Memorial Hospital. She was thrilled for her brother. As Dan said good-bye to Jane that day, it never crossed his mind that it might be the last time he would visit her.

A few days later, Dan flew to Calgary, and his father joined him as a spectator. Dan was warming up a night or two before his signature race, the 500 meters, when he saw his dad standing at the side of the ice. When Dan skated over to him, his father said, "Son, I have to go, Mom wants me home. . . . Jane's not doing well." Dan replied, "Yeah, of course you have to go."

Dan had to compete in his second Olympics in less than twenty-four hours. He had been on top of the skating world, truly unbeatable, until that moment. Now he couldn't even keep his skates steady under his feet. At 6 A.M. on the day of the race, a knock came on the door of Dan's room in the Olympic Village. It was Valentine's Day, a day meant for love, but he answered to find a member of the American delegation telling him his mother was on the phone. "She told me Jane's blood pressure had really dropped overnight," he explained. "Jane was still with us, but they didn't think she would make it through the day. I had them put Jane on and I said a few words [Jane was unable to respond], and then I talked to my mom— what should I do? Should I skate? I didn't know. We knew Jane would have felt so bad if I didn't even go out there and give it a shot."

Dan returned to his room, reeling. He spent the next few hours thinking about Jane and wondering when he would get the call that said she was gone. Dan's brother Jim, who was also in Calgary, got a pass to enter the village and be there with him in those uncertain morning hours. About 10 A.M. the phone rang, bringing the sickening news that Jane had passed.

"Then it hits you again. You spent four hours knowing it would happen, but when it does it really takes it out of you," Dan said.

Later Dan sat in the hallway of the village, his head in his hands. Team USA Speedskating coaches called a meeting, and everybody would be dedicating their performances to Jane. Dan was in shock, rattled and grieving, yet he still thought he could—and should—skate. He convinced himself that he could perform, make his legs work, and keep his skates straight. His mother had encouraged him to compete, and he knew Jane would want him to. Then, according to Dan, a different thought jumped into his mind. "I remember thinking, what happens if I actually win? Will people think I don't care about her or this doesn't affect me at all? I had so many things in my head at once, the last of which were the thoughts that are normally in your head when you go to the starting line."

Looking back now, he can see that there was no way it would be a successful race. But at the time he was on automatic pilot, feeling as if he were controlling someone else's legs, putting them through the motions it took to skate in the Olympics.

It did not go well.

The first thing that happened was that Dan false-started. Skaters are allowed one false start before being disqualified. Dan and his lane partner returned to the starting line. The gun went off for the second time, and both took off. Dan was unsteady in the initial 100 meters, but it was his first step into turn number one that did him in. His skate slid out from under him, and he fell to the ice, sliding quickly into the padding surrounding the rink.

"I felt really numb, almost unfeeling. It certainly didn't feel like I had just lost the gold medal. Jane was the big picture that day, and this became like a side note. But the way it ended was not what I wanted or anyone wanted. When it did happen it was like, really? What more can possibly happen today?"

By now the news of Jane's death was widely known, and sports fans across the globe shared Dan's pain. Everyone could understand falling under such circumstances.

Dan and his family decided to hold off on the funeral until he was able to return to Wisconsin. There were three days before the 1,000. Each day the noose on his body loosened a tiny bit. His legs felt like they were his own, his timing felt right. Dan started the two-and-a-half-lap race with a terrific first 600 meters and had the fastest split in the group. He was leading after two laps, completely relaxed as he moved into the second-to-last inner turn, but with just a half lap to go, on the backstretch with one more turn and nothing but finish line and a medal in front of him, the unthinkable happened again. Dan's right skate did what skaters call "catching an outer." When you speedskate, you bring the skate down slightly on the outer edge of the blade, then push for stride and roll it toward the inner. But sometimes when a skater puts down the outer it just catches and instead of going the way you want it to, it moves you in the opposite direction and there is nothing you can do. You go down. Dan fell just 200 meters from the finish line, a rarity on a straightaway.

"It was the same kind of feeling. 'That did not just happen.' I was speechless. Then I really, really wanted to get home. Just take me out of here. I need to say goodbye [to Jane]," he remembered. But first he had to attend a torturous press conference filled with strangers and their sometimes unfeeling questions. A reporter raised his hand and called out: "Do you feel like you let Jane down?"

A Team USA publicist took over and gave the man a curt response. Dan made his way through the rest of the press conference and then rushed to a waiting plane that a Milwaukee company had provided. At one point on the flight to Milwaukee, Dan and Jim looked each other's way, and the realization of what had just transpired passed between them in one glance. "I will tell you the truth," Dan said, "we looked at each other and we kind of laughed. We were like, 'This was so bad it's unbelievable. What just happened these last four days?'"

Back home, the funeral had become a TV event. There was even a television camera in the church. Dan's first response was anger. He felt invaded and upset and kept wondering, can't they just let us have this moment? Dan did his best to ignore the camera and instead flipped through memories of his dear Jane, the baby of the five sisters. Jane, Mike, and Dan were the three youngest children of the clan and had spent their formative years together while the older siblings were grown and off to college. Jane was the last of the girls to still skate, and she and Dan had spent countless hours chasing each other around Wilson Park and the Olympic Oval. Jane was the least selfish person Dan had ever known. She was always worrying about other people, a natural caretaker. She was also a sensitive soul, and Dan recalled the normal sibling stuff—how he and Mike used to try to make her cry because she would easily do so.

"But she still loved us. We had a great, great relationship."

Now tears were flowing freely in the church, and Dan wondered again how the Olympics could possibly compare to his sister's death. "My parents always taught us perspective," he said later. "Always take wins and losses with the same amount of dignity. If you don't get perspective out of *this*, something is wrong with you."

Dan returned to Calgary after the funeral to watch his friend Bonnie Blair and others compete. Blair won her first gold, in the 500 meters, and added a bronze in the 1,000. Watching Bonnie climb to the top of the skating world was both exhilarating and, in a way, much needed. Dan said, "Bonnie's first gold medal race, her 500 in Calgary, remains my personal favorite Olympic moment of all time. It was just such a lift after so much bad the previous week."

Dan's time on the ice in Calgary was done, but he had become a symbol of just how human athletes really are. At the conclusion of the Games he was awarded the US Olympic Spirit Award for showing courage through tragedy.

Dan's world had been forever changed by Jane's death, but speedskating remained a constant. He knew he would try again for the 1992 Olympics in Albertville, France. He resumed "normal" life that summer of 1988, but he never allowed himself time to properly grieve. When fall came, he enrolled at the University of Calgary as a marketing major so he could study and skate. But being back at the site of the last Winter Games stirred up all kinds of memories and emotions. "That was a really hard time for me," he explained. "I don't know how I got through it. I went through a lot. . . . It was a period of my life that was one of the most difficult."

Dan's sister Joanne came to visit. Dan spoke with the team's sports psychologists. Both of those things helped. He slowly pulled through the dark days, always thinking of Jane, but it took most of the year. Meeting and marrying future wife Robin helped him a lot too. By 1992, four years after Jane's death, twenty-six-year-old Dan had finally found his way back to a good place mentally and was in top form physically. Dan and Germany's Uwe-Jens Mey swapped spots on the top of most podiums in the months leading up to the Olympics. Each set a new world record in the 500, Mey first and then Dan one week later. They were the two best sprinters in the world, and both should have easily medaled. That is why Dan's performance in the 1992 Olympics is something he still describes as bewildering.

The trouble began with a tactical decision that, in retrospect, might have been an error. Dan and his coach, Peter Mueller, decided to rest Dan, thinking the downtime would give him a huge boost come the Olympics. Team USA flew to Italy to train for two weeks before the Games, but Dan lightened up on the workouts. It didn't turn out the way they had hoped.

To cut costs, the French Olympic Committee held the speedskating events outside, at a venue that they planned to repurpose into a football field with a running track. The weather was poor, and several events were postponed in the hopes of better ice, which never came. Times were slower than at Calgary. (After Albertville, the International Olympic Committee would never again allow speedskating to be held outdoors.) Dan's first race, the 500, was held in rain and wind, which made for soft ice. Still, Dan skated well, with a time of 37.46, 0.01 below the rink record. He had been the first of the favorites to skate, and now he sat back to watch the others. In the next pair, a largely unknown Japanese skater named Junichi Inoue beat Jansen's time by .2 seconds, and that was just the start. Two more skaters surpassed that, including Dan's friend and rival, Germany's Uwe-Jens Mey, who took the gold, and another Japanese skater, Toshiyuki Kuroiwa, who wound up with silver. Inoue got the bronze.

For Jansen, there had been no mistake, no slip, not even a bad feeling about the way he had performed. That's why finishing fourth despite being one of the top two favorites was such a stunning turn of events.

"I felt so confident, and it was really a shocker. Finishing fourth is not terrible, but this time I should have gotten gold or silver, and I knew it. Still the most baffling of my Games for me in terms of performance. In '84 I was happy to be there. In '88 I had the issues. But '92 . . ."

Once again Dan's dream was over in under 40 seconds, less time than it takes most people to walk to the refrigerator and ponder what to eat. It's one of the cruelties of speedskating. You get one blisteringly fast chance, and that's it for four more years. Following the 500, Dan was completely derailed, and his 1,000 was not even a battle—he finished twenty-sixth.

"I checked out, I was gone," Dan explained. "I knew I didn't have the stamina for some reason; I was probably too flat from laying off too much. I'm not proud to say it, but I think after the 500 it was done for me. I just completely died the last lap, and that was it."

Dan had now been to three Olympics, favored to win in two of them, and he had no medals to show for it. For all of his accomplishments in World Cups (he won forty-six races) and other international events, he knew that people remember the Olympics. The entire thing left a pit in his stomach, yet he reminded himself of what was important in life: health and family. He realized that if he never won a medal, it would be okay. His sister's death was a constant reminder of what mattered and what was peripheral.

Dan likely would have competed again in 1996 if there had been a Games then, but it turned out he didn't have to wait that long. The International Olympic Committee voted to stagger the Summer and Winter Games, and the next Winter Games be would in 1994, just two years away, in Lillehammer, Norway. Dan would be twenty-eight when he headed to his fourth Olympics.

Dan and Robin soon learned they were expecting their first child, and it was Robin who suggested that naming the baby Jane would be a powerful and lasting way to honor Dan's sister. Yet Dan hesitated at first. "I always worried about what other people might think about it. Are they going to think I'm dragging this thing out? I finally realized this is one where you can't worry about what other people think. This is about honoring your sister."

In 1993 their little girl entered the world and was christened Jane Jansen. The next year Dan headed to Lillehammer for the 1994 Games, which he had already decided would be his last. His support group now included his wife, one-year-old daughter, parents, and several siblings and their spouses. Once again, Dan had been on an absolute tear heading into the Olympics. Nobody else had skated under 36 seconds in the 500 meters, and he had done it four times already, meaning the five fastest times in the world all belonged to him. He could have skated the 500 at 85 to 90 percent of his capabilities and still won a medal.

Race day was Valentine's Day, February 14—the anniversary of Jane's death. Dan had been well aware of that coincidence for a full year and didn't let it distract him, although the media talked about it. In fact, Dan felt great in warm-ups. The top skaters would skate early in the competition (this has since been changed to reverse order, so the best skaters go last), and Dan was in the second pair. There would be just one run for each skater. This meant one shot—one 36-second blast of adrenaline—to secure a medal. Even a tiny mistake would blow your chances. But Dan had a good, clean race going. He got to the last outer turn and thought to himself, "I can skate a 35 [seconds] here, I know that." Normally skaters accelerate in the second half of the turn, just after the apex. In his excitement, perhaps Dan tried to push it a bit too early. He gave it a strong nudge, too strong, and he knew immediately.

"As I did that, the ice actually broke away. It wasn't a slip like in '88 where my left skate just slipped. This time the ice actually chipped and broke. It was an instant of, *oh, shit*. I tried so hard to get it back right away, it was like a panic. The whole turn I just kept slipping. Where you gain all your momentum, I lost all my momentum."

His hand touched the ice, and although he didn't fall, he knew coming down the last 100 meters that it wasn't going to happen for him, again. An indescribable feeling washed over his body, the thought that maybe, for whatever reason, it just wasn't meant to be for Dan Jansen in the Olympics. He knew he was the best 500-meter sprinter in the world, and he had done everything he could: his attitude was good, he was skating well, he wasn't scared or nervous, he was confident. It just didn't happen. Looking back, he wonders if he was overconfident. But his immediate thought at the moment was that fate had a cruel Olympic plan for him. He didn't even want to skate his next race, the 1,000, a few days later. He was fed up. Plus, he explained, "I was uncomfortable because I knew my friends, my competitors, felt sorry for me and I just didn't want that. It was an awkward feeling."

It took about an hour of fuming before Dan was able to shake the idea of blowing off the 1,000. He was not going to do that. As one of the top five or six guys in that field, he wasn't an outright favorite, but he knew he had a chance. Three days later came the 1,000, his last Olympic race. This was it: his final opportunity to medal, to prove something to himself and everybody else.

Yet as he got on the ice for warm-ups, he didn't feel good. His timing was off, and he did some quick brainstorming as to what to do about it. The solution came in the form of a stationary bike in the locker room. Dan reasoned that in other international races outside of the Olympics, the 500 and 1,000 were run back-to-back with no days in between. His body was used to the feeling of skating a 500 right before a 1,000, and now his body was not properly warmed up. He jumped on the exercise bike to try to simulate a 500. He hammered away on the bike, exerting his body to the point that he would have in a sprint race.

With ten minutes to go before the 1,000, he got ready to move to the starting line. So many things were flooding his mind: his new baby, his family. He remembered what a great night the Jansens had had at dinner the evening before. In fact, Dan had told them all, "Whatever you do, have a blast tomorrow because that's what I'm going to do. That's all I can do at this point." Also swimming through his brain was a blunt comment a reporter had made in a big press conference the day before. The guy said, "If you come out of these Games without a medal, you'll probably go down in history as the greatest never to win a medal." Dan responded to him by saying, "Over the last four Olympics, though, I've also had the opportunity to become one of the most successful Olympians ever. It didn't happen that way, but I had the opportunity." He was trying to turn negatives into positives. Searching for one last dose of perspective now, just minutes before his final race, he landed on something he would always pester his mom and dad about when he was a child.

"I used to always ask if we were rich, and they said yeah, we're rich because we have nine kids."

That was all he needed to remind himself that he was still going to be himself the next morning, no matter what happened, and that fame, wealth, or medals were not important if you had a loving family.

He put his toe into the starting mark and waited. The gun went off.

The race felt easy, effortless and in slow motion, exactly what athletes hope for when they are in the zone. He couldn't hear any of his split times due to the deafening roar from the crowd, but his coach, Peter Mueller, was on the backstretch with the time written on a wipe board. When Dan saw the 600-meter split, he knew that if he just held on, he would have a medal.

This time he did not push it more than needed, he did not lose control of his skate, and the ice did not chip under him. The race lasted 1 minute, 12.43 seconds. It was a perfect glide home, and when he looked up there was a big "WR" for world record next to his name. He threw his arms up into the air, his head tilting back, a look of disbelief on his face, and then put his head into his hands. In the stands, Robin started sobbing while Harry pumped his fists into the air and other family members rejoiced. Peter Mueller skated over and hugged Dan, the wipe board still in his hands. But they couldn't fully exhale yet. Thirty more guys still had to skate. Dan knew that only one or two of them had the talent to beat that record time. A medal should be his—but what color? He waited, cooling down on the inside of the track and returning to the locker room. A Korean skater had to do a reskate after being interfered with, dragging out the process even further. Dan was listening over the loudspeaker in the locker room for times. He returned to the ice to watch the last few pairs, and finally it was official. Dan Jansen: gold. His first in seven Olympic races. The main emotion coursing through him?

"Relief, because I knew I had finally skated to my potential at the Olympics."

Today winners attend a flower ceremony on-site and receive their medals later—sometimes that night or even the next day, usually in a specially designed medals plaza. But back then the medals ceremony happened immediately afterward. Dan got to experience the thrill of the national anthem playing. For him. Finally.

"I had been on the podium a hundred times or more, but never at the Olympics, and as corny as it sounds I had never felt more patriotic than at that moment. It was multiplied by about one thousand percent."

His family was in the stands, tears still running down their faces. As the song came to its close he thought about his sister Jane. As the lyrics "the home of the brave" rang out, Dan looked up and saluted the sky. It was a spur-of-the-moment thing, so unplanned that he didn't even realize he had done it. When his family asked him later, "Was that for Jane?" Dan replied, "Was what for Jane?" When prompted about his salute he confirmed that indeed he had been thinking of Jane.

Following the national anthem, an Olympic official told Dan to get his skates back on—he would be doing a victory lap. Dan retrieved his skates from the locker room, then stepped back onto the ice, where he was handed a thick bouquet of yellow and white flowers. Two Norwegian children dressed in Olympic-mascot costumes skated next to Dan. As the lights dimmed, Dan suddenly saw a security guard holding baby Jane over the railing for him to grab. The ice was littered with flowers fans had thrown from the stands, and a spotlight beamed directly onto Dan and Jane. Although it remains one of the most iconic images of the Olympics, Dan's thought at the time was trying not to trip over the flowers or the mascots as he skated in the dark, with a spotlight blinding his vision and his baby and a bunch of flowers in his arms. Somehow all made it through unscathed, and that moment would become one of the most widely viewed images of the modern Olympic Games. It touched souls all over the planet and especially resonated with people who had lost a loved one or overcome obstacles. The official Olympic report for 1994 states, "At that moment there were no Norwegians, Dutch, Americans or people of other nationalities among the spectators, only fans of Dan Jansen."

There was one personal moment Dan was still waiting for. He had yet to see and hug his family. The Jansens had lived through hell together, and this medal represented both joy and pain. Dan first had to go through drug testing and take phone calls from President Bill Clinton and First Lady Hillary Rodham Clinton. Finally he was taken to a room under the stands where the king of Norway was waiting to give his congratulations. Dan was standing in that room, talking with the king of Norway and other officials, when the door opened and in walked his family. His eyes locked with his dad's. "He had this huge smile on his face and he kind of nodded at me and we didn't even have to say anything," Dan remembered. The two shared a bear hug.

One of the most iconic Olympic photos: Dan Jansen, holding
eight-month-old Jane, takes a gold medal victory lap at
Hamar Olympic Hall, February 18, 1994. AP PHOTO/JOHN GAPS III

A few days later, his fellow Olympians chose Dan to be the US flag
bearer in the closing ceremony. He wore a wide cowboy hat, a red, white,
and blue jacket, and a grin that could have stretched from sea to shining
sea as he proudly carried the flag into the stadium. In April he was honored
with the James E. Sullivan Award as the nation's top amateur athlete, an
award some have compared to the Oscars of sports. That same year, the
city of Greenfield, Wisconsin, renamed Squire Park Dan Jansen Park in his
honor. The playground equipment was specially ordered in red, white, and
blue, with a fifty-foot gold-colored flagpole as a centerpiece. Every year

since, Dan Jansen Family Fest has been held at the park, with music, rides, food, and entertainment. One hundred percent of the profits are donated to the City of Greenfield Parks Department.

Dan Jansen's Olympic journey had come to an end. He might not have seen all the successes he had once dreamed of as a kid, but he had won a medal—as he had seen his idol, Eric Heiden, do—and he accomplished far more than that in the hearts and minds of fans. He had become a symbol of hope in the face of tragedy and of perseverance when a setback befalls you.

Dan and Robin had a second daughter, Olivia, but the couple separated two years after the Olympics and divorced in 1998. Robin moved with the girls to her home state of North Carolina, and Dan decided to relocate as well to be near his daughters as they grew up. He married Karen Palacios, a golf professional, and stayed tight with his girls. As for Jane, famous around the world as a baby held in her father's arms, she eventually went to Clemson University and majored in sociology and education. Olivia chose North Carolina State.

Dan's father, Harry Jansen, was diagnosed with symptoms of dementia around 2005. The Milwaukee-area siblings took turns staying at the house to help Dan's mother with caretaking. Harry died in 2015 at the age of eighty-six.

Dan Jansen became a highly respected Olympics speedskating analyst for NBC, usually paired with Dan Hicks at every major event. He is a motivational speaker and started a foundation for leukemia-related cancers that grants scholarships and helps pay when families and siblings can't afford to be with a sick loved one while they're being treated.

Dan was elected to the Wisconsin Athletic Hall of Fame in 1995 and the United States Olympic Hall of Fame in 2004. He was featured in a Visa commercial about traveling full circle from sister Jane to daughter Jane; it draws tears from even the most hardened observers. Jansen's story is one of the most recognizable in all of Olympics history. With the benefit of more than twenty years' hindsight, Dan looks back on his Olympic ride and wonders if it was all meant to be this way in some grand scheme of the universe.

"I've thought about that a lot over the years. I've been asked a lot, would

Lifelong friends Dan Jansen and Bonnie Blair helped each other through tough times. © 2015 JOURNAL SENTINEL, INC., REPRODUCED WITH PERMISSION

you change anything about it if you could? The obvious thing is, bring Jane back and you can have everything back," he explained. "But in terms of the races—as a competitive athlete it's still strange and it's almost hard to believe that I didn't win the 500 at the Olympics because I should have three times. But no, I wouldn't change it because I think it's made me who I am as a person and as a father. I think the response I've gotten from people from around the world—they certainly wouldn't have reached out in the way they have and told me the stories they've told me if I had won everything."

As for being the central character in one of the greatest Olympic tales, Dan still has a hard time wrapping his head around that. "It's odd to hear," he said. "I've heard it a lot, and I very, very much appreciate it, but it's still odd because, you know, it's just my life. Everybody has their stories and their life that they've lived. Everybody has great times and tough times. . . . For me, that's my reality. [It would be] corny if you wrote a movie about it like that, but it was real life and it's . . . amazing."

CHAPTER 13

BONNIE BLAIR

Speedskating, 1984, 1988, 1992, 1994

Bonnie Blair's mother had a feeling about the baby growing inside her. A premonition of a superathlete? A hint that five gold medals were in the future? Quite the opposite.

"My mom was forty-five and my dad was fifty-two when I was born," said Blair. "They didn't have all of the tests we have now. For most of the pregnancy, Mom thought that she was going to have a child that she would need to attend to for the rest of her life. She thought there was a high probability that there would be something wrong with me."

Bonnie was the sixth child born to Charles (nicknamed Chili) and Eleanor Blair. Eleanor had had five miscarriages, and Bonnie's closest sibling was eight years older. On March 18, 1964, Chili drove Eleanor to the hospital to give birth, but he didn't stay. He was too busy taking the rest of the kids to a speedskating practice.

"You have to remember, husbands weren't allowed in the delivery room," Bonnie explained. "Me being the sixth kid, they had already been there, done that, plus there were the five other kids to look after. He dropped my mom off at the steps of the hospital and was like, okay, let us know what happens."

A few hours later he found out via an announcement over the public address system at the rink. "'The Blairs have a new daughter!'" laughed Bonnie fifty years later. "That's how they knew whether I was a boy or a girl."

Bonnie Blair was born into a winter-loving family. BLAIR FAMILY PHOTO

Just three months after the healthy Bonnie Kathleen Blair entered the world, Chili, a civil engineer, was transferred back to Champaign, Illinois, where they had lived before Bonnie was born. Bonnie grew up in a happy household, although she often felt like an only child due to the age gap between her and her brothers and sisters. On the other hand, having so many older siblings provided her with a comforting sense of having numerous parents.

Young Bonnie took to sports quickly and participated in everything from skating to softball, track to cheerleading, and swim team. In fact, that's where her first source of internal conflict was. "I remember the point where I didn't want to do swim team anymore," she recalled. "I thought, 'How am I going to tell my dad?' My insides would just churn. He liked going to meets and timing, and I thought I was going to disappoint him."

Finally, the laid-back man of few words brought it up himself, asking Bonnie what she thought of swimming. "I said, 'You know, Dad, I don't think I want to do this anymore,' and he was like, 'Okay.' That's all he said, okay. I was like, that's it? Okay? My insides have been turning inside out for weeks and that's it? That was easy."

She began to gravitate toward speedskating. The family love of the sport had started by accident long before she was born. Bonnie's sisters Suzy and Mary had been given figure skates as a present, and they were tooling around the local rink when a speedskating coach approached them and told them they should try his sport instead. The girls went home and reported this to Eleanor, who initially pooh-poohed the idea. "But then they were at the grocery store and ran into the guy and my sisters said, 'Oh, there's Dick, he's the guy who says we should be speedskaters,'" said Blair.

Something about the chance meeting convinced Eleanor to let the kids give it a shot, and they joined a local speedskating club. Eleanor looked high and low for white speedskates, as her daughters loved the white boots of figure skates. Eventually, Eleanor figured out they simply don't make white speedskates and bought a more traditional dark color. Still, Suzy and Mary took to it, and eventually speedskating became a family pastime.

Chili, a Yale alumnus, was a good athlete who enjoyed playing basketball. Both Chili and Eleanor were avid golfers. They also liked going onto the ice to skate with the kids but did not consider themselves exceptionally gifted athletically.

After the family relocated to Champaign, they began traveling the Midwest for meets. Almost every weekend from November 1 through March the Blairs piled in the family car and headed to a meet in a neighboring city or state, foregoing vacations and spring breaks. Bonnie remembered, "That's where we spent our money, all of these meets. When people talked about vacations, I was like, 'I've never been on a vacation.'"

Yet Bonnie never felt pushed into the sport. Speedskating was a natural for her, and she thrived on all aspects of it. She looked forward to meets every weekend and couldn't wait for the winter season to start.

During this time Bonnie got to know fellow speedskater Dan Jansen, who grew up and trained in West Allis, Wisconsin, three and a half hours from Champaign. The two families were friendly even before Dan and Bonnie were born. "When there was a meet in Champaign, Dan's brother Dick would stay at our house. If there was a meet in Milwaukee, my brother Rob would stay at his house." Bonnie was one year older than Dan, but the two of them grew up skating in essentially the same age group, and both their fathers timed local races. Bonnie always remembers "DJ" in the blue tights and jersey with an orange stripe that the West Allis team wore.

She was buoyed by a lot of success early on against her peers. But there was one bump. At about age twelve or thirteen the young teen was growing quickly and began to feel like her body would not perform the way she

PIONEERS OF WOMEN'S SPEEDSKATING

Women's speedskating did not make the Olympic program until 1960, thirty-six years after men's speedskating debuted. Long before Bonnie Blair became a household name, many other women came through Wisconsin and took their talents to the ice. Here are some of the women who made huge contributions in the years 1968–1980.

Dianne Holum, 1968, 1972

Chicago native Dianne Holum began training as a teen in West Allis, Wisconsin, shortly after the Olympic Oval opened in 1966. Her first Olympics came just two years later in Grenoble, France, when she was only sixteen. In the 500 meters, she finished in a three-way tie for second place with two other Americans, Jenny Fish and Mary Meyers. They all had crossed in exactly the same time, 46.3 seconds, and all three won a silver medal. Holum also took home a bronze that year in the 1,000. Four years later, twenty-year-old Dianne was back for more in Sapporo, Japan. Dianne was chosen to be the US flag bearer in the opening ceremonies, which she called "an honor that is hard to put into words." She took home her first and only gold, in the 1,500 meters, and capped her skating career three days later with a silver in the 3,000 meters.

Holum retired after the 1972 Games. She wasn't yet twenty-one but felt ready to coach. Her most famous pupils would be Eric and Beth Heiden and Bonnie Blair. She also taught physical education at two Milwaukee high schools and later coached her own daughter, Kristin, in the 1998 Winter Games.

wanted it to. "I couldn't skate my way out of a paper bag," she laughed. "I remember that being a very frustrating time and thinking, do I want to do this anymore? I remember having a lot of people come up to encourage me and tell me, 'Don't worry, you're just going through a growth stage; don't give up on it.'"

Chili also stepped in to give his daughter a pep talk. "He was the one

Sheila Young, 1972, 1976

Like Dianne Holum before her and so many afterward, Sheila Young moved to Milwaukee to be near the Olympic Ice Rink. A native of Birmingham, Michigan, Young competed at the 1972 Winter Olympics in Sapporo, Japan, at the same time as Holum. While Holum was winning her first gold, twenty-one-year-old Young finished just one spot from the podium in her event, coming in fourth in the 500 meters. The following year Young did something amazing: she won World Championships in both speedskating and cycling in one year. Then in 1976 she burst onto the Olympics scene, becoming the first woman to win three medals at a Winter Olympics as she took gold in the 500, silver in the 1,500, and bronze in the 1,000. She and her husband, Olympic cyclist Jim Ochowicz, lived in Waukesha, Wisconsin, for many years, and their daughter, Elli, was a speedskater in the 2002 and 2006 Games. Sheila later became a middle school physical education teacher in northern California.

Leah Poulos-Mueller, 1972, 1976, 1980

How many people can say they've had their face on a box of cereal? Leah Poulos did just prior to her second Olympics in 1976, when she was featured on the front of the Kellogg's Corn Flakes container. Leah, who hailed from Northbrook, Illinois, and trained in West Allis, competed in three Olympics, collecting silver medals in the latter two (1976 in the 1,000 and 1980 in the 500 and 1,000). She married gold medal–winning speedskater Peter Mueller (who coached Dan Jansen and Bonnie Blair) and became a lawyer in the Milwaukee area.

that put the idea in my head, maybe I could go to the Olympics, maybe I could win a medal," Bonnie said. It was profound advice from a man Bonnie deeply respected but rarely heard much from.

"We would go back and forth to Chicago for meets and I would think, did he even talk to me this weekend? He just was a very quiet person," she explained. "But the thing is, when he did say something it always seemed to have an impact. He was very involved—he was at every practice and meet I ever had. Maybe he was so quiet because he was in a family where all of the females demanded so much talking space. He didn't have a chance to get a word in edgewise!"

While in high school, Bonnie made the US National Team. This led to more training, more meets, and packets of training programs sent to the house. It also meant being encouraged to train at the outdoor Wisconsin Olympic Ice Rink near Milwaukee. Just as Bonnie's parents began to look around for a host family, one appeared almost magically before them. The corporate lawyer for Chili's civil engineering firm lived in Elm Grove, Wisconsin. Bill and Rita Denny had six kids, most of them grown, and they were happy to open their home for Bonnie. "They became my Milwaukee family," Bonnie said. "My parents would come and stay with them sometimes too; we basically moved into their house and spent Christmas and other holidays with them."

She would live with the Dennys for weeks at a time, putting in long hours at the rink. Then after high school Bonnie's sister Angela moved to Milwaukee with her husband, and Bonnie lived with them. She took some junior college courses in the summer, but it was clear where her focus was.

In 1984 nineteen-year-old Bonnie qualified for her first Olympic Trials. Her dad's confidence that she could make an Olympic team came back to her in a crystal-clear moment as she prepared for her races. She was being coached by Eric Heiden's old coach, Dianne Holum, as well as Mike Crowe. As Bonnie recalls the trials, "They were taking something like five [athletes] to the Olympics in the 500, and I'm guessing I finished third." Bonnie made the trip to Sarajevo for that race, the 500 meters. From the moment she got there she felt powerful emotions about being at her first Olympics. "It was kind of like being that kid in a candy store," she later told a writer for the website Olympic.org. "You can't believe you're here, this is unbelievable, just total excitement and thrill with every aspect that went with the Games, from Opening Ceremonies, walking in, to the crowd. I was able to pick out my mom and my two sisters who were in the crowd. And that just brought tears to my eyes. It was just so overwhelming to think, 'OK, the whole world is watching this.'"

As the week went on, she was thrilled by fellow athletes she met in the cafeteria of the village, a little overwhelmed by the guards with machine guns, but overall loving the entire experience. Then came her race. On February 10, 1984, she skated a time of 42.53, which landed her in eighth place in the 500. She was more than a second behind the gold medal winner, Christa Luding-Rothenburger of East Germany, but that mattered little. It felt like a victory for the nineteen-year-old. "If you had seen me cross the finish line, you probably would have thought I had won, because I was so excited with this result that I had. It was way above my expectations," she said.

The '84 Olympics were a wonderful learning experience and gave her a chance to get over the thrill and the nerves of just being there, a lesson that would greatly help her four years later. Having her mother and two of her sisters there was also very meaningful. She didn't know it yet, but it was only a tiny taste of the contingent that would follow Bonnie in future Olympics. The media would dub them "the Blair Bunch" as the group swelled to twenty-five in Calgary, forty-five in Albertville, and sixty in Lillehammer.

After her experience at Sarajevo, Bonnie knew she would do anything to return to the Olympic stage. She spent the next four years training, pushing herself, and dominating others in competitions.

As 1988 approached, both Bonnie Blair and Dan Jansen were getting ready for their second go at the Olympics. Both had monstrous amounts of talent and high hopes. These Games were expected to be a breakthrough moment for both of them. Bonnie was staying at the Jansens' house on that heartbreaking day when the phone call came to tell them that Dan's sister Jane had been diagnosed with leukemia. "Talk about your heart being stabbed," remembered Blair.

Bonnie was dealing with her own family medical crisis. Her father had been diagnosed with lung cancer and had already begun chemotherapy and radiation. Still, Dan and Bonnie headed to Calgary with the rest of Team USA. Bonnie remembers her reaction when Dan found out Jane had died. "I remember seeing him in the hallway kind of crouched down and just crying. It was one of those things where there wasn't anything you could do except give him a hug and wish him well. He decided to skate. A lot of people [ask], should he have skated or shouldn't he have skated? I'm not sure if there would have been a doubt in my mind whether I would have skated too. I guess I wouldn't have realized that there would be an option."

When Jansen fell in his first race, the 500, Bonnie's heart dropped. "It was very upsetting to our whole team. We were all pretty close even though it's an individual sport. We train together and live under the same roof for eight months out of the year. It was a hard time on our team."

Jansen would slip again four days later in the 1,000. Bonnie had yet to skate her first race. As she prepared to take the ice on February 22, she had to try to put DJ's falls out of her thoughts. "I went back to my dad, who is strong-minded, and I was somehow able to put it out of my mind for the race," she said.

One of the first to compete was the gold medal winner in the 500 in Sarajevo, Christa Luding-Rothenburger, who immediately set a world record of 39:12. Bonnie was a few pairs later. "Going to the starting line, not only do I know that I have to go faster than I ever have, but I have to [skate] a world record to even beat it," Blair remembered. "My coach came up to me before the race with his little pad of paper, telling me, 'You know, that one lap you did earlier this week was good enough to beat that time.' I looked at him and said, 'I know,' and I just skated away from him. He was so nervous that he was making me nervous. I knew I had the ability to beat the time that she posted, but you've still gotta make it happen."

Bonnie lined up at the start with thoughts of DJ, her dad, the world record, and her own long journey all dancing in her brain. But she bore down and focused on nothing but the mechanics of the race. One hundred meters in she heard the announcer yelling out the split time, and she knew she was $\frac{2}{100}$ths of a second faster than the East German, Luding-Rothenburger. She was on pace to win.

"I really don't remember anything else except crossing the finish line. I wound up beating her by that same $\frac{2}{100}$ of a second [39:10]. I could cry now just thinking about it, the emotions were so powerful. I immediately started crying. One of the first long track coaches I had was on the backstretch, and I stopped and gave her a hug. I hugged my boyfriend. One of the other East Germans came by and stopped me and said, 'That was not a race, it was a dream,' and they caught that comment on camera. She was right—it was a dream."

Bonnie's supporters were all in one area—twenty-five strong, and including Chili, who attended despite cancer treatments. Bonnie clearly remembers the awards ceremony held just a short time later in the rink. She had a good view of most of the Blair Bunch. "My sister Angela was crying. My sister Suzy had a real huge big grin on her face. My brother Rob was standing next to his best friend and giving him a high five. My sister Mary was the loud, crazy, and wild one, standing up, yelling and screaming and going absolutely crazy. Then I saw my mom. She still looked scared to death, as if I were still racing. To see so many emotions, it was actually exactly what it felt like for me—so many emotions all rolled into one."

She still hadn't been able to get a clear view of her father or to hug anyone in the family. She was hustled off to drug testing and then scheduled for media interviews. But she cut away for a moment right after testing and found Chili and Eleanor. "The smile on my dad's face was priceless. I had never seen my dad smile a smile that big, ever. That was the moment that was like, 'Oh my Gosh, I won a gold medal.' He was sick, and for him to be there and witness that first medal was very special."

Bonnie was overjoyed with her own success, but almost immediately after seeing her parents she thought of Dan. "If I could share this medal with him . . ." she recalled, her voice trailing off. "I wish there was a way I could have been able to do that. I thought, God, he's been so successful, and to have this all happen. I just wanted to share it."

Four days later Bonnie won a bronze in the 1,000 meters as well. She left Calgary with the first two of what would eventually be six medals, five of them gold, over the next four Olympics, making her the most decorated female Olympian in Winter Games history. She won gold medals in the 500 and 1,000 in both the Albertville and Lillehammer Games in 1992 and 1994. She was the first US athlete, male or female, to be crowned at the top spot in the same event three times in a row, the first American woman to win five golds. She was the *Sports Illustrated* Sportswoman of the Year in 1994 and was inducted into the US Olympic Hall of Fame. Every race was special for its own reasons, but none could ever top that first gold—especially the sight of her father's face.

Chili Blair died on Christmas Day, 1989, a year and a half after watching his daughter win gold and two days after he had been out at an ice rink

Speedskating came naturally to Bonnie, and she was happy to put her swimming days behind her. BLAIR FAMILY PHOTO

timing races. He had dinner with the family, went to bed, and was gone within twenty-four hours. Officially it was pneumonia, although cancer was certainly a factor. Eleanor passed away in 2004.

At her last Olympics, in Lillehammer in 1994, Bonnie shunned the tradition of waiting to see family until after drug testing and interviews and instead climbed into the stands with her skates on to hug the Blair Bunch. Family meant everything to her, and she was incredibly moved when three hundred people, including old friends from Champaign, showed up for one of her final competitions at the Pettit Center one year after Lillehammer. The Blairs enjoyed a beer tent set up in the parking lot to create a tailgating atmosphere. It was a rocking good time.

Blair retired a few months later at age thirty-one. Meanwhile, she had found her soul mate. Dave Cruikshank was a fellow speedskater, five years younger than Bonnie, but someone she had always been friends with. "I remember once at O'Hare Airport [as the team left for a meet], Dave's mom telling me, because I was the oldest on the team, 'You take care of my son Dave.'" The pair got married and had two children, Grant in 1998 and Blair in 2000.

Retirement was not a difficult transition for Bonnie. She felt she had gone out on her own terms, and she stayed involved in the sport for three more years as Dave trained for his fourth Olympics (he competed in 1988, 1992, and 1994 with Bonnie and again in 1998). They would often do training bike rides and other workouts together before the '98 Games.

Bonnie does recall a time, in the fall of her first retirement year, when the smell of wet leaves reminded her of Germany, and she thought to herself, "I should be at a World Cup right now!" She called a skating friend to wish her good luck as she left for the World Cup season, and the floodgates opened. Bonnie cried into the phone, explaining to her buddy that she was feeling nostalgic about the end of her career. But overall, Bonnie recalls most of those emotions passing quickly. The births of her children refocused her life on being a mom.

While Bonnie's career brought her fame and adulation, it also took a physical toll. She had a difficult delivery with Grant, and the doctors told her that her muscles couldn't relax enough after having been so honed during her time as an elite athlete. For years after the birth of the children she suffered from stress incontinence. She couldn't bend down to pick up a laundry basket or go out for a run without leaking urine. It's a private matter, to be sure, but one Bonnie is comfortable sharing now.

That wasn't always the case; for years she lived in silence about it. But after two years, "I finally had the guts to say something to my OB/GYN," she explained. That led to a fairly easy twenty-minute surgery with transvaginal tape to fix her bladder. "I was so excited to get my life back that I was ready to shout from the rooftops. People live in silence with this, and they don't have to."

Bonnie and Dave are happily settled in Delafield, Wisconsin, and their two children have grown up to be great athletes. Grant was drafted in 2014 by the United States Hockey League and committed to play for the Wisconsin Badgers. He has hopes of the Olympics and the NHL. Blair was a state champion gymnast in middle school until a wrist injury led her to

Bonnie, daughter Blair, husband Dave Cruikshank, and son Grant
show their Olympic spirit at home. BLAIR FAMILY PHOTO

dabble in speedskating. Bonnie is on the other side of the parent-athlete
dynamic now: driving the kids to and from practices, organizing their gear
and schedules, and cheering from the stands. She says they must follow
their own paths, and it must come from their hearts. She models their
upbringing after her own childhood.

Bonnie was named to President Obama's official delegation for the
closing ceremony of the 2014 Games in Sochi, Russia, along with Wisconsin native Eric Heiden. She started a charitable foundation, supports the
American Cancer Society and the Alzheimer's Association in memory of
family members, and is a motivational speaker. She joined the Pettit Center board of directors after retirement. There was no doubt in her mind

ALMOST AN OLYMPIAN: DONALD DRIVER

When Donald Driver came to a fork in the road of his athletic career, he became a record-setting Green Bay Packers wide receiver. But he could just as easily have chosen the other path and pursued an Olympic career. In addition to being a standout football player, Driver was a stellar track and field athlete at Alcorn State University in Mississippi. In his specialty, the high jump, he had an Olympic-caliber leap of seven feet, six inches. This qualified him for the Olympic Trials for the 1996 Games, which were to be held just a short dis-

Donald Driver went from high jumps to Lambeau leaps. MIKE MORBECK/WIKIMEDIA COMMONS

tance away from Alcorn State in Atlanta, Georgia. Four years later he likely would have qualified for Sydney, Australia, as well.

But knowing the devotion needed for any professional sport, Driver had to make a decision: was he an Olympian or a football player? He turned down the invitation to the trials and kept on catching the pigskin. A seventh-round draft pick, he went on to become the Packers' all-time leading receiver in yards and receptions. Some say the high-jumping abilities helped him scale the wall after a touchdown when the fans beckoned him to do the Lambeau Leap. We'll never know what Driver the high jumper might have accomplished on the world stage, but Driver the football player sure kept the fans entertained.

that she would settle in Wisconsin for life. "I never thought about moving elsewhere," she explained. "I wanted to be by the Pettit and to give back."

There has been tragedy in her life. Of her five siblings, only two remain. But overall Bonnie retains a highly positive and optimistic outlook on her world. "Life is good," she said. "Family members were taken from me way too soon, but that's life. I can't dwell on that, and I don't think they'd want me to. I miss them all dearly. My parents having me at such an older age, the chances of them having been around very much longer were not great. We're here and we're healthy, and I'm enjoying the ride with my kids and following them."

Sometimes she still can't believe her own success. Her home is decorated with Olympic memorabilia. Wooden Olympic rings adorn the deck near the hot tub, and every medal is displayed in a coffee table she had made, also in the shape of Olympic rings. She likes to look at them and remember those happy times.

"You never want to take anything for granted. I loved what I did. Passion for something can take you a long way. That was a driving force in my success—I loved what I did. I had frustrating times, but through it all I never lost the love for the sport."

CHAPTER 14

MIKE PEPLINSKI

Curling, 1998

Curling is one of the oldest team sports in the world, dating back to sixteenth-century Scotland. The game has been described as shuffleboard on ice. It was on the Olympic program at the first Winter Games in 1924 in Chamonix, France, but was then demoted to a demonstration sport. Finally in 1998 in Nagano, Japan, curling returned to the main stage for both men and women. At least six Wisconsin natives took part, and through 2014 more than twenty Olympic curlers had come through Wisconsin. That 1998 group included Wisconsin native Mike Peplinski.

The majority of elementary school kids across the United States do not have curling as an option for a sport. But Wisconsinites are lucky; dozens of curling clubs are active in the state, and the headquarters of USA Curling is located in Stevens Point. Peplinski grew up in Centerville, where the curling club was founded in 1947 and has an active juniors program. Mike began curling in fourth grade, and by the time young Mike was in middle school, the Centerville Curling Club had close to a hundred participants.

Mike's mother was a part-time secretary for a local newspaper, his father worked for the railroad, and his brother would grow up to run a local bowling alley. A natural athlete in every sport he tried, Mike remembered, "I was very active in high school, playing three varsity sports [plus] curling. I knew that I wouldn't be able to play the others for the rest of my life, so I pushed myself to excel at curling."

Twenty-one-year-old Mike Peplinski hugs his mother after winning a Junior National Championship. COURTESY OF MIKE PEPLINSKI

He also believed he'd be healthy and strong forever. "As a high school athlete you think you're invincible," he explained.

By age seventeen, Mike was traveling the world for curling competitions. When the team he was playing for lost in the finals of the national championships that year, the team that beat them asked Mike to travel with them. In 1994 he was part of the first US team to play an Eastern Bloc country (Bulgaria) and the first to face Russia. But during this time came the first hint that he was not invincible. In 1994, when he was nineteen and a sophomore playing baseball and curling on the side at Viterbo College in La Crosse, he noticed strange symptoms. His socks left marks on his skin that did not disappear for hours, and he was fatigued nearly all the time. When he ran for baseball, he felt himself moving more slowly than he had ever felt in his life.

Eventually a series of tests revealed a kidney condition called idiopathic membranous nephropathy. Mike's kidneys were functioning at only 70 percent. As he absorbed the shocking diagnosis, he continued to curl and play baseball, and in 1996 he proposed to his girlfriend, Michelle, at a curling club, using curling rocks to spell out "Will you marry me?"

Almost immediately the young couple was hit with more bad news. Doctors told them Mike might not be able to have children and suggested a fertility bank. During this time, Mike's doctors treated his disease with medication and an improved diet. Despite his declining kidney function, as the 1998 Olympics approached Mike was one of the top curlers in the nation, having won back-to-back titles at the junior national level. His team won eight straight games in the 1997 trials tournament to secure its position as Team USA—and Mike left for Japan with his kidneys now at a dangerously low 25 percent function.

Peplinski was just twenty-three years old and would be the team's vice-skip (the player who discusses strategy with the skip, or leader) in Nagano. His age put him at least fourteen years younger than the rest of the US curling team. But he was assertive, and that dynamic created a different kind of relationship among the "rink" (a curling term for team). As Mike explained, "Not being friends exactly, we could be very honest with each other on things we thought could be improved on. It was an interesting dynamic. We all had a lot of confidence in ourselves and shared our opinions."

Despite his age, Mike was in the worst health of anyone on the team. He needed six medications at the Olympics, including a diuretic that was on the banned substance list because it can mask other drugs. That necessitated a waiver from the IOC. There was only one good side to all of this: the national media caught on to his story, bringing much more attention to curling than the sport normally enjoys. Mike appeared on *Good Morning America* and on TNT and CBS, among others, to talk about the importance of organ donation.

Team USA played in an eight-team round robin starting on February 9, 1998. They finished 3–4, their best two games coming at the wrong time to medal, and just missed the podium, coming in fourth. Switzerland took the gold, Canada the silver, and Norway the bronze. Mike said, "It was devastating. I wanted to show my friends and family a medal forever. Now, the most common joke I hear from friends is about finishing fourth."

Despite the disappointment, Mike Peplinski stayed in Nagano after the

WISCONSIN SKI JUMPING

Wisconsin might not be Colorado in terms of topography, but it boasts many hills, thanks in part to the Ice Age glaciers that shaped its landscape. Combine that hilly terrain with frigid and snowy winters and a love of challenging winter sports, and you get a ski-jumping legacy that has produced several Olympians.

Norwegian immigrants brought ski jumping to the Eau Claire area in the 1880s, and by 1887 Eau Claire had a ski jump at the Big Heart Silver Mine and a ski club, the Dovre Ski Club, that held one of the country's earliest ski tournaments. In 1922 a group in Westby in Vernon County founded the Snowflake Ski Club and built a wooden jump. The Snowflake Ski Club's first tournament, on February 8, 1923, drew nearly two thousand spectators, and every business in Westby closed for the afternoon. Today Westby continues to support the Snowflake Club with zest, and the club has more than five hundred members—in a town of two thousand. The Snowflake Ski Club is one of two remaining all-volunteer, large ski-jumping clubs in the Western Hemisphere.

Also in the early 1920s, Scandinavian students at the University of Wisconsin–Madison built a ski jump on what is now Observatory Drive. Competition was overseen largely by Dr. H. C. Bradley, who raised the funds needed to construct the steel jump and installed another jump near Shorewood Hills, west of campus. Bradley was always on hand with a pocket filled with ribbons for the winners. The success of these early jumps led to the creation of the Blackhawk Ski Club and the purchase of more land near Middleton. The club remains strong today.

In 1933 the Flying Eagles Club was formed in the Chippewa Valley.

US was done curling and watched the women's hockey gold medal game, featuring fellow Wisconsin native Karyn Bye. He attended the closing ceremonies too, but his strength was zapping fast as his health situation became even more perilous. Doctors told him his kidney function was now at 14 percent. He would need a transplant.

Dale Severson, an Olympic alternate in 1956, goes flying off Blackhawk Ski Club's Tomahawk Ridge jump in Middleton in 1958. WHI IMAGE ID 98793

In 1969 the club built a revamped ski jump to replace the 1887 version; the Silver Mine Ski Jump rises 351 feet above the Chippewa River and is considered one of the largest ski jumps in the country. The Flying Eagles Club is the longest-running junior club in the nation.

The 1940s saw another Wisconsin jump erected, this one on the Anderson farm in Vernon County. Olympic champions Peter Haugstad of Norway (1948 Olympics) and Arnfin Bergmann of Canada (1952 Olympics) jumped on Anderson Hill, and the US Olympic team used it as a training hill in 1952 and 1960.

Ski jumping Olympians with Wisconsin connections include Anders Haugen (the first American to win a ski jumping medal, in 1924), LaMoine Batson (1924 and 1932), Jimmy Hendrickson (1936), Joe Perrault (1948), Willis "Billy" Olson (1952 and 1956), Lyle Swenson (1964), Bill Bakke and Dave Norby (1968), Reed Zuehlke (1980 and 1984), Kurt Stein (1992 and 1994), and Clint Jones (2002 and 2006). Dale Severson of Eau Claire was a 1956 alternate.

When Mike returned to the United States, the Peplinski family huddled up. Later Mike told the *Baltimore Sun* about the decision they made: "It was up in the air whether my wife, sister or mother would give me a kidney. My mom went for a walk, came back and just said, 'I'll be your donor.' I always say that she gave me one life. And now, she's giving me another.

Peplinski goofs around with members of the last team he was on before the Olympics. Blue ring: Peplinski, yellow ring: Shawn Rojeski (who won bronze in 2006), black ring: Craig Brown (alternate in the 2014 Olympics), green ring: Jon Brunt, red ring: Cory Ward. COURTESY OF MIKE PEPLINSKI

And she says she'd do anything for her son. I'm an optimist. My thought is that after the transplant I'll get better."

Unfortunately, things did not go as planned. Peplinski's mom was well into the matching process when doctors handed her some devastating news of her own. She had a milder version of the same kidney disease her son harbored and would not be allowed to donate. Mike's wife, Michelle, and Michelle's brother and father all offered to be tested. Amazingly, all were perfect matches. Peplinski's father-in-law, Bill Brendel, decided he did not want his children to undergo such an operation and volunteered to be the donor. One of his kidneys would go to Mike.

"The surgery was in the summer of '98. It went very well," Mike said. "I immediately felt better since I had a healthy kidney. As with most surgeries, I was moving slow [afterward] but really felt very good."

Then came the best gift of all for both families. Despite the doctors' warning about Mike's fertility, Michelle was pregnant. A beautiful, healthy

FATHER-DAUGHTER CURLING DUO

One of Wisconsin's most distinctive curling stories belongs to Wally Henry and Debbie McCormick, who are not only coach and athlete but father and daughter.

Native Canadians Wally and Ginny Henry moved with their two children from Saskatoon to the small town of Rio, Wisconsin, thirty miles north of Madison, in 1978. Young Debbie, a preschooler at the time, spent a lot of time hanging out at the Madison Curling Club while her parents competed there in league play. Debbie, her brother, Donnie, and other kids were allowed to play on the ice after the adults were finished. But Debbie didn't take to it right away. "I did not love the game until I was invited [at age fourteen] to go to an international tournament in Scotland with a team from Madison," she said. "I was competing for Team USA for the first time. [Seeing] my last name and Team USA on my jersey and curling jacket, I thought that was so cool. I met kids my age from all over the world who loved the sport. When I came back to the United States I was addicted!"

Debbie competed at an impressive four Olympics, in 1998, 2002, 2010, and 2014. And she almost made a fifth, barely missing making the team in 2006. In 2002, her father was Team USA's assistant coach; the team flirted with a medal but finished fourth. Eight years later, Wally Henry was the head coach as the Olympics returned to his home country for the Vancouver Games. He and Debbie desperately hoped to medal this time, and being back in Canada would have made it especially sweet, but the team finished tenth.

Still, the unique father-daughter dynamic was a storyline that fascinated the media. For Debbie, it was never a big deal. "He was my mentor and coach from the first time I stepped on the ice," she explained. "My dad is an amazing coach. He is knowledgeable, patient, calm, understanding, and his smile makes everything okay." They shared some funny parent-kid moments during those times together, of course, like when the curling team sang aloud to hip-hop music on the way to games.

Having your father coach you in the Olympics is something special. Wally Henry is at far left next to his daughter, Debbie McCormick, and the rest of the 2010 USA curling team, which also included Wisconsin's Nicole Joraanstad (fourth from left) and Tracy Sachtjen (second from right). MICHAEL BURNS JR./ USA CURLING

Debbie noted with a laugh, "As you can imagine, some of the lyrics are not what a father wants to hear his daughter sing!"

One of Debbie's favorite memories is a curling event at which their team lost a close match. Traditionally, the coach stands next to the alternate during the ceremony. "My dad ignored the tradition and stood next to me on the podium. He said to me, 'There is no other place I would rather be right now but standing next to you.'"

Debbie transitioned out of competitive curling to sell curling equipment. Both she and her dad still live in Wisconsin, and both curl recreationally. Wally Henry retired from the admissions department at Herzing University and is on the United States Curling Association staff as the Junior Men's High Performance Team coach. Debbie looks back on her shared experiences with her father with great fondness. "I feel very lucky and blessed to have experienced four Olympics with my dad, twice as dad and twice as coach," she said.

daughter, Matelyn, was born in 1999. The entire experience spurred Mike to promote organ donation, and a photo of Mike curling appeared on a poster promoting National Donor Day. Mike went on to a fulfilling life as a husband, father, and fourth-grade teacher in Eau Claire, Wisconsin, public schools. He never competed in another Olympics, although his "rink" attempted to make it in 2002 but failed to get past the US Olympic Trials. Mike still enjoys speaking about his Olympic experience and curling. "Every four years as the Olympics rolls around, curling gets great publicity, and a large amount of people want to try the sport," he said. "I have spoken at Olympic Day events, encouraging today's youth to follow the Olympic ideals through their own competitions. Sharing my Olympic story with the grade-school kids at my elementary every four years is really a joy."

In 2012, Mike faced another obstacle: a cancerous tumor was found on one of his native kidneys. Luckily, surgeons removed the entirety of the cancer, and he could count it as one more thing he had successfully overcome.

Not surprisingly, Mike Peplinski's nickname is "Pep." And those are the kinds of talks he gives to children and adults, not only about the Olympics but about the importance of signing your donor card or volunteering to be a living donor, as his father-in-law did. "I was given the gift of life. I try not to take anything for granted and to be a positive influence in everything I do," said Mike.

CHAPTER 15

BEN SHEETS

Baseball, 2000

Baseball has a rocky Olympics history. First introduced to the Games in 1912, it began as a demonstration-only event, such a poor stepchild to other sports that at first it was played simply as a one-game spectacle by those already involved in other Olympic endeavors. America's favorite pastime was finally given full status for the 1992 Summer Games in Barcelona, only to be banished altogether starting with the 2012 Games in London for a multitude of reasons including concerns about steroid use, a lack of worldwide popularity, the need to cap the number of sports at any given Olympics, and Major League Baseball's refusal to bend its schedule to allow professional players to take part. But before baseball was sent to Olympic-sports Siberia, Ben Sheets of the Milwaukee Brewers had a spectacular shining moment.

The Milwaukee Brewers drafted Sheets out of Northeast Louisiana University (now called the University of Louisiana–Monroe) in the first round, tenth overall, in 1999. One year later, Big Ben was still mowing down batters in the minor leagues, trying to work his way to the majors, as the 2000 Summer Olympics approached. Although the International Baseball Association had opened the Olympic doors to professional players that year, Major League Baseball did not allow any of its big leaguers to miss that much time, so the US team consisted of minor league talent. In that pool Sheets was considered a star.

"From Day One, we knew if we had one player to build around, if we needed to have somebody who could win the gold medal for us, that player was Ben Sheets," USA Baseball executive director Paul Seiler said at the time. "We had an ugly group. We didn't have a Ferrari, but if we had one, it was Sheets."

The US had never won Olympic baseball gold. They finished fourth in 1992 in Barcelona and took bronze in 1996 in Atlanta. At the 2000 Games, in Sydney, Australia—the third Games in which baseball was a full sport—there was one clear favorite: Cuba, the two-time defending gold medalist, a team that had never lost a single game in the Olympics. Although some considered Cuba's power to be slipping a bit thanks to many of their top players now competing in the US major leagues, Cuba did return eleven players from the gold-medal squad in Atlanta to try to do it again. Many predicted the United States would finish no better than third.

The twenty-two-year-old Sheets was known as a prankster on the team, a lighthearted guy from Baton Rouge, Louisiana, who liked to have fun. But he was absolutely deadly on the mound. Sheets pitched twice in the round robin, beating Japan and Italy each by a score of 4–2. It was also during the round robin that Cuba faltered, getting upset by the Netherlands 4–2 for their first-ever Olympic defeat. Perhaps there *was* a crack in their armor. Cuba still managed to trounce the US 6–1 when the two met in the preliminaries, a game that featured a hit batter, retaliation in the form of interference, and tension between the two clubs that threatened to boil over into a full-blown fight.

In the semifinals, Cuba blanked Japan 3–0, while Team USA barely made it past Korea, winning 3–2 on a bottom-of-the-ninth home run by Doug Mientkiewicz after a two-hour rain delay. The winning run crossed after midnight, and the players were both spent and exhilarated as they mobbed Mientkiewicz when he stepped on home plate.

"[Sheets] came up to me in all the pandemonium and he said, 'You just won me a gold medal. You just won us a gold medal,'" Mientkiewicz remembered. Sheets was that confident that the US would prevail in a rematch with their rivals. He would be handed America's hopes along with the ball for the gold medal game on September 27, 2000. "We had it set up a long time ago that he was going to pitch this game," manager Tommy Lasorda said after Team USA won gold, "because we knew he was that good."

One of baseball's legendary managers, Lasorda had spent twenty sea-sons with the Los Angeles Dodgers, winning two World Series titles. The seventy-three-year-old took Sheets out to dinner that night before the 7:30 P.M. first pitch. "I said to him, Ben, you're gonna pitch the biggest game of your life tonight," Lasorda recalled. "I said, Ben, you are going to go to the major leagues with Milwaukee. I think you'll even win twenty games. You might even be a Cy Young award winner [best pitcher in base-ball], but everybody in America is going to remember you for this game that you're going to win tonight. And he looked up to me and he said, 'Who are we playing?'"

Sheets was joking, of course. Every sports fan on the planet knew who was meeting who for the gold medal showdown that evening. Friction rippled in the air, from both the near fight in the last game and each club's intense desire to put the other in its place. Cuba had beaten the US twenty-five of twenty-eight times they faced each other in previous international tournaments and were 7–0 against the US in the Olympics in previous years.

Yet this game started in Team USA's favor. Mike Neill blasted a first-inning home run off Cuban starter Pedro Luis Lazo for a 1–0 lead. Sheets took the mound with that edge. He gave up one hit in the bottom of the first but then struck out Cuba's first baseman looking, and the US held on to the 1–0 advantage after one. People in the stands could feel a momen-tum surge. This game had an entirely different aura about it than the previ-ous US–Cuba matchup, but there was still a lot of baseball to play. In the second inning, Lazo surrendered a double to US designated hitter John Cotton, and Cuba's manager had already seen enough. Lazo was yanked.

From that moment forward, Sheets delivered near perfection. He would yield just two more hits the entire game while walking no one. His command was impeccable, and his fastball reached 98 miles an hour. He rarely went deep into the count and had thrown just 25 pitches after three innings. Sheets struck out five, but most importantly, he did not allow a single run. The defense behind him was sublime, too, with every player at the height of concentration and discipline. The US pushed across three more runs in the fifth inning and held a 4–0 lead heading into the ninth.

"The way Sheets was pitching," US leadoff hitter and second baseman

Brent Abernathy said after the game, "There was no team in the world that was going to score four runs off of him. To do what he did at his age against that team is just unbelievable."

Sheets struck out the first two batters in the ninth. Cuba was down to its final out. The third and final hitter whacked it to left field. As Ben whipped around to watch, and the eyes of thousands of spectators followed, left fielder Mike Neill slid to his right and made a snow-cone grab, barely holding on with the tip of his glove, to end the game. It was a complete-

Ben Sheets pitched a complete-game, three-hit shutout for the gold medal. AP PHOTO/ELAINE THOMPSON

game, three-hit shutout; Sheets had needed just 103 pitches to dispatch the world's powerhouse baseball team. The final score: 4–0. Ben had been right in his confident assertion that the US would win gold.

As Neill held on, just barely, to the final out, Lasorda was watching eagerly from the dugout. He threw his arms into the air, while on the mound Sheets instinctively sank to his knees with relief and joy, his arms also rising to the skies.

Ben bellowed several loud and guttural *whooo*s and was just getting back to his feet when his teammates descended on him in chaos. They had beaten the mighty Cubans to establish a new world superhero in baseball. Lasorda and his assistants rushed out to join the others. Lasorda was wearing a microphone for television and could clearly be heard saying, "We did it, we did it! We came for the gold and we got it!" to anyone and everyone within earshot. Then Lasorda pulled Sheets in close for a bear hug and gushed, "Atta boy, Ben. You did great!" Emotion choked his voice.

DAVE NILSSON

Brewers catcher Dave Nilsson also competed at the 2000 Olympics, playing for his native Australia. He had an excellent individual performance
as a catcher and designated hitter, leading all Olympic players that year
in hitting and slugging percentage, but Australia's record was just 2–5 in
its home Olympics. Four years later, Nilsson made a repeat showing for
the Aussies. This time they took home silver, losing the gold-medal game
to Cuba, who had bounced back from their defeat in Sydney to ascend
again to the top of the baseball world.

The team took laps on the field holding American flags, then briefly
retired to the clubhouse to change into their USA sweat suits for the medals
ceremony on the field. Tears streaked many of their faces as the flag was
raised and the familiar strains of the national anthem echoed from the
stadium speakers. They were not embarrassed to cry. There had never been
a better moment to do so.

Lasorda and the other coaches were not given medals, which in all
Olympic sports are reserved for athletes. After Lasorda watched the team
he had gotten to know so well being honored with the highest award there
is in sports, he said, "I got my gold medal when I saw them put the medal
around their necks. I got my medal when I saw them raise that flag. I got
my gold medal when they played the national anthem."

As Sheets wrote his name in Olympic lore that night, the team that had
drafted him could not have been happier. "He has a burning desire to be
a major league player," Milwaukee Brewers farm director Greg Riddoch
said at the time. "He rose to the occasion in the biggest game of his life.
That tells you all you need to know."

Unfortunately, Sheets's career never lived up to the potential Lasorda
had seen. Ben made his major league debut for Milwaukee less than seven
months later, on April 5, 2001. He pitched eight seasons for the Brewers
but never won more than thirteen games and was plagued by shoulder and

elbow injuries throughout his time in baseball. He made the all-star team four times, but the closest he came to the Cy Young Award was eighth in voting in 2004. Eventually, the elbow required what's known as Tommy John surgery, replacing a ligament with a tendon from another part of the body. Sheets left the Brewers for free agency in 2008. He finished his career with one year each in Oakland and Atlanta, where he won just four games for each club.

Ben Sheets retired from baseball in 2012. He and his wife have two sons, and Ben became a volunteer assistant baseball coach at his alma mater, the University of Louisiana–Monroe. He was inducted into the Brewers Wall of Honor in 2014 for pitching more than 1,000 innings.

Ben Sheets's career may not have unfolded the way he would have liked, but he will always have that gold medal and the respect of the nation for what he did on a September night in Sydney, Australia, when the underdog toppled the favorite and left American spectators in chills. No other US baseball team made it to a gold medal game after that. The best they could do was a bronze in 2008, and then baseball was removed from the Olympic calendar, leaving Sheets's heroics all the more indelible.

CHAPTER 16

Karyn Bye

Hockey, 1998, 2002

Spectators looking at their hockey programs in River Falls, Wisconsin, in the 1980s saw only the initials and the last name: K. L. Bye.

Keith? Kurt? Kevin? Surely this had to be a boy. After all, the athlete in question had short hair and zipped around the ice scoring goals at will for the varsity hockey team. What a shock it must have been to learn that K. L. stood for Karyn Lynn.

Karyn deliberately called herself by those anonymous initials to avoid any hassles that might come if the opposing team—or anyone else in the arena—knew that she was the only girl on the ice. She just wanted to blend in. Yet Karyn's parents would sometimes overhear others whisper: "There's a rumor about a girl on the team! Which one is it?" These amateur detectives usually guessed wrong, pointing at one of the guys whose longer locks stuck out of his helmet. Sometimes, just to mess around, the cheerleaders for Karyn's team would gesture to #23—#23 was the largest boy on the club and sported a full beard and moustache—and say, "That's the girl, right there."

This had been Karyn's world for almost as long as she could remember. Born and raised in River Falls, near the Minnesota border, she made her first trip to the city's Hunt Arena for open skating with her dad, Chuck, and her brother, Chris, one Sunday afternoon in 1975, when Karyn was just four. Little Karyn was hooked. Soon, her dad was perfecting the art of flooding the backyard. It took many tries before he realized that just letting a sprinkler go all night was not going to create much more than an ice sculpture. He eventually learned to drive their truck over the snow to pack it down and then spread water evenly over the top. Karyn would race home from school, throw down a fast snack, and lace up her skates. She couldn't wait to get on that ice, and she didn't want to get off.

"My feet often got so cold that when I finally came inside for some of Mom's hot chocolate, tears of pain ran down my cheeks as my toes thawed out. Nevertheless, I would proceed to skate again the following day no matter how cold it was," she remembered.

In 1978, Karyn was seven, and nine-year-old Chris was playing for the River Falls Youth Hockey Organization. One night when Chris was sick, Karyn's father asked her if she would like to go to practice incognito, pretending to be Chris. After all, they already had the team jersey with the name Bye on the back.

"As we drove to the practice, the last thing Dad said to me was, 'Don't talk to anyone,'" Karyn said. "I stepped onto the ice with my head down so no one would see my face. After about ten minutes Chris's teammates figured out it was I instead of Chris, [but] I loved the hockey practice! Later, on our drive home, Dad asked me if I would like to play hockey on a regular basis. Without hesitation I said, 'Yes!'"

There were no girls' teams in the area, and Karyn would be the only female on the ice not only that night, but every night during her eleven years playing hockey in River Falls. She might have been the first in the history of the city, period. With her tomboy background, this did not seem like a big deal to her, and she didn't realize the barriers she was knocking down. Her parents, Chuck and Diane, were worried at first, but after watching in awe as their daughter scored a goal in her first game, most of their doubts vanished.

Women's hockey was first documented in 1889 when Lord Stanley of Preston, Canada's governor general, supervised the flooding of his lawn. Lord and Lady Stanley and their children, including two daughters, spent many a winter day zipping around the ice playing hockey as a family. Lord Stanley was so instrumental in hockey that the Stanley Cup trophy, given to the winning team of the National Hockey League finals, was named for him.

The earliest photographic evidence of a woman playing hockey dates from one year later, in 1890, when one of those daughters, Isobel, was pictured with a stick in her hand on a sheet of ice. The following winter an account in the *Ottawa Citizen* told of a women's game between two unnamed teams. In 1920 women's college teams began to form in both the United States and Canada, but they largely died out during World War II because of two factors: women had to turn their attention elsewhere to help the war effort, and the rise in popularity of the men's game led to decreased ice time for the opposite gender. In the 1970s, when Karyn Bye was racing through snack time to get to her backyard rink in River Falls, college teams had just started to spark up again at the club and varsity levels, mostly in the Midwest and East.

In 1980 fellow Wisconsinite Eric Heiden was winning his unprecedented five gold medals in Lake Placid, but eight-year-old Karyn was fixated on every game of the Olympic hockey tournament. Between periods she would go to the basement for a spirited contest of floor hockey with Chris and sometimes younger sister Kjellrun. Karyn always pretended to be #6, Bill Baker, a former Minnesota Golden Gopher who was playing for that 1980 Olympic hockey team. She was over the moon when Baker and his teammates beat Russia in the semifinals of the Miracle on Ice. But Karyn couldn't cheer for a women's Olympic team. There was none. That would not come until eighteen years later, and little did she know she was destined to be part of that history-making moment.

Meanwhile, Karyn's training continued to take shape with hockey camps, a new pair of inline skates for summer training, and nonstop competition. Karyn put in tons of extra work to keep up with her male peers. At night before bed, she would perform repetition after repetition of pull-ups and push-ups in her room to build strength. One thing she did not have to worry about was the reaction of her teammates, though. The boys not only welcomed her, they looked after her as well. "I had grown up playing hockey with the same guys, so they accepted me on the team," she said many years later. "If any of the opposing players tried to hurt me, it was like I had nineteen brothers to protect me."

Playing for the River Falls Wildcats boys' high school team, "K. L." was given her own locker room to change in for home games. For away games,

Karyn Bye (right) with her brother, Chris, and sister, Kjellrun, in 1980. Her father gave them the USA jerseys for Christmas in honor of the men's Miracle on Ice team. COURTESY OF KARYN BYE DIETZ

when space was not always as accommodating, Karyn waited outside the locker room until her teammates were done showering and then dashed in for her own shower before boarding the bus. It was not a big deal to anyone on the club, but interviewers from newspapers and TV stations often wanted to know how she handled the locker room situation. "One day I decided to have fun with a reporter," she said, "and told him I showered with the boys. You should have seen the look on his face. It was priceless!"

In the 1987–88 season, Karyn was the hockey team's second-leading scorer with 7 goals and 11 assists. She also played softball and tennis at River Falls High School and went to the state tennis tournament three years. But hockey was her sport. She made varsity as a sophomore and was second team all-conference as a junior. In her senior year her coach named her captain, a measure of the respect he felt she had earned. Karyn flourished in sports and school and graduated in 1989 as a member of the National Honor Society.

By that time, many East Coast colleges offered scholarships for female hockey players, and the summer between her junior and senior years Karyn attended a girls' hockey camp in Massachusetts attended by scouts from these schools. Harvard, Dartmouth, the University of New Hampshire, Northeastern University, and Providence College recruited Karyn, but only three came through with athletic scholarships: UNH, Providence, and Northeastern. She ultimately decided to move to New Hampshire and join the UNH Wildcats squad. It would be the first time she had ever played hockey with women. As fate would have it, when she got to the locker room on day one the only jersey that fit her was #6. Bill Baker's number, the jersey number of the player she had once emulated while goofing around with her brother in the basement, now resided on her back.

A major difference between the men's game and the women's was the lack of checking or body slamming an opponent into the boards. Karyn took a little time to adjust to that, in her first game winding up in the penalty box three times for too much physical behavior. But she eventually found her groove, honored as the university's rookie of the year in 1990 and becoming the leading scorer during her four seasons at UNH. She tallied 164 points in 87 games as a star forward. Then in November of 1992, Karyn's senior year, came a major announcement from the International Olympic Committee: they would offer women's hockey as a full medal sport beginning in 2002. But the IOC also offered the organizers of the 1994 Games in Lillehammer, Norway, and the 1998 Games in Nagano, Japan, the option of including the sport on their programs if they had the time, space, and inclination. Norway declined, but Japan accepted. The first women's Olympic hockey event would be just six years away, in 1998.

Bye graduated from UNH in 1993 with a BS in physical education. She wanted to continue playing hockey, but her choices were very limited. Then she heard that she could compete for two more years at Concordia University in Montreal if she attended graduate school there. It was a no-brainer. Bye packed up and moved to Canada, where she earned her master's degree in sports administration and competed on Concordia's hockey team.

"Basically, I was able to play six years of college hockey compared to most athletes who only get to play four years," she said. "I was nervous about going to a different country, but it was an incredible learning experience. Unfortunately for me, I had studied German in high school. It was a challenge at times to learn French. I received many parking tickets because I couldn't read the parking signs. At a hockey tournament in Quebec City, I thought I ordered a hot chocolate at the concession stand. Instead I received a hot dog. All I could do was laugh."

During Karyn's Montreal years, women's hockey was making strides in the United States. In 1994, Minnesota became the first state to sanction girls' ice hockey as a high school varsity sport. Wisconsin would not follow suit until 2001, but it was clear that hockey for women was growing, and Karyn was on the cutting edge.

Starting in 1992, Karyn played for the Women's National Team during the summers. In the 1994 World Championships, Team USA faced Team Canada in the finals in Lake Placid, New York. The US lost 6–3, leaving Karyn with a strong feeling of determination. "I realized we had a lot of training to do to be able to beat the Canadians and make a run for an Olympic gold medal," she said. "We had only four years to prepare."

Karyn graduated from Concordia in 1995 and moved back to River Falls. She lived with her mom and dad to save money while working at her father's law office and going to a local fitness center to lift weights every chance she had. Nearby Hastings High School offered her the chance to skate with their boys' team during practices, and the manager of Hunt Arena, where Karyn had learned to skate as a four-year-old, told her to come by any day and he'd have ice time for her.

It was pleasant being back in her familiar surroundings, but by 1996 Karyn wanted more routine and competition. She consulted with USA Hockey, and together they decided that she could relocate to Lake Placid to work out at the Olympic Training Center, where speedskaters, bobsledders, lugers, and many others were training for the '98 Games. But there were few hockey players. Most had opted to do as Karyn had been doing, remaining in their hometowns to train. Without many people to play hockey with, Karyn focused on strength training and bike sprints during the day and at night joined nearby North Country Community College's hockey team for practice.

Although they were not as organized in one place as they could have been, the Women's National Team competed together for tournaments, including one in China in 1997. It was an eye-opening experience. The players' luggage did not arrive with the flight, and they had to live in their same clothes for two days. The coal soot was so bad in the city of Harbin that Karyn and the rest of the team wore surgical masks to protect their lungs. The bathrooms in the locker room flooded more than once, and the food consisted of everything from cow tongue to an entire duck. Still, it was a cultural experience the girl from western Wisconsin was grateful for, and she would never forget seeing the Great Wall of China, Mao Zedong's tomb, and Tiananmen Square. Hockey had given her the opportunity to travel the world and absorb many tastes, smells, and sights she never could have afforded or imagined on her own.

As the 1998 Nagano Games approached, USA Hockey hired Ben Smith as head coach of the women's team. Smith had been a men's assistant coach, and at first Karyn was skeptical of his coaching women, but his knowledge of the game soon won her over. When Smith was asked once what the contrasts were in coaching men's and women's hockey, he said, "Well, I guess the only difference is the fingernail polish and ponytails."

In the summer of 1997, Karyn moved with the other US women's team hopefuls to Boston. The entire group trained at Boston University and played at night against men in a local league. No one had officially made the Olympic roster yet. The group of fifty-four athletes would be cut to twenty for Nagano. In August, at the end of the Boston experience, it was time to cut the roster by more than half, to twenty-five. Coach Smith called everyone in to a gym to read off the names of those who were still standing. Karyn was grateful to have a last name so close to the beginning of the alphabet. "I heard my name early on and felt a tremendous sense of relief and accomplishment," she recalled. "I had survived the first cut."

But there was still a final cut to come months later. Competition among the women was fierce as fall and winter bore on. Each tried to shine in every practice and game. In December, they faced Canada and Finland in the Three Nations Cup tournament in Lake Placid, a round robin, and for the first time in years Team USA beat their talented northern neighbors. The Olympics were now just a few months away, and the Americans knew they would be facing the Canucks again soon enough. The two teams had split their last two matches. It could go either way in Nagano. They were that close.

But first came the matter of the roster. Right after the final horn sounded in the victory over Canada, Coach Smith gathered the team back at the Olympic Training Center to announce the names of the twenty women who had made the team. Nerves were running high.

"Coach named the two goalies first, then the six defensemen, and finally the twelve forwards, including me, who ended up playing right wing," Karyn said. "The first part of my dream had come true. I had made the first-ever women's Olympic hockey team! After congratulating my teammates and consoling those who didn't make it, I called my mom and dad to share the big news. I just remember them saying 'Congratulations!' and 'We are so proud of you!' I could feel their smiles through the phone."

The next month Team USA left for Japan. Karyn was so excited the night before the flight she couldn't sleep. She kept reminding her teammates, "We're going to the Olympics!"—not quite believing it herself. Not only was she fulfilling a life-long dream of competing, she was part of Olympics history.

Upon landing, the athletes went first to team processing, where each person was given a bounty of Team USA gear, including warm-up suits, parkas, jeans, hats, gloves, sweaters, dress pants, bathrobes, towels, and boots. An on-site seamstress would make alterations. "We were being treated like queens, and we loved every minute of it," Karyn remembered.

They checked into the village and began to get comfortable with their surroundings. In the massive cafeteria one morning, Karyn found herself eating breakfast near Wayne Gretzky, considered by many *the* premier hockey player of all time. Gretzky would be playing in his only Olympics, as a thirty-seven-year-old, after Olympic rules had been changed to allow NHL players to compete. For Karyn, it was a surreal moment: "I couldn't believe I was actually eating my oatmeal, egg whites, and orange juice next to one of the greatest hockey players in the world."

Karyn and her team walked into the opening ceremonies wearing their USA gear, including cowboy hats. Entering the massive stadium near the end of the parade of nations was an overwhelming experience on every level. "Chills ran up and down my back," she recalled, "as I tried to jump in front of a camera to say 'Hi' to my friends back home."

Then came the competition, which would consist of a preliminary round robin followed by a medal round playoff. The United States viewed Canada and Finland as the only real threats for gold. Canada was the favorite after winning every World Championship since 1987. The only time the US had prevailed was in the Three Nations Cup in Lake Placid leading up to Nagano.

First for the USA was a matchup against China. It was not much of a contest—the US blanked them 5–0. In the next game, the US got off to a slower start against Sweden but turned on the jets in the second period and wound up winning 7–1. Finland was next. Karyn and the club came out flying but then got into penalty trouble. It wasn't until a focused third period that they pulled away for a 4–2 triumph, giving Team USA a shot of self-assurance. If they could top one rival, perhaps they could take down another. A game with the overmatched host country of Japan amounted to a 10–0 shellacking, and there was just one team left to play in the round robin: their biggest foe, mighty Canada.

Because the US and Canada had each gone undefeated in the preliminaries, it was already settled that they would face each other for the gold. The next game would not matter in the end but would send one team to the finals on a high and the other scrambling to change the results when it truly counted.

Canada looked dominant, leaping out to an early lead and holding a 4–1 edge in the third period. The US could see the swagger building on the opposite bench and feel a bit of air escaping their own, but something came over all of them, some type of drive, and they scored six unanswered goals in twelve minutes—practically unheard of in hockey—to shock the Canadians and win the game 7–4. Afterward, one of Karyn's teammates taunted Canada's leading scorer, and the rivalry only intensified. The Canadians would go to the gold medal game three days later angry. But Team USA now had momentum and a supreme amount of confidence. They felt there was clear evidence that they could beat the top team in the world and take home the first-ever women's Olympic hockey gold—that is, if they played up to their capabilities and didn't fall on their faces when the largest spotlight on the planet shone on them.

"The night before the gold medal game, I lay in my bed thinking of all the years of dedication and commitment I had put into hockey," Karyn wrote years later. "I had trained my hardest, so now all I could do was step onto the ice and play my best. I couldn't do another push-up, sit-up, bike sprint, or eat any healthier than I already had. Now was the time to have fun and play hard. We had played Canada thirteen times on our pre-Olympic tour and one time in the preliminary round and our record was 7–7 against them. I think Canada felt more pressure than we did because they were favored to win. Our team was relaxed, focused and ready and willing to do whatever it took."

On the morning of February 17, 1998, Karyn woke up at 6 A.M. and ate the same breakfast she did every day—oatmeal, egg whites, toast, and orange juice. The game was not until later in the afternoon, so the morning was devoted to a skate-around, followed by lunch, where Karyn again stuck to her usual pregame ritual meal—chicken breasts, salad, pasta, a roll, water, and milk.

Now it was time for the bus ride to the rink. On the drive they watched a video put together by the team's sports psychologist showing every goal Team USA had scored in the previous fourteen matchups against Team Canada. The motivational technique worked perfectly, and the USA women arrived at the rink ready to explode with energy.

Inside the locker room, Karyn received a huge surprise that both shocked and touched her. Minutes before she took the ice, she was handed a telegram. Wishing her luck on this special day was none other than her childhood hero, Bill Baker, the man who wore #6 in the 1980 Miracle on Ice victory. Baker had heard Karyn talking about him on the news and was moved to reach out. Karyn hung the telegram in her locker with pride, feeling more ready than ever to try to repeat Baker's magical ascent to the top of the podium. She would be doing it in front of family, too; her parents, brother Chris, and sister Kjellrun had made the long journey to Japan and were in the stands.

The US came out strong and utilized two power play goals to go up 2–0 after two periods. Only one period to go and they would wear the gold. But Canada, quiet thus far offensively, finally found the net and scored to slice the lead in half, making it 2–1 in the third period. USA goalie Sarah Tueting made some brilliant saves, and the score remained 2–1 in the final seconds. Canada pulled its goalie in favor of an extra attacker to try to score. They were frustrated and desperate, but it didn't work. Forward Sandra Whyte, the woman who had taunted the Canadians after the preliminary win, scored an empty net goal, and the horn sounded on a 3–1 US victory. The shocked Canadians hung their heads. Team USA went nuts. Not only was it the first-ever gold medal in women's Olympics history, it was the first gold for US hockey, period, since Baker and the 1980 Miracle on Ice team that Karyn had watched as an eight-year-old. The drought had gone on for far too long, but America finally had something huge to celebrate on the ice.

"We jumped on top of our goalies, and all I could hear was 'Get off!'" Karyn remembered. "We were crushing them with joy. My dream had finally come true, and all of my hard work and dedication had paid off. At times I cried, and at times I smiled ear to ear. [At the awards ceremony on the ice] I was so emotional I could hardly stand up. When the gold medal went around my neck my entire body went numb. Whenever I'm asked what it feels like to receive an Olympic gold medal, here is the best way I can explain it: Take the happiest day you've ever had. You probably didn't go to work, but spent time with friends and family. At the end of the day you said to yourself, 'Wow, that was the best day ever.' Now multiply that by 100, and that will put you where I was when I won the gold!"

Karyn's team had not just taken gold, they had dominated, outscoring their foes 36–8. Although Karyn did not score in the gold medal game, she led all scorers overall with five goals and three assists in the tournament and was later named USA Hockey Player of the Year.

As the party continued in the locker room, champagne spraying all over everyone, Karyn called family and friends back in Wisconsin and around the country. Later, she would discover fifty-five congratulatory emails in her inbox from the first few minutes after the victory. Reporters were still waiting for comments.

"I was on cloud nine and could hardly answer all the questions asked by the media," Karyn said. Yet when she did find a moment to share her feelings, she had a great answer for one interviewer: "I want to go home and share my gold medal with the kids. If I was a kid going to school right now, and an Olympian came in and showed me their gold medal, I would be over-

Bye in her second Olympics in 2002. Four years earlier she
helped Team USA to the first-ever women's hockey gold
medal. COURTESY OF KARYN BYE DIETZ

whelmed. I hope they go out there and work hard and know that dreams
come true. Because right here, baby, this is a dream come true for me."

Eventually that night Karyn made her way to find her family at their
hotel. "There were lots of hugs and tears!" she remembered. "And they
were pretty excited to have a closer look at the gold medal. Everyone was
dressed in red, white and blue! It was one day that I'll never forget."

She finally got to bed at 5 A.M. and slept for only an hour. David Letterman had booked ten members of the team to be on his TV show, and with

the time difference, they had a 6 A.M. wakeup call. Still living on adrenaline, Karyn and nine teammates went to the CBS compound in Nagano to read the 'Top Ten Reasons to Win an Olympic Gold Medal.' Letterman's mother was there to greet the women and congratulate them in person. In fact, the line Bye was handed to read for the top ten list included Mrs. Letterman. It said, "Get to do Jell-O shots with Dave's mom."

The talk show experience was another pinnacle moment, but the excitement still wasn't over. General Mills selected the entire team to be on a Wheaties box, an honor reserved for very few athletes. Over the next few days the women attended the photo shoot for the Wheaties box and met Tipper Gore, wife of then–vice president Al Gore. Karyn took in one speed-skating event as a spectator, the only chance she had to see anything else at the Olympics. She then joined her teammates for dinner at a Japanese restaurant where decorum required them to wear slippers and sit on the floor to eat. The green tea ice cream was not a hit, but the closing ceremony a day or two after that was. The athletes were given little white lanterns to hold aloft as fireworks went off around and above the stadium.

The US men's hockey team was experiencing the opposite feeling at these Games, finishing with a 1–3 record. Despite the presence of Gretzky and other NHL players, the team failed even to make the semifinals. Some athletes vandalized their Olympic Village rooms after the final loss, chalking up three thousand dollars in damages and not painting America in a very positive light. The Olympic team with the fewest NHL players on its roster but the best goalie, the Czech Republic, wound up taking gold while a crowd of 70,000 watched in a town square in Prague.

But the USA women were basking in glory, and the coming months would bring more accolades. Karyn returned to a hero's welcome in River Falls. A fire truck drove her down the center of Main Street, past the only theater in town, which had changed its marquee to read: "Congrats on the GOLD Karyn." When Chuck Bye went back to work at his law firm, he could hardly get anything accomplished thanks to the multitude of people who just wanted to talk about his daughter's achievement. The women's hockey team was invited to the White House to meet President Clinton and was honored at the New York Yankees home opener. The Minnesota Twins called and asked Karyn to throw out the first pitch at one of their games.

All of this was overwhelming and wonderful, but for Karyn the best part was seeing young girls suddenly interested in hockey. Nothing made her smile more than having a hockey player in pigtails or a braid, with a bag slung over her shoulder and a stick in her hand, come up to speak to her and to thank her.

Karyn Bye decided to go to one more Olympics, in Salt Lake City in 2002. She devoted the next four years to training while also working part-time for the Minnesota Wild hockey team, promoting her favorite sport. She said later that Salt Lake City was a very special experience as well, especially for the feelings of patriotism after 9/11, but nothing would ever compare to Nagano and that gold. The US faced Canada once again for the top podium spot in Salt Lake City, but this time the Canadians got their revenge, winning 3–2 for the gold. The US took home silver. Team Canada continued to dominate, winning every gold through 2014 in women's hockey. The United States has taken three silvers and a bronze in that time frame. As of 2014, no team, men's or women's, had won it all for the United States since Karyn and the '98 squad.

"Yes, it was disappointing that we lost the gold medal in Salt Lake City," Karyn said later. "But when I took time to reflect, I was very proud to have played in two Olympics and to have come away with two medals, one gold and one silver."

Looking back, the thing Bye appreciates the most about her athletic career is not wins or losses or even medals. It's the lessons.

"Hockey has taught me to worry only about the things that are in my control," she explained. "For example, there is no reason to worry about the referees, how the other team is going to play, or what the fans are going to do. Instead, focus on skating, making good passes, being positive at all times, and encouraging teammates. I've also learned to accept people for who they are. When a person spends seven straight months with twenty-four other women, one learns a lot about them. Not everyone will have the same opinions that one does, but that's all right."

After the '98 Games Karyn was invited to Indiana for the wedding of her athletic trainer from Nagano. Karyn had no idea she would meet the love of her life there, Ohio native Cal Dietz, a former football player and wrestler and a strength and conditioning coach.

They fell in love and married just after the 2002 Salt Lake City Games. Cal Dietz became the head strength and conditioning coach for the University of Minnesota, and the two settled on the Minnesota-Wisconsin border in Hudson, Wisconsin. They have two children, Tatum and Brody.

Karyn keeps the precious gold and silver medals locked up in a local bank but takes them out frequently to show truly awe-inspired audiences when she does public and motivational speaking. She teaches fitness classes around Hudson, is the color commentator for the Minnesota State Girls High School Hockey Tournament, and runs her own hockey camp, Karyn Bye Gold Medal Skills Camp, in Hudson.

Brody followed his mom's footsteps into hockey. Karyn coaches his team and also serves on her city's youth hockey board. Tatum chose swimming. But it is thrilling and validating for Karyn to know that if her daughter, or any other girl, wanted to lace up the skates and put on the helmet, she would have unlimited resources and support everywhere. It has become the norm. And Tatum Lynn Dietz does not have to list herself as T. L. Dietz in any program. No female athlete will feel pressured to use initials to hide her identity, and that is largely thanks to Karyn's generation.

CHAPTER 17

CASEY FITZRANDOLPH

Speedskating, 1998, 2002, 2006

asey FitzRandolph remembers watching Eric Heiden win his medals
in 1980. Casey was just five years old, cheering on Heiden while
watching on the six-inch black-and-white TV in his family's kitchen in
Verona, Wisconsin, just a few miles from Heiden's hometown of Madison.
Casey had recently decided to become a speedskater after switching from
hockey because he didn't like the physical contact and heavy gear required.
He just wanted to skate, and skate fast.

Inspired by Heiden's Olympic success, Casey spent countless winter days
circling the ice at Madison's Vilas Park Lagoon, where the city's speedskating
club held its practices. At nearby Vilas Zoo, monkeys swung by their tails in
an outside enclosure. Casey has described one of his oldest memories of
long-track skating as "gasping for air with the smell of the monkey cages."

Casey and his younger sister, Jessi, showed enormous talent practically
from the moment they laced up their first speedskates. As they got older and
stronger, they needed tougher competition and a better facility, so their
mother, Ruthie, drove from Verona to the Pettit National Ice Center in Milwaukee at least four nights a week, bringing along home-cooked meals, and
sharpening her children's skates in her free time. Casey and Jessi did homework in the van nearly every night. Casey started winning his age group and
even beating older kids. He liked speedskating but admits now that pressure
from his parents also contributed to both his success and his stress.

"The most stressful years in my speedskating career were ten to four-

Casey FitzRandolph holds his first trophy, in the shape of Wisconsin.
COURTESY OF CASEY FITZRANDOLPH

teen. By and large the expectation was I would win. Second place was the first loser, to put it bluntly; second place was failure. It was not a very relaxing position to be in as a twelve-year-old boy in an individual sport that is as black and white, as exposing, as you're ever going to get. You're expected to win and win and win. Mom and Dad weren't exactly like, 'Oh well, off weekend. So and so's good too.' Not that Dad would chew me out, but he was very intense. There was a lot of stress. I don't want to hide that. It's an important part of our story."

When Casey was twelve he contracted a viral infection that zapped his energy and stamina. He started losing races and felt psyched out. Showing remarkable poise for his age, he agreed to see a psychologist. Through hypnosis, deep relaxation, and visualization, Casey was able to change his mental outlook and his results. "I went on to win the indoor and outdoor national championships that year, so it righted the ship," he said.

After that experience, Casey was a believer in the power of mental preparation. Later in his career he would work with another psychologist who helped him visualize himself as a cheetah on the prowl, the fastest land animal in the world. It would help carry him from his early twenties through three Olympics.

Casey kept on winning through high school and in 1993 started college at Carroll University in Waukesha, near the Pettit Center. His goal was to make the 1994 Olympics in Lillehammer, Norway, more for the experience than anything else. Most speedskaters who medal usually do so in their second Winter Games, and he wanted one Olympics under his belt before the 1998 Games in Nagano, Japan. But he missed making the 1994 team by $8/100$ of a second.

Now Casey had no choice other than to rededicate himself to making it to Nagano. "There was no such thing as an alcoholic beverage in my life," he said. "I gained strength by not doing what everyone else was doing. It gave me a psychological advantage. I was thinking 'I have this dream, and it's not a pipe dream, it's a legitimate opportunity.' I was lucky to have a good group of friends. They had my back. Nobody ever peer pressured me. What I was trying to accomplish and how I proceeded toward my goal was respected and totally cool with them."

The college workload, coupled with kicking for the school's football team and skating, became too much, and he left Carroll, skating full-time as 1998 approached. He won the US Olympic Trials held at the Pettit on January 1998 and the speedskating national championships.

Casey was on his way to his first Olympics. But he had a problem leading up to Nagano. The Dutch introduced the clap skate—which was about to revolutionize the speedskating world.

A traditional speedskate has a long blade that protrudes three inches in both the front and back of the boot and is attached at both toe and heel. On a clap skate, the blade is attached only to the toe, so the back of the blade opens and closes like a movie director's clapboard. The hinged blade makes a clapping sound when it closes. The new design allowed the blade to stay on the ice longer, giving athletes more natural push out of their legs and considerably reducing the number of falls.

Dutch athletes had the skate a full season before the Nagano games. As they started shattering records, everyone wanted in on the action. But Casey was one of the world's most talented skaters, and the Dutch knew it.

"The company in Holland that made them would not sell me a pair of their skates," he explained. "'Oh, sorry, we're out, oh, sorry, we're out,' [they said]. It was one frustrating fax to the owner of this company after another. It was, even in hindsight, ridiculous, a total debacle."

This was supposed to be Casey's Olympics. He had already decided that it wasn't going to be a matter of *if* he would medal in 1998 but rather how many and what color they would be. He had consistently been in the top three in the world in the 500 meters and 1,000 meters. As the season leading up to Nagano progressed and other skaters around the world began skating on the new skates, Casey was crossing the finish line outside the top twenty on his traditional skates.

Casey finally got a pair of the new skates less than two months before the Olympics. "We actually put the things together ourselves," Casey recalled. "US Speedskating [officials], who were becoming equally frustrated because some of our athletes couldn't get skates, finally approached the Easton Aluminum Company for help. Easton was an Olympic sponsor and gladly took on the challenge of creating the blade and clap mechanism for us. So I took the newly created blade with clap mechanism and attached it to the boot from my traditional skate after removing the old blade. Two to three months prior to the Olympics we are sitting in Bonnie Blair's driveway drilling and screwing and gluing our hopes together. I was way behind the eight ball."

"And there comes the psychological aspect as well—the panic and 'Oh my God, I have two months to get this figured out. I've spent my whole life preparing for this and now this is going to happen? You've got to be kidding me,'" Casey recalled thinking.

Every country was scrambling to find clap skates for their athletes, some faring better than others. And the countries that were successful didn't share any information with other countries. Recently retired superstar Blair and other former athletes from several countries who wanted to help the next generation filed formal protests against clap skates with the International Skating Union, speedskating's governing body. They pointed out that speedskating laws say you can't have a mechanical advantage. Even more importantly, they said, if the International Skating Union did approve the clap skates, they should wait until after the 1998 Olympics to do so to give everyone a fair chance to train on them for the next four years.

"But the ISU was run primarily by 'good old Dutch boys' whose country had the technology," Casey maintained. The clap skate stayed in for the Nagano Games, and Casey, who had been looking forward to counting his medals, finished sixth in the 500, seventh in the 1,000, and thirty-first in the 1,500. The US media seemed to view this as a colossal flop, but that's not how Casey saw things.

"The reality of it was it was a huge success coming from where I had been even a month prior," he said. "To get sixth and seventh, I had to skate above and beyond where I had any right being at that point in time. The most important thing I took out of the '98 Games was saying to myself, 'You saw Dan Jansen [fall] and [know] how hard it is when something gets in your head. Forget about sixth and seventh compared to where you were a year ago, and recognize that you used all the energy surrounding the Olympics in a positive way. Consider this a huge success given where you were.'"

Casey returned home with two thoughts about Nagano. "One, a pity party for poor me, I got screwed by the clap skate, yada, yada . . . and two, the Canadians were second, third, fourth, and fifth; all four of their guys beat me in the 500 and it wasn't because they had traditionally been the powers in the world, so they must know something about this new clap skate. I thought, if I'm going to do this and do it right, that means moving to Canada, if they'll let me, to train with people who have figured something out."

Casey had three years to prepare for the 2002 Winter Games in Salt Lake City, Utah. With the memory of Nagano still clear in his mind, he wasn't about to squander his next opportunity even if it meant moving to another country to train. Casey and his new fiancée, Jenn, left for Canada the day after he proposed.

Competing in an Olympics in your home country is a dream that most Olympic athletes never get to experience. When you combine an athlete's brief window of opportunity with the facts that the Winter Games are held every four years and dozens of countries are vying to host, most athletes never get the chance to compete in front of a partisan crowd. The last winter Olympics held in the United States had been in Lake Placid in 1980—Heiden's Olympics. Casey knew he had the opportunity of a lifetime.

He started seeing results right away, and he relished the relaxed, fun attitude the Canadians brought to the ice. They would make bets to see who could skate 100 meters the fastest, often wagering fly fishing paraphernalia. Blasting music in the oval, they danced during down moments. More importantly, Casey's skate times were dropping, and he and Jenn felt very good about the move. They grew close with the Canadian team, especially fellow athlete Jeremy Wotherspoon.

As the Winter Games of 2002 approached, Casey and Canadians Wotherspoon and Mike Ireland were sweeping the podium at national and international events. Casey has estimated that they won sixty-five out of roughly seventy-two medals given out in November through January of that stretch of World Cups and World Sprint Championships in the 500 and 1,000 meters. The three became best friends and best competitors, pushing each other to reach their potential.

In one of the last tune-up races before Salt Lake, Casey slipped coming out of the final turn but nevertheless finished with the best time of his life. His confidence soared. If he could make a mistake and still perform like this, the sky was the limit. He narrowed his focus on not just winning gold but setting a new world record. The Olympics were going to be his playground, and he was ready to tackle the challenge. Yet in his most private moments he battled the demons of self-doubt. Casey knew that the Olympic stage usually sent athletes in one of two directions: you either elevated yourself to the top performance of your life, or you choked. Fear of failure lives in every athlete, and Casey had to work through the process: What if he failed? How could he make sure that he didn't? He continued to practice visualization and relaxation and added Athletes in Action, a Christian organization, to his list of important commitments.

"The catalyst for me was the recognition that, no matter how hard I trained, when the moment of truth came, there were going to be things out of my control," he explained. "It would have been overwhelming to go to the Olympics and feel that my success or failure would dictate my life and who I am as a person. I was working hard to make something happen but also recognizing that it might not happen, and guess what? If it doesn't happen the sun's still going to come up and Jenn's going to love me and life will go on. So I reached out to the Lord and acknowledged that my fate was ultimately in his hands."

By accepting the worst-case scenario, Casey was able to focus on the best. He viewed the buildup to the Games as a time for mental as well as physical prep, and he and his psychologist used all the tools they had, including visualizing the perfect race over and over again, until Casey could play it like a movie in his head.

Finally, the 2002 Winter Olympics arrived. The 500 meters had once been just a single race, but in 1998 the Olympic Committee made it a two-day event, with each athlete competing in two races and total time determining the winner. The IOC made these changes because, in theory, the participant who had to skate the inner track in the last corner was at a disadvantage, as the speeds being skated on the new clap skate made it nearly impossible to hold that corner without slowing down or falling. The solution was two races so that each competitor would skate the inner corner in one race and the outer corner in the other to level the playing field.

Day one of competition, February 11, saw Casey execute a flawless first race on the inner lane. The kid from Wisconsin was sitting two-tenths of a second in front of the rest of the field. That might seem like nothing to people outside of the sport, but in elite speedskating it's a lifetime, equating to about 5 meters. Casey knew he was off to a great start, but his heart was heavy. His friend and training partner Jeremy Wotherspoon, who had shared so many meals and laughs with Casey and Jenn, had slipped and careened to the ice face-first just 30 yards into his race, his Olympic medal dream squelched in a hail of ice chips.

Casey felt sick for his friend, but he had to stay mentally sharp. The US skaters were staying in a house in the neighborhood adjacent to the Utah oval instead of at the Olympic Village, so they could have home-cooked meals, avoid germs, and add to the home ice advantage. Casey was glad to be sharing the space with Kip Carpenter, a fellow Midwesterner who also trained at the Pettit Center and who sat in third place after day one. The two of them tried to joke and keep things light even as they recognized that each was on the verge of achieving a lifelong dream. The distance from family proved to be a good thing, as Casey was able to talk himself into a good sleep the night before race day.

The second leg of the 500 was set for early afternoon on February 12. This was the first Olympics after 9/11, and security had never been tighter. The rink was cordoned off within a one-mile radius, helicopters circled overhead, and police dogs sniffed every bag. It took the FitzRandolph family a long time to make it through the various checkpoints to their seats.

As he did warm-up laps with his favorite music in his ear, Casey made eye contact with his fiancée, sister, mother, and father. "They were all looking a little pale and serious," he remembered. "I tried to get their attention and smile. It made sense that they would be white as ghosts because they had no control. I can understand. I remember watching Jessi race, and it was much harder being a spectator. But I felt so relaxed and confident it was almost surreal."

He saw that Jenn had on her lucky cheetah gloves to symbolize Casey's visualization of himself as a cheetah. The family was well armed with a collection of cowbells and horns, and many of them sported USA tattoos on their cheeks. Casey was grooving to the beat of Van Halen's "Right Here, Right Now" and Montell Jordan's "This is How We Do It." He liked to listen in that order, the first song to get him pumped up and the second to put him in exactly the frame of mind he wanted to be in when he heard the starter's commands.

Now the rink quieted as the final pair, Casey and Kip, stepped to the line. But the race was not destined to go without a hitch.

"The gun went off, and the first 300 meters went well. As Kip and I entered the final turn of the race, Kip went from the inner to outer lane [the skaters are required to switch lanes as they go so each skates an equal distance]," Casey explained. "At the beginning of the corner each lane is marked with a big orange construction cone to prohibit skaters from cutting the corner. At the Olympics they have a ten-pound television camera mounted inside the cone to get shots of skaters coming down the backstretch. Kip misjudged his entry to the corner and leaned into the cone with his knee, and it scooted into my lane."

This came at the most crucial part of the race. The cone spun in front of Casey and hit his leg. He didn't realize Kip had bumped the cone, so his first thought was, "How the hell did I misjudge *that* turn setup so badly?"

It all happened so fast that Jenn and the family didn't even catch the cone movement with the naked eye; they just saw Casey stumble. It wasn't until the replay that they realized what had occurred. With the winning margin so small, any slip in this event usually spells doom for the athlete.

Casey felt his balance sway for just a moment, but all the mental repetition he had done, seeing himself skating the perfect race, paid off in this most imperfect moment. "You need to picture where you're going to be about ten yards ahead so that your body can actually do it in the split second it takes you to get there. I thought, 'Oh boy, that was bad,' but then I was able to think about how I wanted to look in ten yards. I struggled through the first half of that corner a little bit, but I righted the ship."

The 500-meter race takes between 34 and 35 seconds. Casey needed a 34.82 to win the gold medal. He crossed in 34.80, sixth place in that second race but enough to give him the top spot overall by $\frac{3}{100}$ of a second over Japanese competitor Hiroyasu Shimizu. The 5-meter edge Casey had enjoyed after day one was sliced to the equivalent of a skate blade. That's what he won by—a streak of metal, less than a blink of an eye. If you superimposed Casey and Shimizu coming across the line at the same time you'd have a hard time knowing who was first without the benefit of slow-motion replay. Carpenter kept his hold on third. Casey had set an Olympic record, but the hurtling cone had cost him a shot at the world record. That mattered little. Jenn knew right away he had won when the 34.80 flashed across the jumbo scoreboard, and she started screaming.

"He did it, he did it!"

The family went into a joyful frenzy.

Casey himself was so deep in a zone that he had no clue that he had just taken gold. But he was about to find out from his childhood idol, in an unlikely twist of fate. Heiden, US Speedskating's team orthopedist, was one of the first people Casey saw, standing at center ice.

"I crossed the finish line, and because that race hadn't gone as well, I didn't know where I sat overall," Casey said. "The crowd went crazy. I [had been] paired with Kip, who was also in medal contention. I knew something good had happened, but what did it mean? Did it mean we flip-flopped and he won gold and I won bronze? I didn't know. Of course the finish line of the 500 is at the end of the straightaway and the scoreboard is on the middle of the backstretch, so you have to turn your body to see it, which isn't easy when you're going so fast. On the scoreboard there are all kinds of splits, your 500 meter, your lap split, your 100 meter opener, and then there's total times or plus and minus and too many damn numbers! You can't really focus on it because you're still going 40 miles per hour. I'm thinking, 'What happened?' Finally I caught eyes with Heiden on the inside of the track and I did one of these 'What happened?' gestures, and he gave me a big thumbs-up and a big smile. He was walking toward me fast, and I said, 'Me?' and he said, 'Yeah'—and that's when I knew I'd won gold."

Jenn was desperate to get to the ice and hug her fiancé. A cameraman from NBC who saw the family jumping up and down gestured for them to follow him to ice level. There was only one problem: a huge wooden wall had been erected around the oval to prevent people from doing exactly what the FitzRandolphs were attempting—rushing the ice. The wall was so high Jenn could barely see over it on her tiptoes. As she hopped up and down trying to get a view over the wall, her six-foot-two-inch friend Jeremy Wotherspoon approached. He hoisted Jenn up onto his shoulders, and she started snapping pictures of the dramatic minutes following Casey's victory.

Jeff FitzRandolph had raced to the ice right after the victory as well, video camera in one hand and US flag in the other, telling a security guard on the way, "That's my son, he just won gold!" He still couldn't get to Casey, so he passed the flag to Nick Thometz, Bonnie Blair's old training partner who was now director of the oval in Salt Lake City, and said, "Please give this to Casey."

Casey took a victory lap with the flag waving at his side. Jeff was still videotaping, as close as he could get to the ice.

"Way to go, Case!" he screamed, pride swelling in his throat as he watched his son go by. He moved close enough to shake Casey's hand, a poignant moment as the fingers of father and son reached out to touch each other over that tall security wall. The family was overwhelmed with happiness, but it didn't all hit Casey right away.

"It was fairly surreal," he said. I thought, 'All right, I won. I performed,

Casey's father, Jeff, got this flag to his son right after Casey won the gold. COURTESY OF CASEY FITZRANDOLPH

I handled the glitch.' It wasn't until the medals ceremony that the full spectrum of emotions hit me."

First he had more interviews with NBC. Casey tried to put on a brave face, but he still felt despondent that neither Wotherspoon nor their training partner Mike Ireland had medaled after the three of them had owned the podium for months. Jeremy stood just off to the side as reporters peppered Casey with questions.

"If you look at me [in pictures and video from the day] I don't look like someone who just won a gold medal," Casey acknowledged. "I look more like I'm about to cry, for two reasons. Not only was it truly humbling, but I also knew what Jeremy and Mike must be feeling. If they taught me anything they taught me that it's not about a gold medal and beating people. It's about seeing how good you can be and reaching *your* own full potential."

Next it was time for the medals ceremony for the day's winners. Everyone made the ten-minute walk to the Medals Plaza and prepared for another surge of elation. The plaza, which held 10,000 people, was packed. Casey, silver medalist Hiroyasu Shimizu, and Kip Carpenter waited in the green room as other medal ceremonies took place. Because Casey's was the only gold medal won by a US athlete that day, their ceremony would be last to build up emotion in the home crowd.

Finally the skaters were brought onstage to the cheers of thousands. The noise was deafening. Jenn's and Casey's families were in the stands, bundled against the Utah cold and screaming until they were hoarse. It was a magical moment. Casey FitzRandolph was about to be presented the first gold medal won by a US speedskater at the 2002 Salt Lake City Winter Olympic Games and the first in the 500 since Heiden won in 1980. When the first notes of "The Star Spangled Banner" rang out, emotion flooded him.

"I remember being sentimental and then excited and then relieved; that may have actually been my strongest feeling: relief," he said. "I was relieved that it was over but also relieved I had accomplished something I always felt I could but never knew for sure I would. Then I was thankful and proud. Proud of two things—not so much of the gold medal itself but proud of what I had gone through to win the gold medal and also very proud to be an American. It was five months after September 11, and it was very patriotic."

He felt another emotion, this one unexpected—a tinge of depression. "I remember thinking, 'I just found this pot of gold at the end of the rainbow, now what do I do?' Or to put it another way, 'I just climbed the highest mountain peak and it meant everything to me. Now what?' Nothing I could do the next day, the next year, very possibly the rest of my time on this planet would ever match this."

A flurry of activity followed the medals ceremony, including seeing US Olympic Committee sponsors and celebrating with friends and family. Casey was interviewed by Jim Nantz for NBC's late night coverage, and just hours later as morning broke, living on adrenaline and no sleep, he was featured live on "The Today Show" and several radio broadcasts. Jay Leno's people called, asking him to fly to Los Angeles. Scheduled to compete in the 1,000 meters three days later, Casey declined. Then David Letterman's representatives asked him to appear after the 1,000, and Casey and Jenn made plans to fly to New York the day following the race.

Casey wound up finishing the 1,000 meters a disappointing sixth. In retrospect he wonders if he should have further limited the post-500 rat race. Nevertheless, for a few weeks Casey and Jenn lived the jet-setting life of stars. They met James Taylor backstage at a concert and did a flurry of other interviews and appearances. Even after he returned to Wisconsin people would point at him in the grocery store. "It was like being in a fishbowl," he said. "It gave us a new appreciation for what real celebrities have to live with every single day. I can't say I'd want that life. It's a pretty heavy price to pay."

Casey took a year off to figure out his next move. He decided he wanted to give the Olympics one more shot and began to prepare for Turin, Italy, in 2006. He and Jenn moved back to Canada to train. But his first race on February 13, 2006, the 500 in Turin, did not go well. He slipped 50 yards in, and "that was it, game over."

He was in eighteenth place with a time of 35.78 after the first race. Although he was faster to the finish, finishing eighth at 35.34 in the second race, it wasn't enough; he wound up twelfth overall, and five days later, on February 18, he landed in ninth place in the 1,000 meters, crossing the finish line in 109.59.

Now the Olympics were truly behind him. What is life like for an athlete after his or her time is done? For Casey, it was unexpectedly difficult.

Casey retired from speedskating competition at age thirty-one. Like many Olympic athletes, Casey had forgone college graduation and a career path in pursuit of his dream. He hadn't earned a degree and was now almost a decade behind his peers in the workforce. Luckily, two businesses that had sponsored his speedskating career invited him to jump on board. He settled on a career in business insurance, first with Wausau Insurance and later with M3 Insurance in Madison. It was a great opportunity but a huge learning curve for a guy who admittedly didn't even know what property and casualty insurance was. Plus, working in the real world changed the very structure of his life.

"You go from being able to physically exert yourself on a day-to-day basis in order to find satisfaction and control, to having to sit and think 95 percent of the time," he explained. "That's a huge change, and all of a sudden not using your body as much chemically changes you too. I had success at the ultimate level, which you can't duplicate. How can you proclaim that you are the best in the world at selling insurance as a matter of fact? You can't. So really you're not duplicating anything from your former life."

Speedskating is black and white: the clock doesn't lie. Casey suddenly felt as if he were living in a murky grey. How was he to measure success? Everything about this new civilian lifestyle took time to adjust to, and he struggled to find his place.

Even as Casey and Jenn raised their two children, Sawyer and Cassidy, Casey's transition to this new life was amplified by the fact that he had been hardwired for so many years to think about himself first. "One of the traits that allowed me to be the best at what I did was being self-centered," he said, "and Jenn didn't realize how difficult that is to change. Neither did I, to be honest, as I still am fairly self-centered. I do a lot of good things for other people in the world and I have a good heart, but when I'm not trying to make a positive difference in our community and country, I tend to focus a lot on what Casey is doing and on Casey's goals and dreams and priorities. I think she thought—we both thought—that would go away more quickly after I was done skating."

The challenges to their marriage nearly pushed Casey and Jenn to the breaking point. But Casey slowly came to a realization. It took a lot of deep self-reflection. "I remember thinking the grass must be greener somewhere else. But then I reminded myself the grass always looks greener when you're not looking at it through your magnifying glass. It was a tough period for us for close to two years. I finally decided that I didn't want to leave my family. That I wanted to be with Jenn and raise our children and move forward together as a team."

On the heels of that rocky patch came the news that Casey's little sister, Jessi, had stage IV breast cancer. "There was a period, I didn't even tell Jenn all of it, but I actually took a small dosage of antidepressants. I remember having a real hesitancy, thinking we're too drug dependent as a society and I don't want to rely on a drug to be happy in my life. . . . I took half the suggested dose for about three months, then weaned myself off and have never had a desire to take them again. It wasn't something I was proud of, but in hindsight I think it actually helped because I literally couldn't sleep. My anxiety and stress levels were through the roof."

Casey also leaned on his faith to help him through that shaky stretch. He felt a connection with God most when outside in nature. An outdoorsman for as long as he could remember, Casey had always wanted to own a piece of land. He and Jenn bought land and set about planting 20,000 trees

LIFE AFTER THE OLYMPICS: SUZY FAVOR HAMILTON

Suzanne Marie Favor began running as a child on the trails by the Plover River near her home in Stevens Point, Wisconsin, collecting sticks as she went to build forts with her three older siblings. Running was more than just easy for her—she was a born superstar. Suzy won eleven state titles at Stevens Point Area Senior High, twenty-three Big Ten titles, and nine NCAA crowns while on the track and field team at the University of Wisconsin. The Big Ten Female Athlete of the Year award, which she won in 1988, 1989, and 1990, was named in her honor. She made the Olympics three times but had disappointing showings in

Suzy Favor-Hamilton, seen here in 1992, was a high school and college star but eventually admitted to falling on purpose at the Olympics. KIRBY LEE/IMAGE OF SPORT—USA TODAY SPORTS

1992 in Barcelona (1,500 meters) and 1996 in Atlanta (800 meters).

Shortly before her final Olympic appearance, in 2000, Suzy's brother Dan committed suicide. Suzy wanted nothing more than to honor him with a victory. She was leading the 1,500 meter final with 200 meters to go. The finish line was within sight, just 30 seconds away. Then suddenly, shockingly, and for no apparent reason, she slowed and broke stride, tumbled to the turf, and fell as other competitors shot past her. At first Suzy indicated it was some type of injury. It was only many years later, after therapy, that she was able to admit the truth.

She had come to the starting line filled with self-doubt and anxiety, partly due to a lack of energy because her tiny physique (104 pounds) did not hold up well in the grueling Olympic format in which runners had to complete two qualifying races just to get to the finals. She knew she couldn't hang on, even for 200 more meters. She felt herself losing ground. She began hyperventilating. Panic struck as she realized she would not win, not for her brother or for anyone else. Runners began passing her, and disappointment and shame coursed through her body.

"Coming around that last corner, the anxiety gripped me so bad," she explained. "It told my brain, 'Just fall. That's the easiest solution. Just fall and this will all go away.' That was the only way out. I remember it so clearly. I remember my cheek hitting the track. I remember the thoughts I was telling myself. It was completely negative: 'You're an idiot. Everybody is staring at you right now. Look at what you did.' Just being so cruel to myself."

Suzy eventually toured as a motivational speaker, telling her tale, and addressing the reality of being an elite athlete, including how well-intentioned loved ones can harm your psyche.

"Your whole life, you're told how great you are, from your coaches to your friends to your parents' friends. I had to be the perfect child, in my mind. The [self-inflicted] pressure to win was great."

Life after the Olympics is not something fans often think about when they watch the Games, but the transition away from the spotlight and downshifting from life as an elite athlete can be difficult. Suzy married, had a daughter, and became a real estate agent in Madison. But she was leading a double life, flying off to work as a high-priced call girl for an escort service.

"I take full responsibility for my mistakes. I'm not the victim and I'm not going that route," she told the website The Smoking Gun, which broke the story in 2012. "I'm owning up to what I did. I would not blame anybody except myself. Everybody in this world makes mistakes. I made a huge mistake. Huge."

After the story came out, the Big Ten removed her name from its conference Female Athlete of the Year award, and Suzy retreated into privacy.

"[I'm] focused on getting well and making amends to my loved ones," she told the *Milwaukee Journal Sentinel* in 2013. In 2015 she published her memoir, *Fast Girl: A Life Spent Running from Madness,* in which she chronicled her struggle with bipolar disorder. She lives with her husband and daughter in Los Angeles, where she teaches yoga and speaks publicly on mental health issues.

to create new travel corridors giving animals food and cover. They planted a variety of food sources and even dug small ponds to provide drinking water for the wildlife. Casey bought a tractor and tended to every part of his new land. It was the final piece that brought Casey back from the dark place he sometimes went to. "It was a lifesaver, almost literally," he stated.

When he thinks about his intense, win-at-all-costs childhood, Casey sees many pros, like the work ethic instilled in him from kindergarten. But there are cons.

"At age forty I feel like I've worked for thirty-five years. . . . My body feels the effects. I'm nine years into my second career now at forty, and I wonder if I had started in my twenties and put half the effort into a professional career that I did into speedskating, where would I be now? Would I be making half a million bucks and we wouldn't have the stress that we have now about finances?"

When asked if he would go back and change any of the past, Casey FitzRandolph took a long time to answer. He looked down, deep in thought, as if he were flipping through a photo album that contained single snapshots of every important moment of his existence. His eyes were far away as he pondered the question.

"No . . . but it's so hard to answer because if my childhood was different, then my perspective on life would be different as well. The bottom line is, the experiences were great, there were a lot of perks and there were some cons, but being able to say I was the best in the world at what I did is something almost no one can say. I'll take that as a source of pride to my grave. That is priceless to me."

CHAPTER 18

CHRIS WITTY

Speedskating, 1994, 1998, 2002, 2006, and Cycling, 2000

Chris Witty's story is as much a story of personal triumph as it is a tale of Olympic stardom. Witty lived for years with an unspeakable secret that she broke free of only later in life.

Christine Witty was a year old when her parents, Walter and Diane, moved with their four children to West Allis, Wisconsin. She was the only girl of the siblings. The first person to welcome the family to the neighborhood was a neighbor who Walter and Diane soon trusted so much that they gave him a spare key. They could not have known that he had been convicted of molestation a few years earlier and had been given probation and psychiatric treatment.

It wasn't long before the neighbor turned to little Chris. The sexual abuse began. After each incident, he would warn her: "Don't tell your dad. Don't tell anyone." And she wouldn't. She was terrified and confused.

Sports became an escape for Chris. She zoomed around on her bike, racing against her brothers, pretending she was a race car driver, usually winning. Her favorite sports involved speed—biking, running, and skating, perhaps seeking something that made her feel in control of her own body, perhaps instinctually trying to flee.

Chris donned a pair of one of her brothers' figure skates at the age of nine or ten. At her first race, the 500 meters, her mother came to watch. Chris flew so far ahead of the pack that she was able to cruise up to Diane and take her skates off before the second-place finisher even crossed the line. Chris had naturally explosive legs and the perfect build for the sport. A coach with the West Allis Speedskating Club noticed the amazing little skater and asked her to consider joining his team. Chris had been thinking of becoming a basketball player, but she realized she had some serious talent on blades and agreed.

At the age of eleven, after seven years of the silent horror of abuse, Witty and her sixth-grade classmates watched a video about sexual abuse. It would change her life. Suddenly she had a name for what was happening to her, and she knew she could say no. She was empowered. The next time the neighbor tried to touch her, Witty told him to stop. To her amazement and relief, the abuse ceased, but she still didn't have the courage to tell anyone what she had endured. Friends and family always thought Witty had a distant quality about her. She kept to herself and was quiet a lot of the time, which she can explain now was because she didn't trust anybody.

Money was tight for the Witty family, and Chris nearly had to give up skating. Her father lost his job as a welder when the Allis-Chalmers factory, where he worked manufacturing tractors, shut down. Even after Chris outgrew her secondhand skates, she kept shoving her feet in, knowing there was no money for a new pair. Chris and her brother Mike began saving up their paper route money at age twelve to help with skating expenses. She was willing to do whatever it took to stay in the sport, even if that meant sleeping in hotel rooms with five or six other skaters to cut costs. Somehow, she managed to scrape by and stay on track.

In 1994 Witty had progressed so far in speedskating that she made her first Olympic team at the age of eighteen. She was going to Lillehammer. This would be Bonnie Blair's final Olympics, and the spotlight was trained on Witty's fellow Wisconsinite. Chris skated in just one event, the women's 1,000, along with Blair. Bonnie took the gold, shattering history in the process as it was her record fifth gold medal. Witty, one of the youngest competitors, skated to twenty-third place out of thirty-six competitors.

After '94 Chris took up cycling, one of her old childhood joys, as a way to cross train for speedskating. She was so good she won a spot as an alternate on the Olympic team competing at the 1996 Summer Games in Atlanta. That same year, the abusive neighbor pled guilty to second-degree sexual assault of a girl who was only four years old. Witty knew the young-ster and had been her babysitter. This news crushed her. She couldn't help thinking that if she had spoken up earlier, this other child could have been spared the nightmare of abuse. Chris buried her guilt and depression, again remaining silent.

As 1998 approached, speedskating was turned upside down by the in-vention of the clap skate. Just as Casey FitzRandolph had discovered, the new skate, with its blade that opened freely from the back, required an entirely different kind of acceleration, speed, and form. Chris was less than pleased, telling the *New York Times*, "It was such a pure sport before. Now we've gone to mechanics. You can't sit back and whine. But I think the Olympics might not be as honest as they should be."

Like FitzRandolph, Witty had to scramble to practice with the new skates. Witty's coach, Gerard Kemkers, attempted to sum up for the *New York Times* the frustrations everyone was feeling with less than a year until the Nagano 1998 Games: "The I.S.U. [International Skating Union] is not taking control. They should give everyone an equal start, not some three- to six-month headstart. It's a nervous time. . . . The people in the best physical and mental shape should win the gold medal, not the people with the best spring system."

After a period of controversy, Team USA accepted the reality that clap skates were there to stay. Soon they saw the remarkable results for them-selves. Witty set a new world record in the 1,000 on clap skates, while other skaters who had previously sworn disdain were now singing the praises of a skate that made them go faster.

Chris went to the 1998 Games in Nagano at the age of twenty-two, clap skates in her luggage and a medal on her mind. She was also dealing with heavy expectations from a country hungry for the next speedskating phe-nom. No one was sure if this next generation of speedskaters could take the reins from Bonnie Blair and Dan Jansen, but their hopes started with Witty. She was a new generation, complete with a pierced navel, a tattoo on her hip of a Notre Dame Fighting Irishman (based on her Irish heritage, not an allegiance to the university), and two earrings in her left ear. The feisty free spirit with the undisclosed childhood pain would compete in three distances, the 1,000 being her specialty.

Her first race was the 500 meters, held on February 13 and 14 at the Nagano venue called the M-Wave. Not known as a sprinter, Witty had some mistakes and slips and finished tenth, still the top American but nowhere near twenty-seven-year-old gold medalist Catriona Le May Doan of Canada. Witty was disappointed in her showing but had a good practice the next day. The day after that was the 1,500.

Marianne Timmer of the Netherlands skated in one of the early pairs. She was considered a long shot for a medal but got off to a fast start and held on to break the world record at 1:57.58. She was so shocked, she collapsed into the arms of her coach, Peter Mueller, at the end. Timmer then watched from the sidelines as the 500-meter gold medalist, Le May Doan, surprisingly faded to finish thirteenth. Chris was in the second-to-last pair and clocked in at 1:58.97, a very solid time that put her right in the mix near the top but with no chance of gold. Then she watched the final skater. Thirty-one-year-old German veteran athlete Gunda Niemann was competing alone, as her pairmate had withdrawn due to the flu. Chris was assured a medal; she just didn't know if it would be silver or bronze. Gunda crossed the line in 1:58.66, about three-tenths of a second better than Witty. The gold went to a flabbergasted Timmer, silver to the well-respected Niemann, and bronze to the rising star Chris Witty. Her first medal was made all the more special by having her parents and two of her three brothers there.

"The 1,500 was not a race I expected to medal," she told the *Los Angeles Times*. "I hoped to finish in the top five. I actually surprised myself a lot. I felt great technically and physically, and winning a medal is like having a dream come true. Some of America has been really hard on us. Dan and Bonnie are gone. People didn't think we'd win a medal, but now we have a bronze and a good chance in the thousand."

The 1,000 was three days later, on February 19. The smart money was on Le May Doan, Witty, Timmer, and Franziska Schenk of Germany to duke it out for the top finishes. All had posted times worthy of medals in previous races. Sixteen other pairs went off, and no one dipped below 1:18. Witty and the others knew they could skate a full second or so faster than that. The Canadian, Le May Doan, was the first of the elite skaters to race, and she came in at 1:17.37. Timmer and Schenk were next. Timmer trailed Schenk at the first split, but suddenly, shockingly, Schenk tripped and fell

Chris Witty went to five Olympics in two sports and won one gold, one silver, and one bronze. © 2015 JOURNAL SENTINEL, INC., REPRODUCED WITH PERMISSION

to the ice, her face buried in her arms, a horrible end to her dream. Timmer not only stayed on course but dropped the leading time to 1:16.51. Now Timmer was in the pacesetter's car for gold, with Le May Doan behind her.

The final contender was Witty. It was up to her now, whether she would medal at all, and what color it would be, to be decided in the next minute and change. Witty took off with a charge and pushed herself as hard as she could. She matched Timmer's split times, but in the final lap she did not put on the push that Timmer had. Chris crossed in 1:16.51, 0.28 slower than Timmer, equivalent to the snap of a finger. It was a silver medal for the twenty-two-year-old Witty. She left Nagano with two medals.

Witty would be back at the Olympics sooner rather than later. She returned to cross training on a bicycle after the Winter Games. That childhood love of bikes had never gone away. Witty got so good so quickly—first place in the 500 time trials at nationals and fourth in the World Championships—that she made Team USA outright and was headed to Sydney, Australia, for the 2000 Summer Olympics just two years after taking silver and bronze in the winter. She started thinking about a cycling medal. "I'm hoping I can squeak past a few people," Witty told an interviewer. "I'd love to get gold. Anything can happen at the Olympics. People can come out of nowhere."

Witty was only the ninth American athlete to compete in both the Summer and Winter Games (fellow Wisconsinite Connie Carpenter Phinney was another, and only three people had medaled in both). In Chris's favor was a lack of expectations. She wasn't under pressure to perform or carry the hopes of an entire sport, yet she knew how the Olympics worked from a media and hype standpoint, so she was confident she wouldn't be intimidated. She had a clear and calm sense of purpose. She wasn't a gold medal favorite and was up against the likes of four-time world sprint champion Félicia Ballanger of France, but she would give it her all.

"If you had the opportunity, why would you pass it up?" Witty said of cycling in the Olympics, adding with a laugh, "Plus, it's good training for speedskating."

Chris was entered in just one race, the 500-meter time trial, and she was the only US representative in the new event. Seventeen cyclists had qualified and would do two laps each inside the Dunc Gray Velodrome, a closed facility with a track sloped at about a 45-degree angle for cycling on a banked course. On Saturday, September 16, 2000, the women took their turns. Although Witty finished in a very impressive 35.230 seconds, Ballanger blew the field away at 34.140, and three others sneaked ahead of Witty in the standings. She finished fifth. For training for such a short time, this was remarkable, but she had not been able to join the super-elite group of athletes who've earned medals in both the Summer and Winter Games. Witty never went back to the Summer Games.

Her focus back on the ice, Witty trained for 2002, but she had a problem. In the months leading up to Salt Lake City she couldn't figure out why she was constantly fatigued. Finally seeing a doctor, she was told she might have had mononucleosis earlier in the year and was still battling the effects.

It was now only weeks until competition, and her spirits sagged. And her body wasn't the only thing feeling weighed down. Witty's mind was reeling with the news that her childhood abuser had recently been released from prison after a four-year sentence and had, in fact, moved right back across the alley from Witty's parents, no longer required to wear a monitoring bracelet.

"So then I was thinking he really is free," Witty told the *Orange County Register* years later. "So it was eating away at me before the Olympics."

Overcoming mono is one thing. Overcoming demons is quite another. Witty finally confided in Team USA's sports psychologist. He advised her that the best thing to do was to forget the past until after the Olympics but made her promise to see a counselor immediately afterward.

"And I think he kind of lifted a weight off me," Witty said. "It made it OK to just focus on the event, and I did that."

As both the media and Chris's competitors started to find out about the mono, many assumed she would not be physically able to contend for a medal. They didn't know Chris well enough. Shaking off her illness, she skated in three races, the 500, 1,000, and 1,500. It was in the 500 that she really shone. Witty was paired with old rival Catriona Le May Doan of Canada. Le May Doan got off the line quickly but slowed in the final lap. That's when Witty soared with a final split of 28.90 to come across the line not only as the leader but as the first woman to break 1:14. Her time was 1:13.83, an amazing mark. There were several pairs to go, and Witty watched nervously. World record holder Sabine Volker of Germany was in one of them. She could also go under 1:14, Witty knew, and she did, clocking in at 1:13.93, a tenth of a second slower than Chris. Witty exhaled as she held on to win her first and only gold medal—not only in world record time, but in a most unexpected fashion following her sickness. With everything she was dealing with, both publicly and personally, this was a triumph of epic proportions. To put it in perspective and show how far and fast speedskating was changing with the clap skate, Witty's time was more than five seconds faster than Bonnie Blair's winning 1,000 mark eight years earlier in Lillehammer, and good enough to have won the men's gold medal in 1992 in France. It was huge news and the worldwide media mobbed Witty in the postrace press conference. But she still wasn't ready to open up about her deepest emotions and childhood scars.

"Every reporter, they want you to fit into every little cliché, you know," she explained, "whether it's God, family, country, and I never went with any one of them, but in the back of my mind I was going, 'I wish I could really tell them what's making me tick right now in my life. I wish I could tell them what's really going on.'"

Chris took fifth in the 1,500 that same Olympics, and just one month later she kept her promise to see a psychotherapist. Beginning to peel back the layers, she started to feel better, but not all the way. She searched her soul for what was missing. Finally, the last piece of the puzzle of her healing clicked into place. She would need to go public. Starting in 2004, just before her final Olympics in Turin, Italy, Witty opened up in several interviews, telling the truth about her past. It was time. "Abuse of any kind thrives off of secrecy," she said. "And that's why it exists and why it will continue, so I just felt like if I started talking about it, maybe other people would talk about it and it can be prevented."

She was embraced by those who loved her and by other victims of abuse, and she was immediately inundated with emails and letters from people sharing their own stories. Witty spoke at a fundraiser for a counseling center in Milwaukee and to other groups around the country, always drawing a large crowd. Her goal was to let children know that abuse was not their fault and that there was a way to stop it—tell someone. Opening up wasn't easy for her with so many years of suppressed emotions, but this felt as good as anything she had done at the Olympics. "It's an accomplishment that's as big if not bigger than winning the gold medal," she told the *Orange County Register.*

Witty finished twenty-seventh in the 1,000 and twenty-eighth in the 500 in Turin, but there was a much bigger moment for her. The Team USA captains chose Chris to carry the Stars and Stripes into the stadium at the opening ceremony. It's an honor bestowed upon only one athlete each Olympics and truly one of the top acknowledgments from fellow athletes.

"I can't imagine a bigger honor than this," she said at a press conference before the Games. And to NBC News she said, "Think about our team. We have so many great successful athletes. To lead a team like this is a true honor, and to represent not just our team but our country at that moment is amazing to me."

She might never have been happier or more free than she was on that night, leading hundreds of US athletes into the opening ceremony with a shy grin on her face, her eyes alive with light and yet strangely peaceful.

Witty retired after 2007. She continued to speak on behalf of abuse survivors and relocated to the Netherlands with her partner, fellow women's speedskater Frouke Oonk. In 2015 Chris gave birth to a baby boy she and her partner named Rhys. It was a crowning moment in a new life far from home, across the ocean both literally and figuratively, from her past.

"There are ghosts that will follow you around your whole life," Witty said. "I think I've met a few of those ghosts head-on."

CHAPTER 19

PAUL HAMM

Gymnastics, 2000, 2004

Wisconsin's Paul Hamm was involved in one of history's most controversial Olympic moments. It happened in 2004, twenty-one years after a set of twins was born in Waukesha, Wisconsin.

Born to Sandy and Cecily Hamm in 1983, Paul and Morgan Hamm always acted like little monkeys. The two began swinging from the rafters of the family barn at an early age and fashioned a pommel horse out of a maple tree. Their father was an All-American springboard diver, and their older sister, Betsy, was the first to get involved in organized gymnastics. Paul decided to follow her, and six months later, Morgan jumped aboard. Sandy and Cecily could see right away that the boys were budding talents. They began researching coaches and eventually tracked down another Sandy, Sandy Maloney, who had been a US national gymnast in the 1970s and 1980s. Maloney, who had been toying with the idea of becoming a rock musician, took one look at the twins and changed his mind. He took over coaching them when they were eight.

"Gymnastics became a part of me," Paul said. "Some kids throw themselves into comic books; for us it was gymnastics." The Swiss Turners Gymnastics Academy in Milwaukee became the Hamms' second home, and as they grew to their full height of five feet six inches, they trained day and night in between studies at Waukesha South High School. By the time the two were seventeen, US Gymnastics head coach Peter Kormann was hailing them as geniuses. "I've never seen anybody who's got everything—the

Paul and Morgan Hamm got their gymnastics start swinging from the rafters of the family barn. JERRY LAI—USA TODAY SPORTS

smarts, the talent—especially in people so young," Kormann said at the time.

Both Paul and Morgan made the US team headed to Sydney, Australia, for 2000, making them the first set of gymnastics twins ever to compete at an Olympics. They had a modest showing: Paul came in fourteenth in the individual all-around, and Morgan was fifty-seventh. Team USA finished fifth in the team event, out of medal contention.

As has happened for so many Olympians, it would be their second go-round that would be the breakthrough.

In the year leading up to the 2004 Games in Athens, Greece, Paul became the first American to win the all-around title at the World Championships. He was poised for Olympic greatness and knew a gold medal was his if he performed up to his capabilities with no mistakes.

There would be two major competitions at the Games, team and individual, and athletes had to compete in the floor exercise, vault, parallel bars, high bar, rings, and pommel horse. Team USA sat in second place after the qualifications, with Paul and Morgan two of the six athletes trying to win America's first team gymnastics medal in twenty years.

The team finals were first. After five rotations, the US was in third behind Japan and Romania. America would need a strong showing on the high bar to move up. A Romanian athlete helped the Americans' cause immensely when he suffered a bad dismount that led to an ugly fall and a very low score—but then Paul nearly fell, too. Feeling incredible pressure to perform perfectly, he slipped on a release move and barely held on, giving him a score of 9.462 in what was considered one of his top events. The Romanian's spill moved the US into second place, however, and only Japan remained on the bar.

The Japanese made it look easy, breezing through with no one scoring less than 9.787. This wrapped up the gold for them and the silver for the US. It was US Gymnastics' first medal since taking gold in 1984, the year of the Soviet boycott, and only their second since 1932. The president of US Gymnastics, Bob Colarossi, had tears in his eyes as he gushed, "I'm just so proud." Team member Blaine Wilson promised, "I'm never going to take this medal off, never. I'm going to sleep with it, shower with it, eat with it. I'll be an old man and I'll still be wearing it."

With olive wreaths on their heads, Team USA stood on the podium for the medals ceremony. The *New York Times* described how in awe the six gymnasts were. "They examined their [medals] gently, as if they were eggs, as if squeezing them too hard would put cracks in their waking dream." It was not their anthem playing, yet it was one of the most powerful and moving moments of their lives. And there was still hope that Paul might capture gold in the individual.

The event kicked off on August 14. Hamm was back at the top of his game and came out of qualifications in first place, right where he should have been based on world standings. Yang Tae-Young of South Korea was second and Hiroyuki Tomita from Japan third. The qualifying scores would not carry over, but the rankings were still an indication of the pecking order.

On the morning of the finals, August 18, the biggest day of his career, Hamm woke up feeling inexplicably sluggish, sore, and tired. He had to mentally push through warm-ups to get ready for the finals.

BEEZIE MADDEN

Paul Hamm wasn't the only competitor who wasn't feeling well before the 2004 Athens games. A week before competition, one of the elite athletes, Authentic, had a terrible stomachache.

Authentic was not a so-famous-I-go-by-one-name celebrity; he was a Dutch Warmblood gelding and the star of the US equestrian show jumping team that year. His rider, Elizabeth Patton—born in 1963 in Mequon, Wisconsin, and nicknamed Beezie after a grandmother—had been a horse lover since she began riding a horse named Flicka at the age of three.

Now Beezie's prized partner had come down with an alarming case of gut rot, a very serious condition that can mean twisted intestines. International Olympics rules do not allow horses to receive any medicine before an event, so Authentic could not be given anti-inflammatories, the usual course of treatment. Beezie and her husband, John Madden, were desperate for a solution. There was one last hope. John and their veterinarian gave Authentic fluids through a catheter, and the vet did a rectal exam to feel where the intestine was out of place. They encouraged Authentic to roll over twice, and when Authentic stood up the intestine was back where it should be. The stomachache was gone, and Beezie and Authentic went on to win gold in the 2004 team jumping competition.

Four years later in Beijing, Madden won gold in team jumping and bronze in individual jumping. She competed at a third Games, in London in 2012, when she was forty-eight years old. After retiring she could claim three Olympics, three medals, and a stellar run over twelve years. She lives in upstate New York with her husband and a stable of horses.

Beezie's parents still live in Wisconsin. "We burst with pride about her," her father, Joe Patton, once told a Milwaukee television station.

Indeed, the onetime three-year-old who loved horses made a career out of her passion, competing long after many other athletes would have been forced to retire. And Beezie was one of the best in a sport that doesn't get nearly as much attention as the mainstream Olympic events but still takes every bit of discipline, sacrifice, and ingenuity.

Whatever he did seemed to work, as Paul Hamm was in first after the floor rotation with a score of 9.725. The pommel horse was next, and his total of 9.700 kept him in first. The third rotation only solidified his standings: rings, 9.587, first again. To an observer he seemed to have moved past his lethargy, but Paul still felt not quite right. Only three rotations remained, and next up was the vault.

"I just remember running for the vault runway, hitting the springboard, block off the table, thinking something is not right here," Hamm recounted for Team USA's online magazine ten years later. "I was off a little bit. It was probably from being a little tired."

Paul landed the vault but stumbled and nearly crashed into the judges' scoring table.

"It almost seemed surreal," he said. "Did that really just happen? That's not how I had pictured this competition going."

His score was a very low 9.137, and he had suddenly tumbled to twelfth place in the overall standings, a shocking turn of events. He was crushed, thinking that a gold medal was now impossible. The competitor in him roared up, and he talked to himself, repeating over and over that he was not going to give up or go out on a bad note. Silver and bronze remained within reach. He consulted with his coach, and the two determined that if he could score 9.8 or higher in both of the final two events, he might medal. The counseling—both in his head and with his coach—worked. Paul would have the best performances of his life in the next two events.

In the parallel bars Hamm turned in a brilliant showing, outclassing everyone else with a score of 9.837, the best of the apparatus, enough to push him back to fourth place overall. He would later call it the best parallel bar routine he had ever done.

Now it would all come down to the high bar again.

"I hopped onto the bar, did my releases as good as I could do. I thought if I could stick the landing maybe I could pull a silver medal for this," Hamm told Team USA.

Indeed, his landing was absolute perfection. His feet balanced expertly and soundly on the mat, he barely flinched, and he threw his arms into the air, thinking perhaps he had just secured that silver. The scoreboard flashed his points: 9.837.

Forget silver.

Paul Hamm had just become the first American man to win gold in the all-around—and by the absolute slimmest of margins, 0.012, over Kim Dae-Eun of South Korea. Yang Tae-Young, also of South Korea, was in third place.

Hamm was overcome with emotion. Had he really just rallied back from twelfth place to win gold? He went to the podium emotional, exhilarated, and exhausted. He had done it. He had overcome his fatigue and a terrible vault to capture what everyone had believed he would in the first place: that gold medal. He had pushed through the high expectations, set by himself and others, and dealt with the pressure that goes along with being the front-runner. And he had emerged victorious against a brutally tough group of competitors. A boy who got his start tumbling around in a Wisconsin barn had just set Olympics history for his country.

But controversy loomed.

The South Koreans approached the head judge, who was from the United States. They began to argue that the start value for Tae-Young's parallel bars routine had been 9.9, when it should have been 10.0 for the degree of difficulty. If it had been marked correctly, they said, their man would be sitting with the gold medal and Hamm the bronze. The US judge waved them off. The Koreans appealed to the A panel of judges, two men from Colombia and Spain. After a careful review, the judges did note an error in the start value that would support the Koreans' claim. Then the US Gymnastics officials argued that Tae-Young had also had a slip-up in his routine, performing four hangs when only three were allowed. If he had been penalized for this, the 0.2 penalty would have negated any difference in start value.

Back and forth the argument went, the Korean Olympic Committee now saying that other gymnasts had not been penalized for long hangs. The protest landed in the laps of the Fédération Internationale de Gymnastique (FIG), who noted that the rules stated that all protests must be filed during competition, not after. In other words, if the Koreans felt the start value was wrong, they needed to have spoken up about it immediately after Tae-Young's routine, not after the gold medal had been delivered.

Suddenly everyone had an opinion. Sports fans worldwide discussed the situation. Hamm should return the medal to the rightful winner. He should not. Maybe they should both be awarded gold. It went on for days. The South Koreans filed an official protest. FIG's executive committee reviewed the case and released a statement, noting that the start value had indeed been incorrect but refusing to change the results because of the delay before the Koreans protested. Three judges were suspended.

Meanwhile, Paul Hamm still had four medals to fight for in the event finals on August 22 and 23. He was definitely not performing to his elite standard, the stress likely taking a toll. He finished fifth in floor, sixth in pommel horse, and seventh on the parallel bars. Then came the high bar, and with it his final chance for another medal. The last thing Hamm needed was a second controversy. He got one, but through no fault of his own.

Hamm was scheduled to follow the 2000 Olympic all-around champion, Alexei Nemov of Russia. Nemov performed a complicated routine that included six releases, four of them in a row. The audience loved it and thought he deserved a huge score, but the judges came back with only a 9.725. The crowd launched into loud booing that lasted close to fifteen minutes and put a halt to the competition while the judges were forced to reevaluate the score. They eventually upped Nemov's marks to 9.762, but that still kept him out of medal contention for the apparatus, and the booing only intensified.

Through all of this Hamm was warmed up and ready to deliver his bar performance, but all he could do was stand by awkwardly and wait, thoughts of the South Korean protest still in his head.

"I'm going through this controversy and it kind of looks like they're booing at me," Hamm recalled ten years later. "I eventually had to ask Alexei to get up on the podium and gesture to the crowd to calm down. I wanted to compete without the booing [but] I eventually had to begin my routine with the booing there. Once I hopped onto the bar I heard the crowd quiet down, but that was an intense way to begin my competition. The whole situation: you have the comeback, you have the controversy and now this booing—it's almost overwhelming."

Remarkably, Hamm was able to put all of it aside while on the high bar. He performed so expertly that he took silver, his third medal of the Athens

Games and the last of his career. Nemov finished fifth in the bars. Meanwhile, questions were still blazing about the rightful owner of the men's all-around gold: Hamm or Tae-Young.

Strangely, the head of FIG decided to appeal directly to Paul, asking him to return the gold out of the goodness of his heart. Bruno Grandi, FIG president, wrote Paul a letter that he sent to the US Olympic Committee, part of which read:

> I wish to remind you that the FIG Executive Committee has admitted the error of judgement made on the Parallel Bars and suspended the three responsible judges, two from the A panel and the FIG Technical Committee member. Indeed, the start value of the Korean gymnast Yang Tae Young was given as 9.9 instead of 10. As a result, the true winner of the All-Around competition is Yang Tae Young. If, (according to your declarations to the press), you would return your medal to the Korean if the FIG requested it, then such an action would be recognised as the ultimate demonstration of Fairplay by the whole world. The FIG and the IOC would highly appreciate the magnitude of this gesture. At this moment in time, you are the only one who can make this decision.

The US Olympic Committee was incensed. They refused to forward the letter to Paul, instead responding in a letter of their own:

> Your letter states "the IOC would highly appreciate the magnitude of this gesture." You should know that upon receipt of your letter, we immediately contacted the International Olympic Committee and its President, Dr. Jacques Rogge, which expressed its displeasure over the fact the FIG would even consider placing an athlete in such an untenable position and strongly stated they do not support the letter or its contents.
>
> Mr. Grandi, it is important to remind you that your own Federation rules, and your own public statements, clearly indicate that Mr. Hamm is the Olympic gold medalist in the 2004 Individual Men's All-Around. We share and support that viewpoint. The statement in your letter that "the true winner of the All-Around competition is Yang

Tae Young" is not only inconsistent with your rules and public statements, it is incorrect and undermines the very spirit of the Olympic Games.

As stewards of the Olympic movement, we all share a responsibility to protect, and not sacrifice, the interests of athletes. We encourage you and other individuals within FIG, who saw this as an appropriate remedy, to begin taking that responsibility more seriously. Once again, we urge you to immediately retract this unacceptable request.

The Koreans took the dispute to the independent Court of Arbitration for Sports. It wasn't until late September, more than a month after the competition, that the Court of Arbitration met in Lausanne, Switzerland, to discuss the case in what would be a twelve-hour meeting. It took yet another month for the committee to make a formal decision and announcement: Hamm was the gold medalist.

The ruling noted, "An error identified with the benefit of hindsight, whether admitted or not, cannot be a ground for reversing a result of a competition" and that the Koreans had not filed the protest until after the events had ended.

A decade later Hamm reflected on the entire bizarre episode. "There were a lot of things done that I thought were handled the wrong way from various committees. I thought they should have stuck to how the rules were stated. According to the rules that competition was over. Nothing should have been debated, period. . . . And if you look at it, you find that the situation really should stay the same because there's another error that was overlooked during his routine. All those things really made me feel I was the rightful winner of that competition. I still feel that way.

"The other aspect of it is, it's only fair for the other competitors to have an understanding of where the true placements are prior to competing that next rotation. I earned the right after the first day's competition to compete last on high bar, which gives me the ability to see the scores and know what I need to get in order to win the competition."

The judging scandal prompted a major overhaul of the gymnastics scoring system for future Games, making it more streamlined and easier to understand.

Paul Hamm at the Olympic Trials in 2008. STEW MILNE—USA TODAY
SPORTS

After the Games Paul turned his focus back to Ohio State. He won the
James E. Sullivan award for the nation's outstanding amateur athlete for
2004, and both he and Morgan (who had finished sixty-seventh in the
all-around in Athens) were featured in *People Weekly*'s Most Eligible Bachelor section.

Both Hamm brothers attended Ohio State, graduating in 2007. They
continued training in gymnastics during those years, though they didn't
participate on the college team. "I think that there is a part of the college

experience that I wish that I would have had—the team environment, every day working toward the goal of becoming NCAA champions with the guys who are like your brothers. . . . But I did train at Ohio State with my brother," Paul explained, "[and] we were around the Ohio State gymnastics team, so we got a sense of what that was like."

Paul hoped to go back to the Olympics in 2008 in Beijing, China, but he fractured his hand at the US Championships in May of that year. The US team still wanted him and allowed Paul to sit out the trials. They held a provisional spot on the team, pending his recovery, but in late July Paul was forced to concede that the hand plus a new shoulder injury would keep him home.

Out of gymnastics for the time being, Paul entered the world of finance in Chicago but later went back to Ohio State to coach. In 2011 Paul faced a humiliating personal episode. He was caught on camera drunk after being arrested for assault and two other misdemeanor charges. Paul had hit and kicked a taxi driver after refusing to pay a twenty-three-dollar fare. He was recorded on video while handcuffed in the back of a police cruiser saying, "I don't understand. I'm going to kill you guys" and telling the officers that he'd had about eight drinks. The video went viral.

Six months later he publicly apologized. "I sincerely regret what happened," he said in a statement, "and hope to regain my reputation through my actions moving forward."

USA Gymnastics stood by Paul. "I've had several consultations with Paul and believe he is taking responsibility for his actions," President Steve Penny told reporters six months later. "He has expressed a desire to do the right thing. USA Gymnastics will continue to work with Paul regarding his future activities."

Paul got back on the competitive track and considered a comeback for 2012, but it wasn't long before his heart and head told him it was time to quit. "I would hear creaking and certain things like that in my shoulder when I was going out to compete and that really bothered me," he said. "After that, I decided this probably wasn't a wise decision. I didn't want to have more serious problems to deal with later in life if I beat my shoulder up anymore, so I decided to stop and step away."

Hamm went on to coach at a gym outside of Chicago and later earned his MBA at Marquette University back in his home state. It wasn't an easy road for Paul, from humble beginnings in the rafters of a barn to a controversial gold that some still felt belonged to someone else, to his own personal demons. Yet he always found a way to persevere, and he left a deep and lasting mark on USA Gymnastics. Paul Hamm will forever be remembered as the first American man to take all-around gold in a sport often dominated by Europeans and Asians. His success may have had a ripple effect, too; before 2004, it had been twenty years since a US man had earned a medal in gymnastics at the Olympics. From 2004 until 2014, America took home three Olympic medals and seven world championship titles.

"I think the men's program is going to continue to be strong for a long time," summed up Hamm. "It feels good to know we were part of that."

CHAPTER 20

GARRETT WEBER-GALE

Swimming, 2008

A large framed photograph is prominently displayed on the wall of Diane Weber and Mark Gale's living room. In it their three-month-old son, Garrett, floats effortlessly on his back in the middle of a pool. Diane is next to him, watching with joy but not holding on. The picture epitomizes Diane and Mark's approach to raising their children. The couple popped daughter Hillary into a backpack carrier and took her cross-country skiing when she was six weeks old. Diane, a former college swimmer, swam laps every day of her pregnancy with their second child, Garrett, who was born August 6, 1985, in Stevens Point, Wisconsin. She had both of her children in the pool at the age of six weeks.

"Every single day," Garrett said, "even if I was cold after ten minutes. By five months she could drop me off the side of the pool into the water and I would be able to turn on my back and float until she came and got me."

Despite his obvious water affinity, Garrett grew up doing a host of other activities as well, from basketball to golf to skiing. After the Weber-Gales moved to Wauwatosa, on the western edge of Milwaukee, Garrett competed starting at age four for the Wauwatosa West Swim Team. But his first love was zipping down wintry slopes on skis. His initial Olympic memory is watching the Lillehammer Winter Games in 1994, when Garrett was eight and on a family vacation at the Indianhead ski resort in the Upper Peninsula of Michigan. Garrett and his sister would sneak out of their room to watch the ski racing on the TV in the resort's common area.

Garrett Weber-Gale was a water baby almost from day one. COURTESY OF THE WEBER-GALE
FAMILY

"The whole aura about it—the Olympics theme song and these athletes from all around the world—I had never even heard something like that, and the idea of it was just so spectacular," he remembered.

A few years after the family ski trip, still active in a variety of sports and now eleven years old, Garrett was equally riveted by the 1996 Summer Games in Atlanta. "My sister and I spent all day, every day in the den watching. At that point I was like, I want to go to the Olympics. . . . I had no idea what that actually meant or what it would take, but I really believed it."

When Garrett was in second grade, the Weber-Gale family relocated one more time, to Fox Point, a northern suburb of Milwaukee, where Garrett would attend Fox Point schools and Nicolet High School. He joined the Fox Point swim team and spent all summer at the pool just three blocks from his house. He loved the freedom he felt, diving and bobbing in the water with his sister and friends. After dinner, the whole family would go back to the pool for an evening swim. Coaches began to take notice, telling Garrett's parents that their son possessed a gift and encouraging year-round practice. However, Diane and Mark were hesitant. Very conscious of burnout, they did everything to make sure Garrett was well-rounded and not overly burdened with one sport. Thus, the future gold medalist did not commit to swimming full-time until he was already in high school—unusual for an Olympian, most of whom start honing their craft in early childhood. For Garrett, giving up other sports would be eye-opening. He realized, "Wow, if I go year-round I can get so much faster. I started going more often and got faster, working harder and got faster."

Wisconsin speedskater Dan Jansen had an indirect influence on the rising star during Garrett's formative years. Although they competed in very different sports and in opposite seasons, something Jansen stated in a television interview stuck with Garrett. As he recalled later, "He said if he loses focus on what's specifically in front of him in a race, if he ever listens to the crowd or sees something, then he knows he's never going to have as great a race as he could have had because his focus is not on the task at hand. That always resonated with me. Okay, if I want to be as good as I can be, I have to just not worry or even think or allow those things outside to come into play. I think that's one of the reasons why I was so focused. I didn't get into trouble in high school, I didn't do some of the social things teenagers do, because I had this one-track mind: I am going to the Olympics, I don't need this other stuff."

This philosophy would carry over to races. When he was in the starting blocks or powering his way through the water, Weber-Gale would always remember how Jansen stayed focused and eliminated all distractions. For Garrett this meant narrowing his mind so much that he did not register a single noise or glimpse of the crowd until his fingers touched the wall and his head emerged from the water after the completion of the event.

As Garrett's star continued to rise, he and his family began to feel that Wisconsin didn't provide the swimming opportunities that warm-weather, water-crazy states could offer. Garrett had grandparents who lived in Fort Lauderdale, Florida, where famed coach and 1956 Olympian Jack Nelson coached and mentored many Olympic swimmers. After Garrett met Nelson and trained with him during vacations, he knew he had to spread his wings beyond Wisconsin borders.

"Every time I'd go down there it was a blast. I would get better and I would learn new training techniques," he said. For the next three summers he went to swim camps, one at Kenyon College, training with Mike Bottom and Jim Steen, and later at the Arizona Sports Ranch. Then his mother called the head coach at the University of Texas for recommendations, and he suggested Nova Aquatics in Irvine, California, and Circle C in Austin, Texas.

Following his junior year at Nicolet, Garrett spent the entire summer in Austin, where he was coached by Randy Reese. He sliced his times even further as he gained confidence and strength. He begged his parents to allow him to stay in Texas, and the family reached a compromise: Garrett would spend the first semester of his senior year there and return to Wisconsin for his second semester. "That year, when I came back," Garrett said, "I broke the national high school record in the 100 freestyle, and that's when I really realized, I can really go to the Olympics. I was competing with the top college guys, and I was only seventeen."

He graduated from Nicolet but skipped the ceremony for a swim meet in Dallas. Choosing the University of Texas for college would be a continuation of everything he knew and all the people he had come to trust in the Lone Star State. Enrolling at UT in the fall of 2003, he had less than a year until the US Olympic Trials for the 2004 Games in Athens, Greece. But although he worked his tail off, it was not meant to be. He missed making the team by one place.

"I was eighteen, the youngest guy in the finals by three years," he explained. "I was seeded seventh going into the finals. I only had to move up one place to get to the Olympics because they take six for the relay. I got seventh. My coaches and I changed my game plan before the race. I usually went out really fast for first half of the race and then hung on. But since I was the smallest guy out there, they said, 'Why don't you go out a little slower, and you'll have a better second 50?' As soon as I touched the wall I had the worst feeling you can ever have, which was that I had more gas left in the tank. I could have gone faster."

He looked up at the big scoreboard above his head and saw the results. Immediately the tears came. He was inconsolable on the pool deck, convinced his swimming career was over. Then his coach approached him. He said, "I want you to look at the scoreboard right now and promise yourself you'll never feel this type of disappointment and pain again."

This would prove to be such a huge motivator that for ten years afterward, any time Garrett woke up tired or cranky or just didn't have the oomph to go practice, he thought back to the image of that scoreboard and his name in seventh place, on the outside looking in.

"I never missed a morning practice again," he said. "I was a freak. [In retrospect] it was the best thing that could have ever happened to me."

He went back to classes and swimming at UT and reset his laser-beam focus on one thing: Beijing in 2008. And then a medical problem blindsided the family. At a routine physical in the UT training room in 2005, the doctor's face registered concern as the blood pressure cuff slowly deflated on Garrett's arm. His blood pressure was 213 over 100, "so high I was at risk of having a stroke or a heart attack."

No one was sure why his blood pressure was so high. Doctors stopped him from working out on days when those numbers were at their peak. Specialists ran tests but could find no direct family link or other cause. The otherwise healthy young man was given a choice: medication, diet, or relaxation techniques. He decided to attack the problem on all three fronts. "I hated the idea of going on medication," he explained, "because I'm tested by three different drug-testing organizations, but I was urged by doctors to go on a low dose."

He added a nutritionist and a sports psychologist to his regimen. Mark and Diane bought their son—who could barely boil water—private cooking lessons. It would be the start of a life-changing journey with food. Immediately Garrett saw his blood pressure drop. He was relieved but also rattled by how close his own body had come to betraying him.

Like the 2004 Olympic Trials disappointment, discovering his high blood pressure would turn out to be a blessing in disguise. Garrett's wholesale and all-in change to healthy eating lowered not only his blood pressure but also his swim times. "I didn't realize how big a benefit nutrition was," he said. "I might not have ever taken what I put in my body as seriously, and that was a ticket to my success. . . . I never was the biggest, strongest, or most talented. I was just a freak for doing all of the little things right. I knew the little things would add up to a big difference."

In March 2008, with the Olympics quickly approaching, Garrett had an amazing meet in Texas. He was now ranked second in the world in the

FROM GOLDEN EAGLE TO GOLD MEDAL WINNER:
DWYANE WADE

Another favorite of Wisconsin sports fans made a splash at the 2008 Summer Games in Beijing: former Marquette University Golden Eagle Dwyane Wade.

In his first two years at Marquette, Chicago native Wade was one of the most decorated basketball players in school history. With his 1,281 career points, he ranks twentieth on the school's all-time scoring list, and he recorded a career 19.7 points-per-game scoring average. Wade was the first Marquette player since 1978 to earn the Associated Press's First Team All-America honors.

After Marquette wowed Wisconsin sports fans by reaching the Final Four in 2003, Wade burst onto both the NBA and Olympic scenes nearly simultaneously. He was drafted in the first round by the Miami Heat, and in his first NBA season he was chosen to represent the United States at the Summer Games in Athens, Greece, one of just a few rookie players selected. Unfortunately, nine of twelve NBA players chose not to make the trip, some due to injury and others for personal or professional reasons. This left the team short on experience, and it proved to be a disappointing showing for US basketball. The team lost in the first round to Puerto Rico and then to Lithuania. Their third loss in the semifinals made a bronze the only medal option, and they wound up with that third-place crown. Wade later summed up the experience, saying, "Being on a losing team and not being able to help much kind of tainted us [rookies]. But it was a great experience."

In 2008, USA basketball was back, this time with a chip on its shoulder. Wade joined veterans Kobe Bryant, Jason Kidd, and a group of younger NBA All-Stars in Beijing on a quest to capture Olympic gold. The team handily beat seven others to get to the gold medal game, which is still considered one of the best ever in international play. The matchup against Spain was a dogfight until the final minutes. Wade sank his fourth 3-pointer with 2:04 left, sealing Team USA's lead and the much-desired gold. The team reveled together arm-in-arm, full of pride after becoming "the Redeem Team." "We did this together as a team, which is what makes it feel that much better," Wade told reporters later. He scored 27 points in the gold medal game and led the team with a total of 128 points in the Olympic tournament. Wade was considered the most valuable player for Team USA, and commentator and silver medalist Doug Collins said as much when he proclaimed, "Team USA plays its best ball when Wade is on the floor."

Wade was chosen to participate in the 2012 London games, but he withdrew due to knee damage requiring surgery in the NBA off-season. However, he went as a spectator, bringing along his young sons to see his good friends play ball. "I'm a competitor, so when I watch the games, I'm like, 'Oh, I could have helped the team there,' or 'Oh, I would have done this or that,' so in that sense, I wish I was there," he said in an interview. "So, yeah, it's hard not to be out there with the guys."

Still, two Olympics and a gold medal were great additions to Wade's collection of achievements, which would also include three NBA Championships, one MVP title, and ten All-Star appearances through 2015.

Other notables from Marquette University basketball include Frank McCabe, who brought home a gold medal from the 1952 Helsinki games, and Naismith Award winner Butch Lee, who competed for his native Puerto Rico in 1976. Lee was not invited to try out for the US team despite his accolades in the NCAA, but when Puerto Rico and the US faced off, he got a little bit of personal redemption, scoring 35 points. Puerto Rico could not quite pull it off, losing by 1 point to a US squad that featured five players who would go on to play or coach for the Milwaukee Bucks: Quinn Buckner, Adrian Dantley, Phil Ford, Ernie Grunfeld, and Scott May. (For more on Milwaukee Bucks in the Olympics, see page 57.)

50 freestyle and third in the 100 freestyle. He was on a roll with swimming even as another crisis diverted his attention. A favorite aunt, Toni, was diagnosed with pancreatic cancer. Garrett went to see her in Jacksonville, even accompanying his aunt to chemotherapy. "I remember sitting there thinking, there's no pain I could ever go through in swimming or in any type of physical exertion that would ever be as bad as this," he recalled. He conjured an image in his mind of an armor shield around his body and created almost a mantra: *Nothing can stop me, nothing can hurt me, there's no pain that can have any type of effect on me like what my aunt is going through.*

Garrett graduated from the University of Texas in May 2008 with a degree in corporate communications. He says now that it was the proudest day of his life, even more so than his athletic achievements, because school did not come naturally to Garrett. He had to work for every single grade he got.

By the time the Olympic Trials came around in late June in Omaha, Nebraska, Garrett was poised for a complete and total turnaround from four years earlier. Mark, Diane, and his sister, Hillary, were in the stands, and Garrett thought of something his father always told him: "Trust your stroke, trust your coach, and swim your own race."

Utilizing every tool he now possessed, from his diet to the pain of finishing seventh the last time around to his aunt's cancer battle to his father's words, Garrett blew everyone away. He won the 100 freestyle with a time of 47.78, breaking the US record and becoming the first American to go under 48 seconds, and he won the 50 freestyle with a time of 21.47, another US record-breaking time. Garrett felt practically invincible. He was going to Beijing.

"I was on a high," he remembered. "Everything I had ever worked for came true. Partly it was a relief as well because the Olympic Trials are the most stressful and intense meet in the world, more so than the Olympics because you're racing all your friends."

After the finals in the 100 free, NBC reporter Andrea Kremer stood on the deck of the pool in Omaha and asked Garrett what he was thinking during the race. There was no hesitation. "I told her I was thinking about my aunt who was at home battling cancer. I knew she was at home watching."

Toni passed away just one week after the trials. Family members felt that Toni had hung on just long enough to see her nephew make the Olympic team. Mourning her loss, Garrett was at a crossroads of sadness over Toni's death and excitement about the Olympics.

The US team, which also included heralded swimmer Michael Phelps, who was gunning to win eight gold medals in China, went straight from Omaha to Palo Alto, California. They had two and a half weeks of training there before jetting to Singapore for eight days to get in sync with China's time zone. The team landed in Beijing six days before the opening ceremony. Garrett's first race would be the 400 freestyle relay, three days after the torch was lit. For now, he had plenty of time to enjoy the perks of being an Olympic athlete.

"[It's] like you're on a cloud. You have no worries, everything is taken care of," he said. "Swimming is one of the marquee events, so we have a big delegation and a ton of staff. You go through this shopping area and get all of this gear, [and] you leave with two duffel bags with stuff."

With the swimming events slated to start not long after the opening ceremony, Garrett watched the opening on TV from the village. He did not want to compromise his legs for race day. "[At the ceremony] you have to stand for six hours. The people that did go, like some of the coaches, came back and their suit jackets were completely soaked through in sweat. It was so hot and humid."

Coming out of the Olympic Trials, Garrett and veteran swimmer Jason Lezak had been pretty much guaranteed spots on the four-man 400 freestyle team based on their times. Michael Phelps was essentially a lock, too. Others would have to battle it out for the fourth and final relay spot. The coaches set up one group of four swimmers to compete in the preliminaries and another in the finals. Garrett, Jason, and Michael would definitely not be in the qualifying heat because coaches don't like to burn out their best swimmers; they want them fresh for the final.

Whoever swam the fastest leg of the prelims would join the others in the final. As the three who were already in watched on a TV in the village, they learned that their fourth teammate would be Cullen Jones, a first-time Olympian.

Now that the group was set, Garrett was beyond excited. He woke up the next morning, race day, and immediately went for a swim, saying he felt amazing in the water despite some nerves. After breakfast he was walking back to the dorm in the village when he passed Phelps and his coach. Michael called out to Garrett: "Hey, did you hear what the Frenchies said in the paper this morning?"

Garrett had not heard. The French team, considered the favorite and Team USA's top rival for gold, had made a reference to smashing the Americans. Garrett told Michael not to worry about it, they would take care of it in the pool. This was not the first trash talk coming from the French. For weeks before the Games they told anyone who would listen that they were the best in the world, but Garrett just silently scoffed. The United States had held the world record in the 400 freestyle since 2006, and Garrett felt confident they would retain it, on this, the biggest stage.

"I never once understood how anyone could think they were going to beat us," Garrett said. "We had way faster people. Jason, Cullen, and myself had all gone 47 [seconds, in their respective legs]. They had the world record holder [Alain Bernard had set a record in the 100 freestyle that year in the European Championship] and a couple of other guys who were amazing, but I never for a single moment believed anyone was going to beat us. I knew we were going to win the gold medal."

A bus would take the swimmers from the village to the pool. With Mariah Carey music in his ears and a bag of USA gear over his shoulder, Garrett boarded and looked out the window as the bus moved through the streets of Beijing toward the swimming venue. The facility, known as the Water Cube, was designed with a honeycomb pattern on the sides and roof for a unique look that athletes and commentators alike had been praising. Suddenly Garrett saw the Olympic torch, high above another architecturally innovative stadium called the Bird's Nest, where the opening ceremony had been held and track and field events would take place. Even though Garrett had been in the city for more than a week, he had not seen the torch yet with his own eyes.

"I thought, holy shit, that flame is orange, it's gold. That means we're going to win the gold medal today. . . . Afterward, it came to me that obviously the flame is gold, that's what they all are, but I was seeing signs in all these little things, and I was so [sure] that we were going to win."

Garrett and the team arrived at the Water Cube two and a half hours before race time. There was enough time to hang out and talk, warm up in the pool for forty-five minutes, grab a drink, and change into their team-issued red, white, and blue bib-style swimsuits. Twenty minutes before the 400 freestyle relay, they were finally sent to the call room to wait for their race to be called. As the four swimmers walked down the hallway toward the call room, Jason Lezak, the most veteran of the foursome, suddenly pulled the other three aside. According to Garrett, "He said, 'Hey guys, I've been on this relay many times. A lot of times we'll go out and swim four 100 freestyles individually. When that happens, nothing good ever happens. That's why today we're going to swim the 400 freestyle together.'"

What Lezak had just said struck a chord in all of them. They looked at each other, and Garrett's first thought was, "Oh my gosh, this guy is a god." His second thought: "This [race] is going to get crazy."

The four of them had never done a relay together before, and even though Garrett was brimming with optimism, he was concerned about swimming's equivalent of the "handoff," the moment when one swimmer touches the wall and the next dives in to begin his portion of the race. All swimmers practice relay starts with each other during training, but by some strange fluke Weber-Gale and Phelps had never been paired together. Now Phelps would swim the opening leg, Garrett the second, Jones the third, and Lezak the final. Garrett would have to time his dive into the pool just as Michael's hand touched the wall. If he left early, it would be a false start and disqualify the team.

Four or five Olympic staff people and thirty-two athletes from eight countries, all in the colors of their homeland, waited in the call room to be sent to the starting line for the same race. The space itself was not large—smaller than some American family rooms.

"You can just imagine the intensity in there," Garrett recalled. "The testosterone [was] through the roof. If there was any type of altercation, I think that place would have just exploded. I was thinking the most nasty, brutal thoughts about every single person in there except for the three guys who were with me. I'm sure [my rivals] were thinking the same thing about me."

The call came at last: time to go to the blocks. All thirty-two walked out
to the pool deck, eight groups of four ready to go to war for a gold medal,
television cameras beaming the image around the world. Nervous cheering came down from the packed house. Hundreds of still photographers
in the pits off to the side clicked their shutter buttons madly.

Diane, Mark, and Hillary were somewhere in the sea of faces, but Garrett did not look for them and did not even want to know where they were.
Going back to the Dan Jansen mentality, Garrett bore down on staying 100
percent focused. The US team stepped to lane four. All of the swimmers
across the deck readied at the start, adjusting their goggles and swim caps
and shaking their limbs to stay loose. NBC sports commentator Rowdy
Gaines, a three-time Olympic gold medalist himself, set the scene for the
US as the first swimmer, Michael Phelps, moved into position on the block.
Gaines felt it wasn't looking good for gold.

"How many times have I broken this down over the last two weeks?
Every time I do it comes out France," he told a viewing audience numbered
in the millions. "Americans are certainly capable of doing it but . . . each
one of them . . . has to have the perfect race to be able to beat the French."

Countries are assigned lanes based on qualifying times, with the two
fastest in the middle. The French team was next to the US in lane five. To
the right of the US were Australia, Sweden, and Canada. Next to the French
were Italy, South Africa, and Great Britain. Most everyone felt it would
come down to a battle between lanes four and five. While Garrett may have
been feeling confident, Gaines and US fans were resigning themselves to
silver.

The gun went off, and Phelps dove in for the first leg. He powered his
way through his massive front crawl to the end of the pool and back again
but, somewhat surprisingly, was not in the lead. And neither was France.
Australian swimmer Eamon Sullivan had a brilliant first leg, outracing
everyone and touching the wall about a head before the rest of the field.
He swam the leg in 47.24; Phelps was next at 47.51, a personal best and a
US record. On the deck, Garrett Weber-Gale crouched in the ready position, twitching with adrenaline, waiting for his turn. Now he had to make
his first-ever relay start with Phelps.

Garrett waited for Michael's fingertips to touch the wall. It is a delicate dance because the faster you take off, the better your chances of gaining a hundredth or a tenth of a second on your competitors. Yet officials won't miss a false start, and every swimmer has to be extremely cautious. When Garrett thought he saw Michael's middle finger graze the wall, he did not hesitate, propelling his body forward and into the water, arms churning like a pinwheel in the wind, legs kicking as if he was swimming away from a shark. He would define his future in less than 50 seconds, but almost as soon as he hit the water a dreaded thought entered his mind: "I was like, holy shit, I think I just false started."

He knew he had cut it close, but he couldn't dwell on it now. If he had false started, he reasoned, he would find out soon enough. He must move forward. Garrett heard nothing outside of the motion created by his own arms and legs. The roar of the crowd was muffled in the water. He had to continue racing and make it the best race of his life, for himself, his three teammates, and his country. Turning once again to Jansen's inspiration, Garrett blocked out everything except his own breathing and the maniacal turning of his arms. Later he would find out just how close he had come to false starting: the time from Michael's hand touching the wall to Garrett's diving in was $\frac{7}{100}$ of a second—a razor-thin margin that almost ended America's dream for any medal right there.

Garrett knew he had to make up for Australia's fast first leg, and he did. Thinking of nothing now but speed, Garrett moved at an incredible pace. By the halfway mark, he had pushed the United States into first place, and he kept hold of it during the final 50 meters of his leg of the race. Garrett touched the wall in 47.02 just as Jones dove in. He had more than done his part. Now it would be up to the last two racers. Jones was considered the slowest leg of the four, but if he could just hold on to the lead, the US would be in good shape for the final sprint. Garrett, still panting with exertion, quickly hoisted himself out of the water to watch the end. He and Michael began screaming encouragement to Jones. But the last man added to the relay team could not hold the edge. France's Fred Bousquet pulled ahead.

Jones swam in 47.65. Bousquet was a full second faster at 46.63. Suddenly it was France's race to win. The prerace favorite was living up to its own hype with a half-second lead heading into the final leg. America's last hope was Lezak, who faced formidable competition in the French anchor leg, the youngster Alain Bernard. Bernard and Lezak each towered over six feet with powerful strokes, but Bernard was the gold medalist and record holder in the 100 freestyle, while Lezak had the bronze. Everyone thought Bernard had the edge. As the two neared the halfway point of the final leg, the commentator Gaines told viewers what already seemed obvious about Lezak: "I just don't think he can do it."

"Bernard is pulling away from him," added Dan Hicks, who was partnered with Gaines for the play-by-play. "The United States trying to hang on to second, they should get the silver medal."

Garrett was still standing nervously next to Phelps and now Jones on the deck, watching the event on a video board. The camera shot showed Jason and Alain side by side. What struck Garrett was that Jason's head was all the way down near Bernard's feet.

"Michael and I look at each other and were like, Oh my God, and I know we were both thinking the same thing: We're going to win the silver medal. For us, that would have been a disappointment because we wanted to win the gold. We would have still been proud to win the silver, but I'm a firm believer that everything is based off your expectation. We expected to win gold, and nothing would have satisfied us if we hadn't won gold."

Suddenly, shortly after the 50-yard turn, Lezak did what would become the stuff of legend. It was similar to a mad dash at the end of a track and field event, a final burst, a race car accelerating at breathtaking speed to take the checkered flag in a photo finish. Lezak poured on an almost superhuman bit of power to catch up to Bernard.

"Lezak is closing a little bit on Bernard!" Hicks noted, his voice rising with shock and excitement. "Can the veteran chase him down and pull off the shocker here? Bernard is losing some ground! Here comes Lezak!"

Americans all over the world were hoarse by this point from screaming at their televisions. Butts were scooching to the ends of seats, fists clenching with anticipation. Garrett, Michael, and Jason were almost jumping out of their skin trying to egg on their teammate to victory. Lezak pulled even with 10 meters to go.

As the swimmers came into the final few yards and touched the wall, it was almost impossible to tell with the naked eye. This would require the electronic timing system to determine whose fingers had grazed the wall first. It took just a half second before the results flashed up: America 1, France 2, Australia 3. The next week *Sports Illustrated* would run a photo taken with an underwater camera that showed Lezak's fingers touching the wall about the length of a fingernail ahead of Bernard's.

"The US has done it!" bellowed Hicks. What followed was almost unintelligible as he and Gaines talked over each other, each shouting variations of "He's done it!" and "Unbelievable!"

Garrett had to look twice at the board to make sure he was seeing it correctly—was that 1 really next to US? His body went numb. Lezak was still in the water, catching his breath, but his three teammates were absolutely beside themselves. Garrett doesn't remember much of the next fifteen minutes in a case of what was almost a joyful amnesia. The camera cut to the three on deck, in their patriotic swimsuits, and Garrett's arms instinctually shot up high in the classic "V" victory pose, his mouth wide open in a primal yelp. There may or may not have even been words coming out; Garrett doesn't remember. Phelps reached down to slap hands with Lezak, then opened his mouth and screamed. The French stepped out of the pool to console each other. As Lezak bounded up from the water, he was greeted with a thunderous bear hug from his three teammates. He had just swum the final 100 in 46.06, an unearthly fast time, the fastest relay split in the history of the race. The US total time of 3:08.24 barely nipped France at 3:08.32 and absolutely obliterated the old world record by 4.22 seconds. Australia took bronze. The victory had also kept alive Michael Phelps's goal of eight golds.

"Who's talking now?" Hicks asked as the TV camera panned the sorrowful faces of the French, a reference to the bragging France had done before the Games. Just a few inches away, at the next lane, the hugs continued for the Americans. In the stands, US president George W. Bush was on his feet, cheering. Garrett's dad picked up Lezak's mother, seated near the Weber-Gales, and spun her around. He told her he just might kiss her son on the lips when he saw him. Tears streaked their faces as they watched their sons celebrate what was already being called one of the greatest relay races of all time. A photographer took a picture of Garrett with an arm around Phelps's waist as they both screamed with unbridled glee. It would become an iconic image from the 2008 Games. People later asked Garrett

Garrett Weber-Gale (left) celebrates a thrilling gold medal win with teammate Michael Phelps on August 11, 2008, in Beijing. Later Garrett had only hazy memories of the moments immediately after the victory, because it was all so shocking and exciting. MARK J. REBILAS—USA TODAY SPORTS

if he had planned that moment, the half-embrace with Michael and the yell, and Garrett laughed. If he couldn't even recall everything that had happened, how in the world could he have planned it?

"It was an out-of-body experience," said Garrett. "I was there but I wasn't there. I remember some things. I remember Cullen kept sitting down, and I was like, Cullen get up, we just won the gold medal! I remember pieces of it but that's all."

The fab four did an on-camera interview with NBC and went through what is called the "mixed zone" with reporters from around the world. The awards ceremony was held immediately afterward in the Water Cube. As Garrett stood on the podium with his teammates, an Olympic official draping the gold medal around his neck, he heard his name being called out on his right. It was his mother. He looked over and saw his family for the first time that day.

"The looks on their faces, how excited they were, how fulfilled, that was the best moment of my entire sporting career because I knew how much time and effort and dedication and sacrifice and money they had spent on my whole career. That this was their gold medal just as much as it was mine."

He had always wondered if he would cry at that moment on the podium, but he didn't. In fact, he didn't even sing the national anthem. "It didn't even really cross my mind, to be honest," he said with a slight laugh. "I know the national anthem was playing, [but] I was looking at the stands, my parents, taking it all in . . . I was so wrapped up in the moment just looking around I didn't even think about it."

The accolades were not over. Team USA paraded around the pool in front of the crowd and then were whisked to a press conference with close to four hundred journalists from around the world, with a translator speaking to the athletes through an earpiece. Question after question showered down on the champions, who smiled through it all. They still had not seen or spoken to the French. It wasn't until drug testing later that they ran into one of the French racers, Fred Bousquet, who had swum the third leg. Although he was representing his home country at the Olympics, he competed collegiately for Auburn University in Alabama, and the Americans knew him and thought of him as a good guy. Bousquet pulled no punches when talking about the anchor leg, Alain Bernard.

"He was like, 'God, that stupid young kid Bernard,' because Fred was supposed to anchor the race," Garrett explained. "[Fred] was really experienced and fast and had anchored tons of relays before, but Bernard was the world record holder, and he told the coaches, 'You're going to put me as the anchor because I'm the world record holder and I want the glory of being the anchor' and he just swam it really stupid. If he had swum it differently, there's no way we would have won."

What Bernard had done wrong, according to Garrett, was to swim too close to the Americans' lane marker. This gave Lezak the chance to draft on him—or, in other words, to expend less energy as he rode in Bernard's wake for much of the way, until Lezak decided to pull away.

"If [Bernard] had just gone to the other side of the lane, there's no way we would have ever done it because Jason wouldn't have been able to draft the whole way," Garrett said.

Garrett Weber-Gale had only that one day to celebrate. Still ahead were three more races, and he planned to win gold in all of them. The 50 and 100 freestyles would be individual pursuits, and for the 400 medley relay he would swim with three teammates.

Despite his high hopes, the magic he had felt with the 400 free was nowhere to be found for the 50 and 100 races. "I just didn't feel quite as good there as I did at the trials. I was on fire at the trials. I wasn't as crisp in Beijing. I'm not sure what it was," Garrett recalled. He made the semi-finals in both races but did not make the finals in either.

He had one more race. In the 400 medley relay, the team combines to swim freestyle, butterfly, backstroke, and breaststroke. Jason Lezak, by virtue of his incredible last leg in the gold medal race, would be the free-style competitor in the final. The coaches decided to use Garrett for the freestyle in the preliminary, swimming to get Team USA to the finals.

"It was disappointing, but Jason swam faster than me," Garrett admitted. "He earned the right to swim in the finals. But I [had] wanted to go in there and win four medals. That was a big disappointment to me leaving Beijing."

He would depart with two. Garrett helped push Team USA to the finals of the 400 medley relay, and the Americans went on to win gold. Phelps swam the butterfly leg in the finals to complete his record mark of eight gold medals, one more than Mark Spitz had won in 1972. All of the pre-liminary swimmers earned medals along with those who swam in the finals. Still, Garrett left the 2008 Olympics with a mix of emotions.

"I had these stupid thoughts in my head, like almost embarrassment, like I should have done better. Ninety-nine point nine percent of athletes look back on their career and say, I wish I would have done that differently. [Many] say, I wish I would have focused more on nutrition. There's nothing I can look back on and say I wish I would have done differently."

After the Games, Weber-Gale, Phelps, and Jones attended the ESPY awards, the sports version of the Oscars, put on by ESPN (Lezak was patched in via video conference). Their team's 400 freestyle relay was nominated for "Best Moment" of 2008, an award they would win that evening. In the audience, Pittsburgh Steelers quarterback Ben Roethlisberger, coming off a Super Bowl victory, approached the threesome, looked them in the eyes, and said, "I still get goose bumps when I think about or watch that race. It's the coolest thing I've ever seen in sports."

Los Angeles Lakers star Kobe Bryant echoed that sentiment. He stopped the group to share his story of the Olympics. Bryant had been in Beijing to try to win basketball gold for the United States. He was in his room in the village, not feeling well, when he turned on the TV to watch Olympic swimming. He told them he was screaming and going ballistic as Jason approached the final touch. After the race, while the Americans were celebrating on the pool deck, Kobe told himself, "I don't care how I'm feeling. I'm going out there to play for the US." The basketball team went on to take gold that year. Garrett also met Green Bay Packers quarterback Aaron Rodgers at the ESPYs, and he introduced himself to boxer Mike Tyson when everyone else was too intimidated to do so.

Not long after the Games, Garrett decided to pursue something that had been in his soul for quite some time. He wanted to share what he had learned about properly nurturing the body, and he started a website called Athletic Foodie featuring recipes and tips. As the website grew popular, he was asked to speak about nutrition and write for blogs.

He wasn't done with swimming, though, and continued training for the 2012 Olympic team in London. But Garrett and his coaches made a misstep that he believes cost him his shot. It started when the coaches wanted him to get stronger.

"I went nuts in the weight room," he said. "But we didn't monitor it well, [and] I got so fatigued. It was partly their fault and partly mine. Normally, I would taper off [before a meet] for six weeks. But I really would have needed about ten weeks, and we didn't monitor that closely enough. I showed up for the Olympic Trials, and I didn't have any of my natural speed because I was so broken down." He finished eighth at the trials.

He tried not to regret it, dwell on it, or beat himself up, and he still went to London, working as a spokesperson for companies like Visa, Cisco, and Hilton. But observing the competitions was grueling. "It was probably the worst experience of my life," he said. "I watched the 400 freestyle at the pool, and [the US] got beat by France this time. I wanted to try and find a place to go cry by myself. I was doing everything I possibly could to not burst into tears the whole time. I felt beyond miserable and distraught. I was thinking, I should be here, I deserve to be here."

Garrett had another taste of Olympic-style competition when he entered the Maccabiah Games in Israel in 2013. Garrett, who was raised Jewish, said, "To be honest, it might have been cooler than the Olympics because it has the cultural aspect that the Olympics doesn't have. . . . You see people from all over the world—black Jews, Asian Jews, Jews from China, Malaysia, South America. It was a really cool experience." In 2015 Garrett was invited to light the ceremonial torch to open the Maccabiah Games, held that year in Milwaukee.

After the 2013 Maccabiah Games, Garrett entered an MBA program. He and girlfriend Kara Dockery got married and settled in Texas. Garrett started a business venture at Athletic Foodie selling prepackaged nutritional foods to parents and their young athletes. The decrease in physical exertion was difficult, but he shifted to exercising his mind. Athletic Foodie and cooking have given him a new kind of gratification, one that's immediate: as he has said, in forty-five minutes he can create something really satisfying, whereas in swimming it takes years just to shave a fraction of a second off your time.

Garrett looks back now on the 400 freestyle with the unique perspective that only three other men share. "People tell me all the time this was the greatest Olympic race there ever was," he said. "It's difficult for me to even really get a concept of it. When you're there you don't really have any idea what other people are thinking or talking about or seeing, and when you're in it . . . it's kind of your life. . . . It's something awesome you did with the four guys and your parents, it's hard to have a concept of millions of people around the world seeing this. I'm a proud American, but it's hard for me to understand people when they tell me that was super touching for their lives and it's only because they're from America."

He's not trying to belittle the moment, just to describe what it feels like

Gold tasted good for the men's 4x100 freestyle relay team at the 2008 Olympics. Left to right: Jason Lezak, Michael Phelps, Garrett Weber-Gale, and Cullen Jones. MARK J. REBILAS—USA TODAY SPORTS

from an athlete's point of view. They were the ones who had to put in every 5:30 A.M. practice, every weight room rep when their arms and legs wanted nothing more than sleep, every party missed to avoid the temptation to drink, every coach yelling split times and haranguing them to go faster. It was truly their medal. To share it with the rest of the world? Sure, they were thrilled to do that, but how can anyone else feel the same depth of emotion?

And there's more. Garrett himself does not want to be remembered as the swimmer who did the second leg of the 400-meter relay in Beijing because he is so much more complex than just those 47 seconds. For a class in his MBA program, he had to write his own eulogy and epitaph. This is what Garrett wrote for his tombstone: "Incredibly loving. Never-ending passion for helping others. He worked each and every day with a smile on his face to make the world a better place."

In his eulogy, he expanded on that theme to talk of other virtues and his love for family and friends. Never once did he mention the word *Olympics* or even swimming. Garrett has worked hard to remain humble. He keeps his medals in a safety-deposit box. His ESPY award remains in a closet. There is no Olympic memorabilia in his Texas apartment. He doesn't even tell new acquaintances about his accomplishments. He has a Midwestern sense of humility, and he never wants to be thought of as arrogant. In another class, he had to write a bio of himself. Garrett talked about his life but again ignored his most famous moment, offering no hint of his Olympic fame.

He sums up the entire experience and his attitude now this way: "I'm super happy and proud and excited [about the 400 freestyle relay]. It's one of the greatest moments of my life, and I'm so happy I was able to be a part of it. It was the greatest honor of my life being able to represent the United States of America at the Olympics, but it certainly doesn't define me as a person, and that's one of the things I'm most happy about."

CHAPTER 21

BEN PROVISOR

Wrestling, 2012

Wrestling is one of the world's oldest sports, with cave drawings of wrestlers dating all the way back to 3,000 BCE and Olympic wrestling starting in 708 BCE. The sport offers two main types: Greco-Roman (in which athletes use only the upper body to attack and hold) and freestyle (using the entire body).

Wisconsin has always had a rich wrestling heritage at the youth and high school levels, and the state can boast an Olympic gold medal (Benjamin Peterson in 1972) and several silver medals (Peterson in 1976, Russ Hellickson in 1976, Andy Rein in 1984, and Dennis Hall in 1996).

World champion Dennis Hall went on to inspire a young neighbor in Stevens Point, Wisconsin, to strive for his own Olympics journey. Hall lived next door to a boy named Ben Provisor. The boy's parents were not athletes—his father had been a musician with the band the Grass Roots—but the young Provisor liked wrestling and soon found himself frequenting the World Gold Wrestling Club, run by Hall.

"First time I saw him, I knew he was somebody who could possibly get to [the Olympic Games]. It was what I saw inside him—his dedication, his heart and how he loved to compete," Hall told a reporter in 2012.

Hall encouraged Provisor to skip eighth grade and live in Bulgaria for a year to train with some of the top Greco-Roman wrestlers on the planet. Provisor grew even more passionate about the sport, but he was not yet a star. Wrestling at Stevens Point Area High School, he never finished higher than third at the Wisconsin Wrestling High School State Championships. Despite this, he dropped out of Northern Michigan University after one year to move to the Olympic Training Center in Colorado Springs. His dream was London in 2012, and he spoke to Hall about it over the phone several times every week.

"I try and help Ben with the mental side of the game," Hall said in 2012. "[At the Olympics] everyone is chiseled—there's not one guy who doesn't look [like] an Olympic athlete. The difference between the guys who win and those who don't is the mental focus they have."

Even as he was encouraging Ben, Hall was nurturing his own dream. At the age of forty-one, he decided to enter the Olympic qualifications himself. He wondered how far he could go; if he still had what it took. Hall and Provisor wrestled on the same day in Iowa City, Iowa, with a ticket to London in the balance for both of them.

Hall's match was first. He was trying to become just the third wrestler to make four Olympic teams. He lost in the first round of the 132-pound Greco-Roman competition but still had a chance in the consolation bracket. It started off well with a win, 3–3, 4–0, 1–0, but his bid came to an end with a 1–0, 0–1, 0–1 loss to Marco Lara of Colorado.

Just a few hours later, Provisor took the mat at 163 pounds, and Hall joined a huge cheering section from Wisconsin in the stands. Provisor breezed through the opening rounds, not yielding a point, which set up a final match with the top seed, fellow Wisconsinite Aaron Sieracki of Richland Center. It was a best of three, and each man won a match. Then came the third and decisive match. The twenty-one-year old Provisor edged the thirty-seven-year-old Sieracki, but only after appealing a judge's ruling that had given Sieracki a point for a final-second push-out. The replay was in Provisor's favor, as it showed that part of Sieracki's body had been out of bounds before the push-out, giving Ben a 1–0, 0–1, 1–0 victory.

"I wasn't 100% positive I'd win the appeal but, hey, I was aggressive the entire time," Provisor told the *Milwaukee Journal Sentinel*. "I never stopped. Always move your feet. Never stop wrestling. That's a lesson to every kid out there. You never know what's going to happen."

Provisor did not let the moment pass without praising Hall for the training and support that got him there. "I owe everything I did to him,"

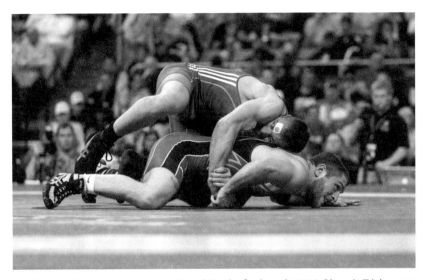

Ben Provisor, in red, wrestles Aaron Sieracki in the finals at the 2012 Olympic Trials. REESE
STRICKLAND—USA TODAY SPORTS

he said. "He's taught me everything, and my mental attitude is the way it
is because of him."

Provisor and Hall put their heads together before the Olympics and
pored over details on all of the international wrestlers, studying their ten-
dencies, strengths, and weaknesses. Hall traveled to London with Ben's
supporters to cheer his pupil on.

On August 5, 2012, Ben beat Alexei Bell of Cuba in the opening round.
But his journey came to an end with a tough match against Zurabi Datunashvili of Georgia in round two. He missed a chance to wrestle in a
wrestle-back (rematch) when Datunashvili lost in the semifinals. Provisor
would return home without a medal. "I wrestled my best, and I'll learn
from this experience," he said. Hall had announced that he would retire
from competing after the trials.

For a while it appeared that those 2012 Summer Games would be one
of the last Olympics to include wrestling. The sport was voted out by the
International Olympic Committee in 2013 and was slated to end in 2020,
but the IOC reversed its decision following a six-month campaign by wrestling body FILA (Fédération Internationale des Luttes Associées, known

in English as the International Federation of Associated Wrestling Styles) to reshape and modernize the sport.

The reinstatement of wrestling to Olympics status marked "the most important day in the 2,000-year history of our sport," FILA president Nenad Lalovic told the Associated Press. "We feel the weight of that history. Remaining on the Olympic program is crucial to wrestling's survival."

Ben Provisor married fellow Team USA wrestler Leigh Jaynes, and they live in Colorado Springs with their daughter, Evelyn, born in 2013. Ben won the Bill Farrell International Wrestling Tournament in 2014 and the Dave Schultz Memorial International in 2015. Since then he has been recovering from hernia surgery and helping coach his wife. "This is a wrestling family, and we hope to keep it that way," Provisor said in an interview in 2015.

CHAPTER 22

MATT ANTOINE

Skeleton, 2014

Friends, family, and competitors call him "Cheese," an affectionate nickname given to honor his favorite state. Matt Antoine hails from Prairie du Chien, a town of 6,000 straddling the western edge of Wisconsin at the convergence of the Mississippi and Wisconsin Rivers.

Matt was born with the surname Antoine-DeJulio to Mary Antoine and Greg DeJulio. He became hooked on fast sports at a very young age, scrambling from bed early on Sunday mornings to watch Formula One auto racing, attracted to go-karts as an older child, and eventually zooming himself down local hills on anything he could find, from sleds to bikes to wagons.

Matt tried basketball, mostly from peer pressure because it was the thing to do in upper elementary and middle school, but he was soon disillusioned by playing time. "I'm a professional benchwarmer," he complained to his mother. Part of the problem was that the coaches always started their own sons. By the time he was in high school, Matt was turned off by traditional sports.

In 2002, when Matt was seventeen, he and his mother watched the Salt Lake City Winter Olympics together on television. Skeleton was back on the Olympic program for the first time since 1948, and there was expanded coverage of the unique sport, as well as many stories on American skeleton slider Jimmy Shea, a third-generation Olympian from Lake Placid, New York, who won an emotional gold that year just weeks after his grandfather, a 1932 speedskating gold medalist, was killed by a drunk driver.

Matt Antoine loved speeding down Wisconsin's hills from a very young age.
COURTESY OF THE ANTOINE FAMILY

Mary Antoine had lived in upstate New York during the 1980 Olympics and told Matt stories about both the Games and the area, but little did she know that Matt would now feel immediately and magnetically drawn to the discipline he saw on TV that combined three of his favorite things: speed, athletics, and winter. Skeleton (also called sliding) is an intense sport that requires an athlete to hurtle headfirst down a sheer mountain of ice at speeds up to 80 miles per hour.

Matt is a quiet person and did not express his new desire to his mother until it was time to choose a destination for vacation that summer, an annual trip for Mary and the kids after Mary and Greg divorced. To her surprise, Matt asked if they could go to Lake Placid, home of one of North America's only skeleton training facilities. It turned out Matt had been on the internet researching skeleton ever since the Olympics. The United States Bobsled and Skeleton Federation was offering tryouts for invitations to sliding schools, and Matt wanted to go and give it a shot. Somehow he knew that skeleton was important to him and would be part of his life. Mary, however, was a bit taken aback.

"I am not an athletic person. I can't even swim," she laughed. Matt's father had done a little skiing, but in general, Matt does not come from a family of athletes. Yet when her son told her of his desire to try sliding, Mary's first reaction was, "Go for it."

She told him she would support any dream he had but that he also had to go to college. Mother and son researched schools within driving distance of Lake Placid and headed east on vacation that summer of 2002 with Matt's brother in tow. Although Matt's only previous experience with any form of sliding was sledding during Wisconsin winters, he was good enough in his summer tryout to join the Olympic Development Center's skeleton sliding school in Lake Placid in November 2002, and he chose to focus on that instead of college for the time being. Matt, the adrenaline junkie, loved the icy track from the first moment. The cold didn't bother him—after all, he was from Wisconsin—and he had little fear of what he was getting into. He felt certain an invitation to the Olympic center's developmental program would be next.

It did not come. This was his first huge blow—trainers at the school told him he simply was not good enough. Matt was at his first crossroads but insisted he wanted to try again. Always supportive of her daredevil son, Mary said that was fine, but he still had to attend college. She would find ways throughout the years, with the help of family and occasional fundraisers, to finance both, but she also made it clear that college was a prerequisite for Matt to get any money from her to support his sliding.

He enrolled at the University of Vermont, forty-five minutes from Lake Placid by ferry across Lake Champlain. That fall of 2003 he had persevered in his training to the point that he was accepted into the developmental program on his second try. But he soon found that those winter rides back and forth on the ferry were more taxing than he had envisioned, and he transferred to the State University of New York at Plattsburgh—still forty-five minutes from his new skeleton home, but over roads instead of water.

School and sliding, sliding and school. It was a relentless schedule. Matt carried twelve credit hours per semester to accommodate his training, but even that became too much as his practice and competitions heated up and he began traveling internationally on the skeleton circuit. Finally, it was clear that an online school would be the best fit, and Matt graduated from California University of Pennsylvania in 2009 with a degree in sports

JOHNNY QUINN

Johnny Quinn had what you call a "cup of coffee" with the Green Bay Packers. That is, he spent a short amount of time—about eight months—in green and gold as a wide receiver in 2008. Quinn was cut shortly after training camp. He went on to the Saskatchewan Roughriders of the Canadian Football League before blowing out the anterior cruciate ligament in his knee. His football career was over, but little did he know that another adventure awaited.

Quinn's agent, who knew Johnny had been a track star at the University of North Texas, suggested that Johnny send a videotape of himself running to the US bobsled team. Bobsled coaches are often looking for athletes with speed and acceleration to be on the "push team." It didn't take long for Johnny to be invited to Lake Placid, New York, and then to be assigned to a four-man bobsled team that eventually made the 2014 Olympics in Sochi, Russia.

Quinn's role lasts just a few seconds. He runs as fast as he can holding on to a bar on the side of the sled. The push team's goal is to give the driver as much of a head start as possible at the top of the bobsled track. Johnny, the driver, and the two other pushers will often scream with exertion as they push the 463-pound sled at the fastest speed they can muster. At exactly the right moment, the pushers jump in, one behind the other, and hold on for the ride as the driver steers to the bottom of the course. The three pushers keep their heads down to minimize wind friction, but this serves another purpose for Johnny, who suffers from motion sickness. As soon as he's safely in the sled he clamps his eyes closed for the ride down the winding, icy track in a precarious sled that can travel up to 118 miles per hour. Quinn has been in several crashes, one of which left a permanent scar on his shoulder.

Johnny's bobsled team did not medal in 2014, but Johnny gained notoriety for something else at those Winter Games. When a bathroom door malfunctioned, Quinn sent out the following message on Twitter: "I was taking a shower and the door got locked/jammed. With no phone to call for help, I used my bobsled push training to break out." He included the

Johnny Quinn made the term "Quinning" (using your strength for even a minor task) popular during the Sochi Games in 2014. KEVIN JAIRAJ—USA TODAY SPORTS

hashtag #SochiJailBreak and a photo of the thin, cheap door with a huge hole busted out of the middle, large enough for a man to crawl through. Many hotels and venues in Sochi were being publicly criticized for being ill-prepared, and Quinn's tweet went viral. It was retweeted more than 29,000 times and was seen by an estimated 10 million people. Later on that Sochi trip, Quinn, teammate Nick Cunningham, and a coach found themselves stuck in an elevator. Nick tweeted a picture of Quinn trying to pull the doors open Incredible Hulk–style while wearing his Team USA–issued sweatpants and sweatshirt. The three men were rescued from the elevator, but the term "Quinning" blew up on social media to describe resolving your problems through physical strength—often applied to more mundane tasks, such as ripping open a package that was taped too tightly.

Quinn has always kept an affection for Wisconsin, taking his fiancée to Lambeau Field to see a game and saying he would be a fan "for as long as Aaron [Rodgers] is around." When asked if he preferred the Packers or the Cowboys, his favorite childhood team, Quinn said with a laugh, "Packers . . . but don't tell anybody in Texas I just said that."

management, wellness, and fitness. It had taken him six years and three institutions, but he had found the college path that was right for him.

Success on the sliding track was also a slow buildup. As Matt got deeper into his twenties he became a two-time national champion with two World Cup medals, set the Lake Placid track record three different times, and was the first to win the Intercontinental Cup Tour, the only US athlete to do so. By this time going by the last name Antoine, twenty-five-year-old Matt had a second major disappointment when he tried out for the 2010 Olympic team in Vancouver but failed to make it. It was a devastating blow to a young slider, and he was heartbroken. In the midst of his setback, a letter arrived from Jimmy Shea, the 2002 gold medalist who had inspired seventeen-year-old Matt to consider sliding. Shea had been following Matt's progress, and now he reached out to Matt personally. The letter said:

Dear Matt,

I'm the only one that has done what you are trying to do [to win a skeleton medal for the US in the modern era]. Your story is just beginning. It's not over. You and John [Daly] will go on to be the best the US has ever seen. Do not let the games hurt or push you away from skeleton. You are the future of the sport for the US. You have the talent to be better than I ever was. You just have to do one thing to get there: never give up. Every problem is an opportunity to guide you to the next step. You will go on to be a champion.

The letter meant so much to both mother and son that Matt consulted it regularly and Mary put a copy of it on her refrigerator. The Antoines sat down together to take a long look at Matt's career. Was he going to push himself all the way, with no regrets? With his mother's advice, Matt decided to test his limits and moved to Colorado Springs, Colorado, to train at the US Olympic Training Center. Motivated by the failure to make Team USA in 2010, he was determined it would not happen again. He set his sights on Sochi, Russia, for 2014.

Yet two years before the Games his body nearly failed him. A lingering knee pain led to the MRI machine, which showed a torn patellar tendon that required surgery. The doctors told Matt that he would have to miss the entire 2012–13 season. This was unacceptable for a guy who always found a way to grasp the positive in any situation. Dedicating himself to rehab after surgery, he was back to running, to the amazement of many, just three months later. In time, he climbed to the top of the world rankings again, and in this go-round, he did not let himself down at the Olympic Trials. He was in, and he jetted to Sochi.

Not far behind were Matt's supporters: Mary; Matt's brother Nick, and Nick's wife, Charlotte; Matt's aunt Margaret; and several other friends of the family, including Charlotte's parents. Matt's sister Elise was unable to get time off from work, and his father, Greg, watched on television back in Prairie du Chien.

Olympic skeleton riders do four runs over two days to determine medals. After the first run, Matt was in third place and his friend and teammate John Daly was in fourth. In race two John posted a really fast time, and the two flip-flopped positions. The final two runs were the next day. Mary and the rest of the traveling party left for the track at 10 A.M. Matt would not race until 6:45 P.M., but they had to make their way to the venue and wanted to be sure they had plenty of time. The entire group was wearing sweatshirts with a logo Matt had designed, and Nick and Charlotte sported yellow foam cheeseheads.

"The Russians at the race were fascinated with the cheeseheads but could not understand why one wore cheese on one's head," remembered Mary.

With the help of a Russian woman, Zhenya, who was assisting their tour group, Mary and the whole gang had been moved from one of the curves of the track to the final grandstand for the third and fourth runs. Zhenya had talked the Antoines, the Dalys, and the family of another American slider, Kyle Tress, past the Russian security guards who were in control of the grandstand, even though their tickets did not allow them in that restricted area. Now they crowded into the bleachers and waited.

After the third run, Matt moved back into third place and John fourth. It looked like Alexander Tretyakov of Russia would take gold and Martins Dukurs of Latvia silver, but a bronze was likely to go to one of the Americans if they could perform well in the final run. It would be only the

Have cheesehead, will travel! Matt Antoine's brother Nicholas (center), Nicholas's wife, Charlotte (right), and Charlotte's mother, Nancy, cheer for Matt in Sochi. COURTESY OF THE ANTOINE FAMILY

second medal for US men's skeleton since the sport was reintroduced to the Olympics in 1948. Emotions were pounding: the culmination of a dream for Antoine and Daly juxtaposed with the difficulty of competing against a friend.

Announcements were coming over the loudspeaker in both Russian and English, and NBC cameras were swarming. "NBC figured out that I was Matt's mom and they asked me if I wanted to be mic'd up," Mary recalled. "I said no. I was afraid what I might say. But the girls [in our party] got a lot of camera time. NBC was always looking for the young, attractive girls."

Mary and the Antoine family were sitting just two rows in front of John Daly's supporters. The families were friendly and had been to many competitions together, but this was definitely awkward as the stakes were so high. "Everybody's very gracious and always wishes each other's sons to do well," Mary said, "but you can sort of imagine what's in the back of your mind. It's difficult. John, Matt, and Kyle had competed against each other for years, and John and Matt flip-flopped in Sochi so much between third and fourth. You realize the fourth run is for all the marbles."

Who would step up and grab the bronze? Only the top twenty slide in the final run, and they do so in reverse order from slowest to fastest. This meant that John Daly would slide just before Matt. Matt was in the waiting area for athletes, getting ready for his turn, as Daly took off running at the top of the hill. Suddenly his sled slipped out of its grooves, a rare event in sliding. The blades underneath shifted and the sled moved sideways; it was all Daly could do to jump on board and hold on for a ride that left him devastated and in fifteenth place overall. In skeleton, tiny thousandths of a second and minuscule mistakes make all the difference.

The crowd in the stands went dead silent, then emitted a collective moan.

"I knew exactly how John's parents felt, how John felt, because Matt had done the same thing in the first run of his first World Cup race at St. Moritz," remembered Mary. "It's a terrible sense of mixed emotions. Knowing how they're feeling, yet at the same time you realize, oh my God! . . . What do I do?"

Matt knew something had happened, but he didn't know what. He hadn't seen it live and needed to focus on his own race. Matt had not been happy with the way two of his previous heats had gone. Warm temperatures had brought on softer ice, and Matt had changed the runners on his sled to accommodate the altering conditions. Although switching any gear mid-Olympics is a gamble, it paid off handsomely. Matt went to the top of the track, put his sled down for the biggest run of his life, and took off. His main competition now for bronze was Tomass Dukurs of Latvia, the older brother of the man sitting in second place, Martins Dukurs. Less than a second separated Matt and Tomass, and Antoine would need a very good run with no mistakes to fend him off.

Matt's supporters did not have the nerve to watch the actual run. Mary focused on the video board closest to them. In the right-hand corner were the competitors' times. The score of the person who was currently sliding would stay green if he was performing at a faster clip than the next-best person. Mary watched for green and nothing else, her heart pounding out of her chest. She knew a solid run would secure a medal. Green, green, so far so good. Still green. The race took 56.73 seconds. As Matt came to a stop, Mary realized the time had never faltered from that magical emerald color.

Matt also knew he had just won a medal. He had been in the sport long enough to recognize the subtleties that separate a run that holds a position versus one where you fall back in the pack. On the last two turns he realized that he was about to complete the dream.

"Once I crossed the finish line I popped up my head, and there is a clock in the outrun that we can see almost immediately," Matt recalled. "I could see it and saw a 1 ensuring that I had held my spot with only two athletes left to go."

He didn't start celebrating yet. He wanted to be absolutely sure that he had seen the clock correctly. Near the bottom of the outrun was another clock, and then came the clincher: he saw his coach celebrating. That confirmed it. His sled was still coming to a stop as realization washed over him. He was going to medal. "I'm usually a very cool and reserved person when I compete but I definitely let out the cheers this time," Matt said.

Mary quickly shifted her eyes from the scoreboard to her son as he was standing up to get off his sled. "You could just see the elation on him and in his body and everything," she said. "It was very exciting. As soon as I realized he had won, my sister Margaret and I hugged each other and we were crying, but then we started cheering."

"Once I came to a stop I jumped off my sled, and my coach ran up yelling and we hugged," said Matt. "I took my helmet off, looked right at my family, and put my arm up pointing right at them. That moment right there was my favorite because if not for them I wouldn't have been there winning that bronze medal. The emotion on their faces, how happy they were, and what this meant to them—I'll never forget that."

Twenty-eight-year-old Matt Antoine had just secured the first men's skeleton medal for the US since he and his mother watched Jimmy Shea take gold twelve years earlier. Could life get any more perfect and full circle than that? In a sport dominated by northern Europeans and Canadians, Matt Antoine had made US history.

Mary and the rest of the Wisconsin fan base were still going nuts. Tears flowed, hugs were passed among them all, feet jumped up and down in joy, and the cold night air filled with screams of jubilation. Matt came over to his family, but security separating athletes and spectators was tight. Nick managed to throw an American flag to his brother, which Matt draped around his shoulders, proud to represent the United States.

A MOTHER'S PERSPECTIVE

What is it like to see your own flesh and blood win an Olympic medal? Whether it's gold, silver, or bronze, a medal is the zenith of what has typically been a decade or more of work, and often one or two parents have been financial and emotional backers, PR gurus, taxicab drivers, healthy food providers, and the biggest cheerleaders along that long and winding road. Some parents have the added layer of concerns about their child's safety.

"People say, Don't you worry about him getting hurt? No, I never worried about him being physically hurt," Mary Antoine said. "He's a very meticulous person. He would always do his research and have everything absolutely perfect. When it came to skeleton, maybe I was naïve, but not really. I figured he would know his equipment, and he would know what he had to do."

Mary decided early on to attend at least one of Matt's races each year. But she also committed to giving him space. "I sometimes think that family is a distraction, [with the athlete wondering], 'Is everything okay, how are things going, are you enjoying yourself?'" Thus Mary did not attend any of Matt's races in the months leading up to the selection of the Olympic skeleton team that would go to Sochi. He was expected to make the team based on his results in international competitions, but Mary still worried that he might feel pressured, thanks in part to a ticket policy that had essentially required her to purchase tickets for the Olympics in July 2013, six months before the Games.

The Russian Olympic organization had released a limited number of tickets to the United States and other countries that summer on a first-come, first-served system. It was potential Olympic families' only opportunity to guarantee seats at the venues where their offspring might be competing. If your loved one failed to make the Olympic team, only the hotel would be refunded; there was no opportunity to opt out of venue or ceremony tickets. Of course, Mary was going to ensure she had the

Matt and Mary Antoine. Many athletes
say that seeing their parents in the stands
chokes them up more than anything else.
COURTESY OF THE ANTOINE FAMILY

appropriate passes if Matt made it, but she worried that ticket purchases might add to Matt's stress. She also stayed away from the World Cup leading up to the Olympic Games.

There was no need to refund the Antoines' tickets for Sochi. When Matt secured his spot on the team, Mary felt more excitement and relief than pure joy. But she knew the elation would come if he medaled.

On Matt's first race day at the Games, Mary was filled with anxiety. "Everybody knew I was a nervous wreck. They all said, 'Leave Mom alone.' I get sort of quiet and withdraw into myself, and to be honest, I say a lot of prayers. I wanted him to do well. I know how crushed he was after not making it in 2010."

After Matt took bronze, the momentousness of it all began to sink in. Mary, the nonathlete, had raised an Olympian. Matt's accomplishment hit her more in retrospect. "Sometimes it will strike me, God, you know, he went to the Olympics!" she said. For eleven years she had been Matt's public relations agent, sending news releases to newspapers and radio and TV stations across Wisconsin and eastern Iowa. The medal was Matt's, a tribute to his dedication and perseverance, but a tiny part of it belonged to Mary—for bringing him into the world, for believing in her son's dreams from day one, and for helping with each milestone, large and small, that led to those grandstands and that wondrous green number on the scoreboard in Sochi.

The gold and silver medalists still had to complete their runs, however, meaning the celebration would not be fully under way for all spectators just yet. The Antoines settled back down, aware of the nearby Dalys and the heartache they felt. Mary and the family watched respectfully as the last two sliders went down and earned silver and gold. Matt observed quietly from a nearby podium until the races were complete. The Russian crowd exploded when their man, Tretyakov, secured gold. For Antoine, it was bronze.

Now the place was in full-blown celebration mode. Standing on risers during a flower ceremony, Matt, silver medalist Martins Dukurs, and Tretyakov were cheered once again, this time by the whole crowd. Seeing Matt beaming, Mary thought to herself, "He's the happiest of all three, and he gets the bronze." The other two did not wear their emotions on their sleeves.

Matt had to go straight to his media responsibilities, so Mary had yet to actually hug her son. A member of the US contingent came into the grandstands to retrieve the family, but security guards, speaking Russian and gesturing, were not going to let them pass. Mary was at her wits' end. "I had no patience anymore. I barreled my way through and said, 'My son won a medal and I'm going through!'" remembered Mary with a chuckle.

Eventually someone was able to explain the situation to the guards, and Mary and Nick were allowed in, but they were kept from Matt while he did hordes of interviews. "The media now owns him," one of the public relations people explained to the Antoines. More impatient waiting ensued. When she finally got close to her son, that long-awaited hug was incredible, though not tearful. "We're very quietly emotional people," Mary explained. "It was a really nice tight hug. Both of us made sure we didn't cry. It was a little bittersweet because of John at the same time."

Matt was also feeling disappointment for his friend John Daly. "It's so unfortunate," he said in a Team USA online article a few months later. "John and I pushed each other to be where we are, and I don't think either of us would've been competing for bronze if it hadn't been for the other person. We've made each other better over the last ten years. My heart goes out to him. That's a really, really tough way to end your race."

But for Matt, nothing could have been better. How many people watch something on TV, say 'I'm going to do that' and then accomplish that goal? The sports landscape is littered with thousands who dreamed a similar fantasy yet failed to follow through for a huge variety of reasons, from motivation to luck. Matt had the perfect combination of timing, skill, and a supportive family that sent the boy from the small town in western Wisconsin to a bronze medal.

Mary and the rest of Matt's supporters were buzzing with energy when they returned to their guesthouse run by a young Russian couple. Although the proprietors spoke no English and the Antoine crew spoke very little Russian, they were able to explain that Matt had just won bronze. The couple, Nickolai and Tanya, put on a celebratory feast with Russian vodka, caviar, cold meats, cheese, and fresh bread.

Early the next morning an NBC van picked up Matt at the village and then got Mary and Matt's brother, Nick. Matt had an entire day of press conferences, television interviews, and photo shoots as well as an appearance on the *Today Show*. Mary and company watched nearby as the *Today Show* hosts interviewed Matt. They also got to meet and take pictures with Bonnie Blair, who was in Sochi as a member of the US delegation. Although celebrities do not often impress Mary, family teased her that she looked awestruck when Bonnie approached.

The medals ceremony took place in Sochi proper, not in the mountains where the sliding competitions were held, in order to garner the largest crowds. Massive numbers of people assembled every night at a grandstand in Olympic Park to cheer the medal winners.

It was drizzling and quite dreary the night of Matt's ceremony, but the weather mattered little. The family went early to secure front-row spots against the barriers while Matt was taken backstage. There were no seats for spectators in the standing-only venue, but tired feet and rain barely registered. Medals for several other sports were given out, and then skeleton was called. Matt had never even touched an Olympic medal, always saying that he wanted the first one he placed his fingers on to be his own. Now he leaned forward from the podium as a Russian Olympic official placed the bronze, hanging from its cloth support, around his neck. His first reaction was that it felt heavier than he had imagined.

The Antoines watched with glee as Matt once again had the largest grin

Matt Antoine receives a warm reception from students during his visit to B. A. Kennedy School in Prairie du Chien, Wisconsin, April 2014. COURTESY OF THE ANTOINE FAMILY

of the three medalists. The Russian national anthem played and the flags lifted, and Mary and the rest of Matt's group found themselves wiping their eyes once again.

It was a surreal experience. Here they were, halfway across the globe, watching Matt do something he had set his mind on as a seventeen-year-old. His medal win had happened at such a fast pace that they had hardly had a chance to catch their breaths or realize the magnitude. And they had seen him win plenty of other races. In some strange ways, the actual sliding had felt much like any other competition. It was easy to forget, so far from US soil and constant Olympic coverage, how many people were watching—and how a medal could change your life. It just hadn't sunk in yet.

The night ended with a return to the USA House, more food and beverages, and nonstop grins on all of their faces. Before Mary and the rest left Russia they bought American-style Ralph Lauren sweaters from that USA House as a thank-you gift for their Russian hosts. Then Mary and the rest of the gang flew home, still high on adrenaline, but also weary from the emotional intensity and the travel.

Back in Prairie du Chien, Mary was overwhelmed with the support she felt from the city. A local business hung up a banner featuring the same logo the family had worn on their shirts at the Games, and that seemed to spark Matt-mania in Prairie. A parade followed, with Matt as grand marshal; he spoke at his old elementary and high schools. Mary was stunned by the number of people who had watched the race and cheered for her son.

Prairie du Chien welcomed home its new favorite son with a rally. Wisconsin governor Scott Walker declared March 14, 2014, Matt Antoine Day, and the next day the city of Prairie du Chien did the same, naming March 15 in his honor.

To get a true sense of how Matt felt, though, go back to Sochi and those moments immediately after the hugging and partying died down, when he said: "It was pure celebration. This is definitely the best moment of my life."

Team USA Medal Winners with Wisconsin Connections

This list was compiled using dozens of sources and is comprehensive through the 2014 Winter Games. A "Wisconsin connection" refers to people who were born, grew up, went to school, or trained extensively in the state. Abbreviations: OR = Olympic record; WR = world record.

Year	Host City	Athlete	Sport	Medal(s)
1900	Paris	Alvin Kraenzlein	athletics	4 gold
1904	St. Louis	Emil Breitkreutz	athletics	bronze
		Archie Hahn	athletics	3 gold
		Oscar Osthoff	weight lifting	gold, silver
		George Poage	athletics	2 bronze
		Phillip Schuster	gymnastics	bronze
		Jerome Steever	water polo	silver
		Frank Waller	athletics	2 silver
1912	Stockholm	Fred Hird	shooting	gold, 2 bronze
1920	Antwerp	Walter Maurer	wrestling	bronze
		Alden "Zeke" Sanborn	rowing	gold
		Arlie Schardt	athletics	gold

Year	Host City	Athlete	Sport	Medal(s)
1928	Amsterdam	Charles McGinnis	athletics	bronze
1932	Lake Placid	Edward Murphy	speedskating	silver
1932	Los Angeles	Helene Madison	swimming	3 gold
		Ralph Metcalfe	athletics	silver, bronze
1936	Garmisch-Partenkirchen	Leo Freisinger	speedskating	bronze
1936	Berlin	Ralph Metcalfe	athletics	gold, silver
1948	London	Lloyd LaBeach	athletics	2 bronze
		Stan Stanczyk	weight lifting	gold (OR)
1952	Helsinki	Ron Bontemps	basketball	gold
		Frank McCabe	basketball	gold
		Stan Stanczyk	weight lifting	silver
		Kenneth Wiesner	athletics	silver
1956	Melbourne	John Bennett	athletics	silver
		George Lambert	athletics	silver
1960	Rome	Bob Boozer	basketball	gold
		George Lambert	athletics	bronze
		Oscar Robertson	basketball	gold
1964	Tokyo	Peter Barrett	sailing	silver
		Harry "Buddy" Melges	sailing	bronze
1968	Grenoble	Dianne Holum	speedskating	silver, bronze
1968	Mexico City	Peter Barrett	sailing	gold
		Larry Hough	rowing	silver

Year	Host City	Athlete	Sport	Medal(s)
1972	Sapporo	Anne Henning	speedskating	gold, bronze
		Dianne Holum	speedskating	gold (OR), silver
		Stu Irving	ice hockey	silver
1972	Munich	Steve Furniss	swimming	bronze
		Harry "Buddy" Melges	sailing	gold
		Tim Mickelson	rowing	silver
		John Peterson	wrestling	silver
		Benjamin Peterson	wrestling	gold
1976	Innsbruck	Dan Immerfall	speedskating	bronze
		Peter Mueller	speedskating	gold
		Leah Poulos	speedskating	silver
		Sheila Young	speedskating	gold, silver, bronze
1976	Montreal	Wendy Boglioli	swimming	gold (WR), bronze
		Quinn Buckner	basketball	gold
		Adrian Dantley	basketball	gold
		Philip Ford	basketball	gold
		Carie Graves	rowing	bronze
		Ernest "Ernie" Grunfeld	basketball	gold
		Russ Hellickson	wrestling	silver
		Scott May	basketball	gold
		Peggy McCarthy	rowing	bronze
		Jim Montgomery	swimming	3 gold, bronze
		John Peterson	wrestling	gold
		Benjamin Peterson	wrestling	silver
		Jackie Zoch	rowing	bronze
1980	Lake Placid	Beth Heiden	speedskating	bronze
		Eric Heiden	speedskating	5 gold
		Mark Johnson	ice hockey	gold
		Leah Poulos	speedskating	2 silver
		William "Buzz" Schneider	ice hockey	gold
		Bob Suter	ice hockey	gold

Year	Host City	Athlete	Sport	Medal(s)
1984	Los Angeles	Judi Brown	athletics	silver
		Connie Carpenter Phinney	cycling	gold
		Barry Davis	wrestling	silver
		Brent Emery	cycling	silver
		Bob Espeseth	rowing	bronze
		Carie Graves	rowing	gold
		Andy Rein	wrestling	silver
		Alvin Robertson	basketball	gold
		Kris Thorsness	rowing	gold
1988	Calgary	Bonnie Blair	speedskating	gold, bronze
		Eric Flaim	speedskating	silver
1988	Seoul	Jeff Grayer	basketball	bronze
		Dave Krmpotich	rowing	silver
		Daniel "Danny" Manning	basketball	bronze
		Jay Mortenson	swimming	gold
		Andre Phillips	athletics	gold
		Herman "JR" Reid	basketball	bronze
		Lynn Roethke	judo	silver (demo sport)
		Scott Servais	baseball	gold (demo sport)
1992	Albertville	Bonnie Blair	speedskating	2 gold
		Darcie Dohnal	speedskating	silver
		Bob Nichols	curling	bronze (demo sport)
		Raymond (Bud) Somerville	curling	bronze (demo sport)
		Bill Strum	curling	bronze (demo sport)
		Mike Strum	curling	bronze (demo sport)
		Tim Somerville	curling	bronze (demo sport)
1992	Barcelona	Cindy Eckert	rowing	silver
		Carol Feeney	rowing	silver

Year	Host City	Athlete	Sport	Medal(s)
1994	Lillehammer	Bonnie Blair	speedskating	2 gold
		Eric Flaim	speedskating	silver
		Andy Gabel	speedskating	silver
		Dan Jansen	speedskating	gold
1996	Atlanta	Kris Benson	baseball	bronze
		Kenny Harrison	athletics	gold
		Dennis Hall	wrestling	silver
		Eric Mueller	rowing	silver
		Gary Payton	basketball	gold
1998	Nagano	Karyn Bye	ice hockey	gold
		Christine Witty	speedskating	silver, bronze
2000	Sydney	Walter "Ray" Allen	basketball	gold
		Vincent "Vin" Baker	basketball	gold
		Sarah Garner	rowing	bronze
		Mari Holden	cycling	silver
		Garrett Lowney	wrestling	bronze
		Kate Sobrero-Markgraf	football	silver
		Gary Payton	basketball	gold
		Ben Sheets	baseball	gold
		Neil Walker	swimming	gold, silver
2002	Salt Lake City	Karyn Bye	ice hockey	silver
		Kip Carpenter	speedskating	bronze
		Joey Cheek	speedskating	bronze
		Chris Chelios	ice hockey	silver
		Casey FitzRandolph	speedskating	gold
		Derek Parra	speedskating	gold, silver
		Brian Rafalski	ice hockey	silver
		Jennifer Rodriguez	speedskating	2 bronze
		Gary Suter	ice hockey	silver
		Christine Witty	speedskating	gold

Year	Host City	Athlete	Sport	Medal(s)
2004	Athens	Dede Barry	cycling	silver
		Rebecca Giddens	canoe-slalom	silver
		Morgan Hamm	gymnastics	silver (team)
		Paul Hamm	gymnastics	gold, silver, silver (team)
		Beau Hoopman	rowing	gold (WR)
		Richard Jefferson	basketball	bronze
		Beezie Madden	horse jumping	gold (team)
		Kate Sobrero-Markgraf	football	gold
		Carly Piper	swimming	gold (WR)
		Andrew Rock	athletics	gold
		Lindsay Tarpley	football	gold
		Dwyane Wade	basketball	bronze (reserve)
		Neil Walker	swimming	gold, bronze
2006	Turin	Joey Cheek	speedskating	gold/silver
		Shani Davis	speedskating	gold/silver
		Molly Engstrom	ice hockey	bronze
		Chanda Gunn	ice hockey	bronze
2008	Beijing	Micah Boyd	rowing	bronze
		Beau Hoopman	rowing	bronze
		Laura Kraut	horse jumping	gold (team)
		Beezie Madden	horse jumping	gold (team), bronze (individual)
		Kate Sobrero-Markgraf	football	gold
		Chellsie Memmel	gymnastics	silver (team)
		Michael Redd	basketball	gold
		Lindsay Tarpley	football	gold
		Dwyane Wade	basketball	gold
		Garrett Weber-Gale	swimming	2 gold

Year	Host City	Athlete	Sport	Medal(s)
2010	Vancouver	Shani Davis	speedskating	gold, silver
		Alyson Dudek	speedskating	bronze
		Meghan Duggan	ice hockey	silver
		Molly Engstrom	ice hockey	silver
		Brian Hansen	speedskating	silver
		Phil Kessel	ice hockey	silver
		Hilary Knight	ice hockey	silver
		Jonathan Kuck	speedskating	silver
		Erika Lawler	ice hockey	silver
		Trevor Marsicano	speedskating	silver
		Joe Pavelski	ice hockey	silver
		Brian Rafalski	ice hockey	silver
		Ryan Suter	ice hockey	silver
		Jessie Vetter	ice hockey	silver
		Kerry Weiland	ice hockey	silver
		Jinelle Zaugg-Siergiej	ice hockey	silver
2012	London	Megan Kalmoe	rowing	bronze
2014	Sochi	Matt Antoine	skeleton	bronze
		Brianna Decker	ice hockey	silver
		Meghan Duggan	ice hockey	silver
		Amanda Kessel	ice hockey	silver
		Hilary Knight	ice hockey	silver
		Jessie Vetter	ice hockey	silver

Carleton Brosius and his tug-of-war teammates on their way to the 1920 Olympic Games in Antwerp, Belgium. THE WISCONSIN VETERANS MUSEUM

Notes on Sources

Introduction

The history of the Olympics is based on the following sources: *An Illustrated History of the Olympics* by Dick Schaap, Knopf, 1963, pages 24–25; *The Olympics* by Sports Illustrated, 1992, pages 12–28; *The Story of the Olympics* by Dave Anderson, HarperCollins Publishers, 1996, pages 9–15; *The Olympics' Strangest Moments* by Geoff Tibballs, Anova Books, 2008, introduction and pages 3–5; *Swifter, Higher, Stronger: A Photographic History of the Summer Olympics* by Sue Macy, National Geographic Children's Books, 2008, pages 13–20; www.olympic.org; www.history.com/topics/olympic-games; and *The Complete Book of the Summer Olympics* by David Wallechinsky, Aurum Press, 1996, page 10.

Chapter 1

Information on Alvin Kraenzlein was gathered during an interview with Kraenzlein's granddaughter, Susanna Tvede, as well as from the following: the University of Pennsylvania online archives at www.archives.upenn.edu; *Washington Post,* June 8, 1913; *Anaconda (Montana) Standard*, January 1, 1928; www.olympic.org; www.sports-reference.com; USA Track and Field at www.usatf.org; britannica.com; *An Illustrated History of the Olympics* by Dick Schaap, Knopf, 1963, pages 59–68; *The Olympics* by Sports Illustrated, 1992, page 28; *The Story of the Olympics* by Dave Anderson, HarperCollins Publishers, 1996, pages 19–20; *The Olympics' Strangest Moments* by Geoff Tibballs, Anova Books, 2008, pages 14–16; an article from the *New York Sun* from January 6, 1928; *Historical Dictionary of Track and Field* by Peter Matthews, Scarecrow Press, 2012; and *Players: 250 Men, Women and Animals Who Created Modern Sport* by Tim Allen, Random House, 2009.

Chapter 2

Margaret Lichter's book *George Coleman Poage: An Olympic Legacy, A Report for the La Crosse Board of Park Commissioners* was invaluable for this chapter, as were articles by *La Crosse Tribune* reporter Betsy Bloom. I also appreciate the input of

Viterbo University professor David J. Waters and La Crosse Director of Parks and Recreation Steve Carlyon. Additional information was gathered from *The Olympics' Strangest Moments* by Geoff Tibballs, Anova Books, 2008, page 19; *An Illustrated History of the Olympics* by Dick Schaap, Knopf, 1963, page 72; www.sports-reference.com; *The Complete Book of the Olympics* by David Wallechinsky, Penguin Books, 1984; www.uwbadgers.com; and *Graduating Class Reunion Book of 1959: Down Memory Lane,* produced by Sumner High School, St. Louis, Missouri, 1959.

Information on Frank Waller came from UW–Madison Libraries (www.library.wisc.edu) and the *Chippewa Herald* online (Chippewa.com).

Chapter 3

Interviews with Oscar Osthoff's grandson John Nugent and great-grandson Patrick Nugent provided much of the background for chapter 3. Additional information was gathered from *A Photographic History of Elkhart Lake* by Peter Laun, Elkhart Lake Historical Society, 2002; www.beerhistory.com; www.sports-reference.com; osthoff.com; and an article by Laurel Walker in the *Milwaukee Journal Sentinel,* August 31, 2004.

Chapter 4

The primary source for this chapter was Marquette University's online archive at www.gomarquette.com. Additional information was gathered from www.olympic.org and an article by Simon Burnton for *The Guardian,* posted February 29, 2012, www.theguardian.com.

Chapter 5

Information on Carleton Brosius came from the Wisconsin Veterans Museum's online exhibitions, www.wisvetsmuseum.com/exhibitions. Additional information came from the Milwaukee Turners at www.milwaukeeturners.org; www.sports-reference.com; *The Olympics' Strangest Moments* by Geoff Tibballs, Anova Books, 2008, pages 45–47; *An Illustrated History of the Olympics* by Dick Schaap, Knopf, 1963, pages 141–143 and 147; and *The Olympics: A History of the Games* by William Oscar Johnson, Oxmoor House, 1992, pages 34 and 35.

Information on Arlie Schardt is from www.sports-reference.com. Information about the Winter Olympics and Eddie Murphy is from the Wisconsin Historical Society at www.wisconsinhistory.org/museum/exhibits/skate; sports-reference.com; *Freeze Frame: A Photographic History of the Winter Olympics* by Sue Macy, National Geographic Children's Books, 2006, pages 12–15; and *The Story of the Olympics* by Dave Anderson, HarperCollins Publishers, 1996, page 32.

Chapter 6
Information on Ralph Metcalfe was obtained through conversations with his son, Ralph Metcalfe Jr., and the following: *The Story of the Olympics* by Dave Anderson, HarperCollins Publishers, 1996, pages 28 and 35–43; *The Olympics: A History of the Game* by William Oscar Johnson, Oxmoor House, 1992, pages 36–37; Marquette University Library's website (www.marquette.edu/library) and the university's archives (www.gomarquette.com); "Illinois Hall of Fame: Ralph Metcalfe" by Mark Rhoads, *Illinois Review,* November 3, 2006 (www.illinoisreview.typepad.com); "Was Jesse Owens' 1936 Long-Jump Story a Myth?" by Tom Goldman, NPR, August 14, 2009 (www.npr.org); "World's Fastest Man: The Ralph Metcalfe Story" by Michael Wittliff, August 15, 2008; "Marty Glickman, Jesse Owens and a Forgotten Story of the 1936 Berlin Olympics" by Peter F. Richman, August 22, 2013, www.bleacherreport.com; "Metcalfe, Ralph Harold," Biographical Dictionary of the United States Congress, http://bioguide.congress.gov; "Metcalfe, Ralph Harold," US House of Representatives, http://history.house.gov; www.sports-reference.com; www.olympic.org; *The Olympics: A History of the Modern Games* by Allen Guttmann, University of Illinois Press, 2002, page 60; *Berlin Games: How the Nazis Stole the Olympic Dream* by Guy Walters, William Morrow, 2006, page 264–267 and prologue; *The Complete Book of the Olympics* by David Wallechinsky, Penguin Books, 1984 edition page 49, 2008 edition pages 48–49, and 2012 edition page 48; and www.jewishvirtuallibrary.org/jsource/Holocaust/glickman.html.

Sources for Helene Madison's story were *The Olympics' Strangest Moments* by Geoff Tibballs, Anova Books, 2008, pages 70–72; *Swifter, Higher, Stronger: A Photographic History of the Summer Olympics* by Sue Macy, National Geographic Children's Books, 2008, pages 23–27; *The Story of the Olympics* by Dave Anderson, HarperCollins Publishers, 1996, pages 25–27; www.olympic.org; the encyclopedia of Washington State history at www.historylink.org; and *An Illustrated History of the Olympics* by Dick Schaap, Knopf, 1963, page 133.

Chapter 7

Sources for the stories of Lloyd LaBeach and Don Gehrmann were the Wisconsin Badgers website at www.uwbadgers.com; "Olympic Runner Don Gehrmann Looks Back at His Accomplishments" by Gary D'Amato of the *Milwaukee Journal Sentinel*, July 24, 2012; www.sports-reference.com; www.cleveland.com; www.history.com; the online Encyclopedia Britannica at www.britannica.com; the USA Track and Field Hall of Fame at usatf.org; www.olympic.org/London-1948-summer-olympics; *The Olympics: A History of the Games* by William Oscar Johnson, Oxmoor House, 1992, pages 76, 77; "London's 1948 Olympics: The Real Austerity Games" by Larry Elliott for TheGuardian.com, posted March 30, 2012; and YouTube videos of the races.

Data for the Milwaukee Bucks sidebar came from the Milwaukee Bucks and the NBA's website at nba.com.

Chapter 8

Buddy and Gloria Melges were the primary sources for chapter 8. Cindy Handel at Melges Performance Sailboats was also invaluable. Other sources were community data at www.usbeacon.com; the University of Wisconsin–Extension (www.uwex.edu); articles in the *Janesville Gazette* from November 9, 2007, and August 18, 2010; *Sports Illustrated* articles by Arthur Zich, August 27, 1962, and Coles Phinizy, August 6, 1973; www.sports-reference.com; www.olympic.org; *Sailing Smart* by Buddy Melges and Charles Mason, Holt Paperbacks, 1987; "Sailing Legend Buddy Melges Reflects on Wisconsin Roots" by Ben Stanley in the *Lake Geneva News*, March 25, 2014; *The Olympics: A History of the Games* by William Oscar Johnson, Oxmoor House, 1992, pages 114–115; and an article by Judy Lawson in the *Capital* newspaper of Annapolis, Maryland, July 13, 1972.

Information on Wisconsin rowers came from www.uwbadgers.com/olympics and from the online magazine www.row2k.com.

Chapter 9

Connie Carpenter Phinney provided most of the information for chapter 9, with additional background material gathered from the Colorado Sports Hall of Fame; an article in the *New York Times* on March 26, 2008; the *Chattanooga Times Free Press* on June 1, 2014; the Associated Press article "Olympics: Madison Native Connie Carpenter Phinney Revels in Being 'Taylor's Mom'" posted at www

.madison.com on July 31, 2012; www.sports-reference.com; the Davis Phinney Foundation at www.davisphinneyfoundation.org; and YouTube videos of Connie's 1984 cycling race.

Information about Nancy Swider-Peltz Jr. and Sr. is from the author's interview with Nancy Jr. for WTMJ, February 3, 2010, and www.sports-reference.com.

Chapter 10

Dr. Eric Heiden provided his insights for chapter 10. Additional information came from *The Olympics: A History of the Games* by William Oscar Johnson, Oxmoor House, 1992, pages 158–159 and 188; *The Story of the Olympics* by Dave Anderson, HarperCollins Publishers, 1996, pages 66–68; Princeton University (www.princeton.edu); *The Complete Book of the Winter Olympics* by David Wallechinsky, Overlook Press, 2002, page 122; multiple articles in the *Wisconsin State Journal* dated February 24, 1980; www.olympic.org; "An Iceman in from the Cold" by Cynthia Sanz for *People* magazine (www.people.com), November 23, 1992; the Wisconsin Historical Society at www.wisconsinhistory.org/museum /exhibits/skate; the *Los Angeles Times*, February 11, 2002; the blog "Like Mother, Like Daughter: Beth Heiden Reid and Joanne Reid" by Teri J. Dwyer at terijdwyer .blogspot.com; an article from March 2013 at blogs.fasterskier.com; "Eric Heiden Still Humble . . ." by Dave D'Alessandro at www.nj.com, February 24, 2010; "Former Speedskating Champion Heiden Is Staying Close to the Ice" by Jeré Longman in the *New York Times*, September 30, 2009; Eric Heiden entry at www.encyclopedia.com; an article by Leonard Shapiro in the *Washington Post*, February 24, 1980; Pettit National Ice Center's website at www.thepettit.com; www.sports-reference.com; the website for the village of Shorewood Hills, Wisconsin, at www.shorewood-hills.org; www.endurancesportsshow.com; "No. 1: Eric Heiden, 1980," by Gary D'Amato of the *Milwaukee Journal Sentinel*, at www.jsonline .com, February 27, 2012; and "Wisconsin Played a Key Role in U.S. Medal Haul" by Gary D'Amato of the *Milwaukee Journal Sentinel*, at jsonline.com, February 8, 2010.

Beth Heiden on a billboard promoting Wisconsin dairy products. WHI IMAGE ID 98793

The Pettit Center provided the chart on pages 87–89.

Information on the 1980 boycott came from a *New York Times* article reprinted in the *Spokane Spokesman Review* of Spokane, Washington, February 26, 1980; www.olympic.org/Moscow-1980-summer-olympics; and *The Story of the Olympics* by Dave Anderson, HarperCollins Publishers, 1996, pages 66–68.

Chapter 11

The following sources were helpful for chapter 11: www.uwbadgers.com, including an article by Mike Lucas; the United States Hockey Hall of Fame at www.ushockeyhalloffame.com; the Canadian Broadcasting Corporation at www.cbc.ca; the British Broadcasting Corporation at www.bbc.co.uk; www.usahockey.com; New York's Olympic Regional Development Authority at www.orda.org/miracle; www.sports-reference.com; the New York Rangers (rangers.nhl.com); YouTube.com videos of games; www.espn.go.com; *USA Hockey: A Celebration of a Great Tradition* by Kevin Allen, Triumph Books, 1997; "1980 Winter Olympics: The Massachusetts Miracle Men" by Joe Gill, www.bleacherreport.com, February 14, 2010; *The Olympics: A History of the Games* by William Oscar Johnson, Oxmoor House, 1992, page 186; *The Story of the Olympics* by Dave Anderson, HarperCollins Publishers, 1996, pages 64–67; *The Complete Book of the Winter Olympics* by David Wallechinsky and Jaime Loucky, Aurum Press, 2009, pages 30–32; "Step Out on the Ice with Mark Johnson . . ." by Eric Barrow for the *New York Daily News*, February 21, 2015; *The Boys of Winter: The Untold Story of a Coach, a Dream, and the 1980 US Olympic Hockey Team* by Wayne Coffey, Crown Publishers, 2005; an article by Benjamin Worgull at www.teamusa.org, September 15, 2014; and the Milwaukee Admirals.

Information for the chart on pages 98–99 is courtesy of the Milwaukee Admirals.

Chapter 12

Chapter 12 is based on interviews with Dan Jansen as well as material at www.sports-reference.com; www.olympic.org; YouTube.com videos of Dan's races; the city of Greenfield, Wisconsin, website at www.ci.greenfield.wi.us; *The Complete Book of the Winter Olympics* by David Wallechinsky, Overlook Press, 2001, pages 105–107; Harry Jansen's obituary at legacy.com/obituaries/jsonline; and

"Ex-speedskater Dan Jansen and Wife Granted Divorce" in the *Chicago Tribune*, April 22, 1998.

Chapter 13
Bonnie Blair provided the information for chapter 13; additional background came from www.olympic.org; *The Story of the Olympics* by Dave Anderson, HarperCollins Publishers, 1996, page 142; *The Complete Book of the Winter Olympics* by David Wallechinsky, Overlook Press, 2000, page 125; *Freeze Frame: A Photographic History of the Winter Olympics* by Sue Macy, National Geographic Children's Books, 2006, pages 39–40 and 87–88; www.sports-reference.com; and www.whitehouse.gov.

Information on Donald Driver came from www.donalddriver80.com and www.widereceiver.com.

Dianne Holum data came from the Wisconsin Historical Society at www
.wisconsinhistory.org/museum/exhibits/skate/ties; www.sports-reference.com; and an article by the Associated Press reprinted in the *Free Lance Star* of Fredericksburg, Virginia, on February 4, 1998. The Wisconsin Historical Society also provided information on Sheila Young and Leah Poulos at www.wisconsin history.org/museum/exhibits/skate/ties.

Chapter 14
Mike Peplinski was the primary source of information for chapter 14, with additional support from www.teamusa.org; www.olympic.org; www.sports-reference.com; the Wisconsin State Curling Association at wi-curling.org; USA Curling at www.teamusa.org/USA-Curling; and an article by Bill Glauber in the *Baltimore Sun*, February 9, 1998.

The history of Olympic and Wisconsin ski jumping was obtained from www
.olympic.org; the Flying Eagles Ski Club at flyingeaglesskiclub.org; the Silver Mine Ski Club historical marker, viewed at wisconsinhistoricalmarker.blogspot.com; the Blackhawk Ski Club at blackhawkskicclub.org; the Snowflake Ski Club at snowflakeskiclub.com; the "Ski Jumping Hill Archive" posted at www.ski sprungschazen.com; "From Telemark to Tamarack: Ski Jumping in Western Wisconsin" by Glenn Borreson, *Wisconsin Magazine of History*, Winter 2013–14; "Westby Ski Jump Has Long, Proud History" by Gregg Hoffmann at www.old

schoolcollectibles.com; "Skiers' Wait: Swenson, Goyen Work and Hope," *Mil-waukee Journal Sentinel*, February 2, 1964; "Historically Yours" by Hans Jorgenson, *Westby Times*, February 7, 2007; "Five Olympic Team Members to Jump," *La Crosse Tribune*, January 23, 1953; "Ski Jumpers Start Young," *La Crosse Tribune*, January 9, 1962; and "Champion Skier Guides Blind Skier to Gold Medal" by Kristine Goodrich, *Shoreview Press*, March 2, 2010.

Debbie McCormick provided the information about her and her father, Wally Henry.

Chapter 15

The following sources provided information on Ben Sheets: "Olympic Baseball History" by the *Washington Post* at www.washingtonpost.com; "Olympics: Will Baseball Ever Return to the Summer Games?" by Frederick Wertz on the Bleacher Report, www.bleacherreport.com, August 10, 2012; www.sports-reference.com; videos of his games on YouTube.com; www.baseball-reference.com; the Milwaukee Brewers at www.brewers.mlb.com; "Retired All-Star Ben Sheets Starts Coaching at Alma Mater" by Aaron Gleeman, posted at www.hardballtalk.nbcsports.com, August 20, 2013; "Remembering the 2000 US Olympic Baseball Team" by Nick Zaccardi, April 2, 2014, at www.olympictalk.nbcsports.com; "Sheets Pitches US to Gold Medal" by John Manuel at www.baseballamerica.com; and "Tommy Lasorda Recalls His Days in Cuba" by Robert Cassidy, April 6, 2008, at www.news day.com.

Information on Dave Nilsson came from the archives of WTMJ-TV in Milwaukee, Wisconsin; www.sports-reference.com; and www.corporate.olympics.com.

Chapter 16

The main sources for chapter 16 were Karyn Bye and *Stories by Minnesota Women in Sports: Leveling the Playing Field* by Kathleen Ridder et al., North Star Press, 2005, pages 255–271. In addition, the following sources were helpful: "US Hockey Women Primed to Bring the Gold Home" by John McClain, posted on the *Houston Chronicle* site at www.chron.com, February 12, 2002; the River Falls, Wisconsin, Hall of Fame website at rfhalloffame.org; www.sports-reference.com; www.usahockey.com; the Wisconsin Interscholastic Athletic Association at www.wiaawi.org; the website of the Minnesota Golden Gophers at www.gopher

sports.com; and *The Story of the Olympics* by Dave Anderson, HarperCollins Publishers, 1996, pages 87–88.

Chapter 17

Research for chapter 17 included interviews with Casey FitzRandolph, Jenn FitzRandolph, Jeff FitzRandolph, Ruthie FitzRandolph, and Jessi FitzRandolph. Much of this material first appeared in the book *No Stone Unturned: A Brother and Sister's Incredible Journey through the Olympics and Cancer* by Jessie Garcia, published by the FitzRandolph family, 2015. Additional information came from www.sports-reference.com; www.wisconsinhistory.org; and "Recognizing Good Fortune, Cheek Shares Gold Medal" by Karen Crouse, *New York Times*, February 14, 2006.

For the sidebar on Suzy Favor Hamilton, the following sources were useful: "Olympian Favor Hamilton Finds True Gold" by Gary D'Amato in the *Milwaukee Journal Sentinel*, July 21, 2012; www.thesmokinggun.com; a blog post by Bob Wolfley at www.jsonline.com, July 3, 2013; an article by Marc Weinreich in *Sports Illustrated*, July 2, 2013; www.sports-reference.com; and *The Huffington Post* at www.huffpost.com, December 22, 2012.

Chapter 18

Chris Witty was the primary source of information for chapter 18. The following were also useful: "Beating Abuse: Speed Skater Christine Witty" by Scott M. Reid of the *Orange County Register*, www.ocregister.com, January 4, 2006, updated August 21, 2013; "Nagano 1998: Olympic Profile; Speed Skater Gives Fear a Long Holiday" by Jeré Longman, *New York Times*, December 16, 1997; a profile of Witty at www.wisconsinhistory.org/museum/exhibits/skate; "Speedskater Witty Earns Bronze for US, Timmer Wins" by Ross Newhan, *Los Angeles Times*, February 17, 1998; "Witty Takes Latest Turn on a Bike" by the Associated Press and posted at assets.espn.go.com; "She's Witty and Fast Olympic Speedskating Medalist Chris Witty Finds Cycling a Perfect Cross-Training Sport" by Gary R. Blockus for *The Morning Call*, www.mcall.com, August 4, 1998; "Chris Witty on Being Named the US Olympic Flag Bearer" posted at www.archive.org, February 9, 2006; www.sports-reference.com; the archives of *The Today Show* at www.nbcnews.com; and "Skating Past Pain: Olympian Hopes to Help Young Victims of Sex Abuse" by Lucinda Dillon Kinkead of the *Deseret (Utah) News*, October 10, 2004.

Chapter 19

Information about Paul and Morgan Hamm's story came from USA Gymnastics at www.usagym.com; www.teamusa.org; www.sports-reference.com; "Twin Gymnasts Go to Sydney" at abcnews.go.com; "Olympic Gymnast Paul Hamm Retires, Says Body Can't Handle Training" posted at www.si.com, March 27, 2012; "After Embarrassing Arrest, Paul Hamm Hopes to Regain Reputation" posted at www.si.com, January 31, 2012; "US Men's Gymnasts Capture Silver Medal" by Juliet Macur, *New York Times*, August 17, 2004; "FIG Asks Hamm to Give Up Gold; USOC Outraged" by Michael Chow, *USA Today*, August 27, 2004; "Despite Scoring Controversy, Hamm Feels Golden," by Robert Hanashiro, posted at www.usatoday.com/sports, August 31, 2004.

Information on Beezie Madden and Authentic came from the article "Madden's Unique Olympics Dilemma" by Jim Capel, posted May 9, 2012, at www.espn.go.com; and www.horsestarhalloffame.org.

Chapter 20

Garrett Weber Gale provided most of the material for chapter 20, with additional support coming from a video of the race on YouTube and "Maccabi Games Bring Israel to Milwaukee" by Annysa Johnson, *Milwaukee Journal Sentinel*, August 2, 2015, page 3A.

Information on Dwyane Wade came from the Marquette University website at www.gomarquette.com; www.landofbasektball.com; "Gold-Medal Game Is Dream Scene for Redeem Team" by Chris Sheridan posted at www.espn.go.com, August 24, 2008; the USA Basketball website at www.usab.com; www.basketball-reference.com; "Kobe Takes Over in the Fourth Quarter, Team USA Defeats Spain 118–107 to Claim Olympic Gold Medal" by David Friedman posted at www.20secondtimeout.blogspot.com, August 24, 2008; and "Miami Heat's Dwyane Wade Visits US Men's Basketball Team at London Olympics" by Michelle Kaufman, *Miami Herald*, August 9, 2012.

Chapter 21

Information about Ben Provisor and Dennis Hall came from the archives of WTMJ-TV in Milwaukee; www.olympic.org; www.sports-reference.com; "Wrestling Reinstated for 2020 Games" by the Associated Press posted at www.espn.go.com on September 8, 2013; "Ben Provisor, Olympic Wrestler, Hones Skills with Dennis Hall, Honors Promise to Late Friend" by Conor Hackett of BSU at the Games, *The Huffington Post* at www.huffpost.com, August 1, 2012; "USA's Ben Provisor, 1st-Time Olympian, Looks Ahead to Rio Games" by Bob Berghaus in the *Detroit Free Press*, August 5, 2012; "Hartford Native Retires but Skips Tradition" and "Provisor Defeats Fellow Wisconsinite to Make Olympic Team," both by Gary D'Amato, *Milwaukee Journal Sentinel*, April 22, 2012; www.teamusa.org; and video of an interview with Ben and Leigh Jaynes-Provisor posted at www.takedownwrestle.com on June 25, 2015.

Chapter 22

Mary and Matt Antoine were the primary sources for chapter 22. Also useful for this chapter were articles and videos at www.teamusa.org; the USA Bobsled and Skeleton website at www.usabs.com; "USA's Matt Antoine Claims Bronze in Men's Skeleton" by Jeff Zillgitt, *USA Today*, February 15, 2014; and "Matt Antoine's Skeleton Bronze Counts as Victory for Him and US Sliding Teams" by Meri-Jo Borzilleri, posted on the Bleacher Report at www.bleacherreport.com, February 15, 2014.

The information on Johnny Quinn came from an interview he did for WTMJ-TV in Milwaukee, as well as "Johnny Quinn Explains How He Busted His Way through Sochi Bathroom Door" by Cindy Boren, *Washington Post*, February 9, 2014; and "Bobsledder Johnny Quinn's Meme #Quinning Sweeps Internet" by Liz Fields, posted at www.abcnews.go.com, February 16, 2014.

Special thanks to Bill Mallon, MD, past president and cofounder of the International Society of Olympic Historians, and the people at www.sports-reference.com for providing information used in the list of Team USA medal winners on pages 251–257. Other sources for the list include www.teamusa.org, www.olympic.org, college websites, Hall of Fame websites, and archived newspaper articles.

ACKNOWLEDGMENTS

This book simply would not have been possible without Julianne Maggiore. Already the best kind of friend, she became the most incredible assistant—researching, fact-checking, tracking people down, writing, emailing and generally being my sounding board. I am indebted to my Wisconsin-turned-Illinois pal for everything from her amazing technical skills to her ever-positive attitude, even when I asked her to handle yet another thankless task.

My appreciation also to Judy Landsman, who stepped in to help with research and offered her keen eye for reading, not to mention encouraging me to escape to the library when needed. Kate Thompson suggested the idea for this narrative and then followed through as a kind and thorough editor. Kate's intelligence is stamped all over this book. To Kathy Borkowski, Kristin Gilpatrick, Diane Drexler, Barbara Walsh, Carlie DeBlois, John Nondorf, and the rest of the Wisconsin Historical Society Press team: whenever I walk into your stately white marble building I find myself feeling calm, focused, and slightly in awe. Those are the exact emotions I have working with all of you.

My family put up with many late nights when Mom's head was buried in an Olympics book. They listened as I tried out chapters on them and allowed me to escape into the past time and again as I wrote and rewrote. To Paul, Jake, and Charlie: thank you. I love you.

You cannot tell a story like this without the help of dozens of people. Every athlete, family member, friend, and photo contributor has my deepest gratitude for taking time out of their lives to help us relive Wisconsin sports history. They all did it out of the goodness of their hearts. Thank you especially to Kevin Butler at the Pettit National Ice Center as well as the Milwaukee Admirals and Milwaukee Bucks for their incredible contributions.

I still remember the first time I became entranced with the Olympics, at age ten. To have this opportunity to recount stories of state Olympians decades later is incredibly moving for me. The Olympics have always been my favorite sporting event and, I think, one of the best things we as human beings do with each other on a global level. I would say that this book is my gold medal, but I simply cannot be that cliché. I'll just say that it was a pleasure, and I'm honored to be a part of telling these amazing tales.

INDEX

Page numbers in *italics* refer to illustrations.

Abernathy, Brent, 153

African Americans, 12–17, *13*, *14*, 31, 35–37, *37*, 40–48, 50–53, *51*, *229*

Ahearn, Dan, 29

Ahrens, Chris, 67

Albertville, France (1992), 116–118, 135, 254

Allen, Bill, 67–69

Allen, Walter "Ray," 58, 255

Amsterdam, Netherlands (1928), 252

Anderson, Dave, 96

Antoine, Mary, 235–237, 240, 241–249, *246*

Antoine, Matt, *ii*, 235–237, *236*, 240–250, *246*, 269; family, 235–237, 241–249, *242*, *246*; Olympics, 241–249; post-Olympics, 250

Antwerp, Belgium (1920), 27–34, 251, 257

Argentina, 58

Athens, Greece: 1896, xi–xii, *xi*; 2004, 198–205, 214, 256

athletics, ix, *xi*, xii, xiii–xiv, 12, 24, 38, 50–55; Bennett, John, 252; Breitkreutz, Emil, 251; Brennan, John, 24–26, *26*, 49; Brown, Judi, 254; crouching technique, 2, *2*, 44; Driver, Donald, 139, *139*; Gehrmann, Don, 49, 53–56, *54*, *56*; Hahn, Archie, 15, 251; Hamilton, Suzy Favor, 185–187, *185*; Harrison, Kenny, 255; Kraenzlein, Alvin, vii, xiv, 1–10, *2*, *4*, 15, 251; LaBeach, Lloyd, 49–53, *51*, 252; Lambert, George, 252; lead-leg technique, 3, *4*, 15; McGinnis, Charles, 252; marathon, 24; medals, xii, 6, 7, 8, 10, 15, 16, 25–26, 31, 38, 40, 44–45, 46, 47, 52, 53, 55, 251, 252, 254–256; Metcalfe, Ralph Harold, 35–48, *37*, *41*, 252; Phillips, Andre,

254; Poage, George, 11–17, *13*, *14*, 51, 52, 251; protests, 7–8, 25–26, 40; Rock, Andrew, 256; Schardt, Arlie, 31, 251; starting blocks, 44, 52; Waller, Frank, 15, 16, 251; Wiesner, Kenneth, 252

Atlanta, GA (1996), 139, 151, 185, 189, 255

Attaway, Marie, 35

Australia, 52, 58, 90, 220; medals, 154, 223; Melbourne (1956), 252; Sydney (2000), 151–154, *155*, 192–193, 198, 255

Austria, 27, 99; Innsbruck (1976), 74, 84, 94, 253

Authentic (gelding), 200

Bailey, Chantal, 88

Bailey, McDonald, 52

Baker, Bill, 98, 158, 160, 165

Baker, Vincent "Vin," 58, 255

Bakke, Bill, 145

Ballanger, Felicia, 193

Barcelona, Spain (1992), 150, 151, 185, 254

Barrett, Peter, 252

Barry, Dede, 256

Bartel, Robin, 98

baseball, 150; Benson, Kris, 255; medals, 151, 153, 154, 155, 254, 255; Nilsson, Dave, 154; Servais, Scott, 254; Sheets, Ben, 150–155, *153*, 255

basketball, 57–58, 214–215, 227; Allen, Walter "Ray," 58, 255; Baker, Vincent "Vin," 58, 255; Bogut, Andrew, 58; Bontemps, Ron, 252; Boozer, Bob, 57, 58, 252; Buckner, Quinn, 58, 215, 253; Dantley, Adrian, 58, 215, 253; Delfino, Carlos, 58; Dream Team, 57; Ford, Philip, 58, 215, 253;

basketball (*continued*)
  Grayer, Jeff, 58, 254; Grunfeld,
    Ernest "Ernie," 58, 215, 253; Jeffer-
    son, Richard, 58, 256; Jianlian, Yi,
    58; Kukoc, Toni, 58; Lee, Butch, 215;
    Manning, Daniel "Danny," 58, 254;
    May, Scott, 58, 215, 253; McCabe,
    Frank, 215, 252; medals, 57, 58,
    214, 215, 227, 252–256; Milwaukee
    Bucks, 57–58, 215; Payton, Gary, 58,
    255; Redd, Michael, 58, 256; Reid,
    Herman "JR," 58, 254; Robertson,
    Alvin, 58, 254; Robertson, Oscar,
    57, 58, 252; Ukic, Roko, 58; Wade,
    Dwyane, 214–215, 256
Batson, LaMoine, 145
Bedford, Ryan, 89
Beijing, China (2008), 200, 207, 213,
  214–215, 217–227, 256
Belarus, 99
Belgium, 27, 33, 54; Antwerp (1920),
  27–34, 251, 257
Bell, Alexei, 233
Bennett, John, 252
Benson, Kris, 255
Bentsen, Bill, 62–64, 67–69
Bergkvist, Gosta, 54
Bergmann, Arnfin, 145
Berkner, Mark, 66
Berlin, Germany: 1916, 9–10, 27;
  1936, 8–9, 41–47, 57, 252
Bernard, Alain, 218, 222, 225–226
Berry, Ken, 98
Besteman, David, 88
Bialis, Valentin, *33*
Blair, Bonnie, *ii*, xiv, 33, 109, 112,
  116, *125*, 127–140, *128*, *138*, 174,
  248; awards, 135; family, 127–129,
  130–131, 133, 135, 136, *138*, 140;
  Olympics, 132–136, *136*, 189, 194;
  post-Olympics, 136–138, 140
Blair, Charles "Chili," 127–129, 130–
  131, 133, 134, 135–136
Blair, Eleanor, 127, 129, 135, 136
Bleibtrey, Ethelda, 27
bobsledding: Quinn, Johnny, 238–
  239, *239*

Boglioli, Wendy, 253
Bogut, Andrew, 58
Bontemps, Ron, 252
Boozer, Bob, 57, 58, 252
Borchmeyer, Erich, 44, 45
Bottom, Mike, 212
Bousquet, Fred, 221, 225
Boutiette, KC, 88
boxing, ix, 12
Boyd, Micah, 67, 256
Bradley, H. C., 144
Breitkreutz, Emil, 251
Brennan, John, 24–26, *26*, 49
Brooks, Herb, 94–98, 100–104,
  106–107
Brosius, Carleton, 27–34, *30*; family,
  29; Olympics, 31, 33–34, *257*; post-
  Olympics, 34
Brosius, George, 29
Broten, Neal, 105
Brown, Craig, *146*
Brown, Horace, 31
Brown, Judi, 254
Brundage, Avery, 42
Brunt, Jon, *146*
Bryant, Kobe, 214, 227
Buckner, Quinn, 58, 215, 253
Bulgaria, 27, 142, 231
Bush, George W., 223
Bye, Chuck, 156–157, 165, 168
Bye, Diane, 157, 165
Bye, Karyn, 156–170, *159*; awards,
  166, 168; family, 156–157, *159*, 165,
  169–170; Olympics, *ii*, 144, 162–169,
  167; post-Olympics, 169–170

Calgary, Canada (1988), 112–116, 133–
  135, 254
Canada, 32, 98, 99, 100, 145, 157,
  160, 162, 164–166, 175–176, 183, 194,
  220; Calgary (1988), 112–116, 133–
  135, 254; medals, 68, 143, 169, 191;
  Montreal (1976), 76, 253; Vancouver
  (2010), 74, 106, 147, 257
Canins, Maria, 79
canoe slalom: Giddens, Rebecca, 256;
  medals, 256

Carpenter, Charlie, 72
Carpenter, Connie. *See* Phinney, Connie Carpenter
Carpenter, Cory, 88
Carpenter, Darcy, 72, 73
Carpenter, Kip, 89, 177, 178–179, 181, 255
Carter, Jimmy, 90, 100, 102, 105
Castleman, Frank, 16
Centerville, WI, 141
Central American and Caribbean Athletics Confederation Hall of Fame, 53
Chamonix, France (1924), 32, 141
Cheek, Joey, 89, 255, 256
Chelios, Chris, 255
Chicago, IL (1904), 11
China, 58, 162, 164; Beijing (2008), 200, 207, 213, 214–215, 217–227, 256
Choisel, Eugene, 8
Christoff, Steve, 103
Clapp, E. J., 16
Clark, Chris, 64
Clinton, Bill, 122, 168
Clinton, Hillary Rodham, 122
coaches, 86, 227; Brooks, Herb, 94–98, 100–104, 106–107; Clark, Chris, 64; Cromwell, Dean, 45–46; Crowe, Mike, 132; Drake, Elvin, 50; former Olympians, 9–10, 31, 47, 56, 83–84, 92, 106, 117, 121, 130, 131, 132, 155, 191, 207; Halvorsen, Finn, 73; Henry, Wally, 147–148, *148*; Holum, Dianne, 83–84, 92, 106, 130, 132; Johnson, Bob, 93–94, 95, 96, 106; Johnson, Mark, 106; Jones, Tom, 50, 53; Kemkers, Gerard, 190; Kormann, Peter, 197–198; Kraenzlein, Alvin, 9–10; Lasorda, Tommy, 151–154; Maloney, Sandy, 197; Mueller, Peter, 117, 121, 131, 191; Murphy, Mike, 1–3, 7, 9; Nelson, Jack, 211; Reese, Randy, 212; Robertson, Lawson, 45; Schotting, Peter, 106; Smith, Ben, 162, 163; Tikhanov, Victor, 101, 106
Colarossi, Bob, 199

Collins, Doug, 215
Colorado Sports Hall of Fame, 81
Connolly, James, xii, 8
Coroebus, ix
Costas, Bob, 86
Cotton, John, 152
Court of Arbitration for Sports, 205
Craig, Jim, 98, 101, 102, 104, *104*, 106
Croatia, 58
Cromwell, Dean, 45–46
Crowe, Mike, 132
Crowe, Peggy, *74*, 87
Crowley, Margaret, 89
Cruikshank, David, 88, 136–137, *138*
Cruz, Chris, 66
Cuba, 10, 52, 152–153, 154, 233
Cunningham, Nick, 239
curling, xiv, *148*; Henry, Wally, 147–148, *148*; Joraanstad, Nicole, *148*; McCormick, Debbie, *ii*, 147–148, *148*; medals, 143, 254; Nichols, Bob, 254; Peplinski, Mike, 141–149, *142*, *146*; Sachtjen, Tracy, *148*; Somerville, Raymond "Bud," 254; Somerville, Tim, 254; Strum, Bill, 254; Strum, Mike, 254
cycling, xi, 131; Barry, Dede, 256; Emery, Brent, 254; Heiden, Eric, 90–91; Holden, Mari, 255; medals, 79, 193, 254, 255, 256; Phinney, Connie Carpenter, 75–81, *80*, 254; Tour de France, 80, 91; Witty, Christine, 192–193
Czech Republic, 99; medals, 168
Czechoslovakia, 97, 98, 100

Dae-Eun, Kim, 202
Daly, John, 240, 241, 242, 243, 247
D'Andrea, Moira, 88
Dantley, Adrian, 58, 215, 253
Datunashvili, Zurabi, 233
Davis, Barry, 254
Davis, Shani, 89, 256, 257
Decker, Brianna, 257
de Coubertin, Pierre, ix–xiv, *x*, 9, 24, 32, 38
DeJulio, Greg, 235, 236, 241

Delafield, WI, 34, 137
Delfino, Carlos, 58
Denmark, 63–64
Denny, Bill, 132
Denny, Rita, 132
Didrikson, Babe, 38–39
Diem, Carl, 42
Dillard, Harrison, 52
Docter, Mary, 87, 106
Docter, Sarah, 77, 87, 106
Dohnal, Darcie, 88, 254
Drake, Elvin, 50
Draper, Foy, 45–47
Dresser, Ivan, 31
Driver, Donald, 139, *139*
drugs. *See under* Olympics
Dudek, Alyson, 89, 257
Duggan, Meghan, 257
Dukurs, Martins, 241, 243, 247
Dukurs, Tomass, 243
Dupuis, Bob, 98
Dupuis, Guy, 99
Dyer, Braven, 48

East Germany: medals, 133
Easton, Lucian, 12, 17
Easton, Mary, 12, 17
Easton Aluminum Company, 174
Eau Claire, WI, 144, 145, 149
Eckert, Cindy, 66, 254
Elkhart Lake, WI, 18–19
Elkhorn, WI, 59
Elm Grove, WI, 74, 132
Emery, Brent, 254
Engstrom, Molly, 256, 257
Erat, Martin, 99
Eriksson, Henry, 54
Eruzione, Mike, 96, 101, 105, 107
Espeseth, Bob, 65, 66, 254
ESPY awards, 227, 230
Ewell, Barney, 52, 53
Exposition Universelle, xi, xii–xiv, *xiii*, 9
Eyser, George, 12

Farooq, Yasmin, 66
Farrell, O'Neil, *33*

Favor, Suzanne Marie. *See* Hamilton, Suzy Favor
Fédération Internationale de Gymnastique, 202–205
Fédération Internationale des Luttes Associées, 233–234
Feeney, Carol, 66, 254
fencing: medals, 31
figure skating, 32, 82
Finland, 99, 100, 103–104, 162, 164; Helsinki (1952), 215, 252
Fish, Jenny, 130
FitzRandolph, Casey, 171–187, *172*, 190; family, 171–172, 178, 180, 182, 184; Olympics, 173–183, *181*; post-Olympics, 183–184, 187
FitzRandolph, Jeff, 180, 181
FitzRandolph, Ruthie, 171
Flaim, Eric, 88, 254, 255
Folk, Torrey, 67
football: medals, 255, 256; Sobrero-Markgraf, Kate, 255, 256; Tarpley, Lindsay, 256
football (American), 139, 238
Ford, Malcolm, 6
Ford, Philip, 58, 215, 253
Fox Point, WI, 210
France, xi, 8, 79, 99, 218, 220, 221, 225–226, 228; Albertville (1992), 116–118, 135, 254; Chamonix (1924), 32, 141; Grenoble (1968), 130, 252; medals, 193, 223; Paris, xi, xii–xiv, *xiii*, 3–9, 11,32, 251
Fredricks, Tucker, 89
Freisinger, Leo, 252
Furniss, Steve, 253

Gabel, Andy, 255
Gaines, Rowdy, 220, 222
Galchenyuk, Aleksandr, 99
Gale, Mark, 209–211, 213, 216, 220, 223
Garmisch-Partenkirchen, Germany (1936), 252
Garner, Sarah, 67, 255
Gehrmann, Don, 49, 53–56, *54*, *56*; awards, 55, *56*; family, 55; Olympics, 53–55; post-Olympics, 55–56

Gengler, Sarah, 66
Georgia, 233
Germany, 9–10, 27, 36, 42–43, 44, 49, 191–192, 194. *See also* East Germany; West Germany: anti-Semitism, 42, 43; Berlin 8–10, 27, 41–47, 57, 252; Garmisch-Partenkirchen (1936), 252; medals, 19, 20, 40, 41, 46, 79, 117, 191
Giddens, Rebecca, 256
Glickman, Marty, 45–46
Goldman, Jane, 87
Gore, Tipper, 168
Goskowicz, Julie, 88
Goskowicz, Tony, 88
Grandi, Bruno, 204
Graves, Carie, 65, 66, 253, 254
Grayer, Jeff, 58, 254
Great Britain, 52, 63, 90, 220; London, 24–26, 49–55, 150, 200, 215, 232–233, 252, 257; medals, 7, 31, 33
Greater New York Irish Athletic Association, 16
Greece, ix–xii, Athens, xi–xii, *xi*, 198–205, 214, 256; medals, 19; Olympia, ix–x, 42
Green Bay Packers, 139, 227, 238, 239
Greenfield, WI, 123–124
Greenwald, Mark, 88
Grenoble, France (1968), 130, 252
Gretsky, Wayne, 163, 168
Grunfeld, Ernest "Ernie," 58, 215, 253
Guay, Paul, 98
Gunn, Chanda, 256
gymnastics, xi; Hamm, Morgan, 197–199, *198*, 206, 256; Hamm, Paul, 197–208, *198*, 206, 256; medals, 12, 199, 202, 203, 208, 251, 256; Memmel, Chellsie, 256; protests, 202–205; Schuster, Phillip, 251; scoring system, 205

Hahn, Archie, 15, 251
Hall, Dennis, 231–233, 255
Halleen, Neil, 65
halls of fame, 10, 17, 23, 53, 57, 70, 81, 92, 124, 135, 155

Halvorsen, Finn, 73
Hamhuis, Dan, 99
Hamilton, Suzy Favor, 185–187, *185*; awards, 185, 186; family, 185, 186, 187; Olympics, 185–186; post-Olympics, 186–187
Hamm, Cecily, 197
Hamm, Morgan, 197–199, *198*, 206, 256
Hamm, Paul, 197–208, *198*, *206*; awards, 206; family, 197; Olympics, 198–205; post-Olympics, 206–208
Hamm, Sandy, 197
Hansen, Brian, 257
Hansenne, Marcel, 54
Harrington, John, 95
Harrison, Kenny, 255
Hauer, Brett, 99
Haugen, Anders, 145
Haugstad, Peter, 145
Hayes, Johnny, 25
Hedstrom, Kristin, 67
Hefferon, Charles, 25
Heiden, Beth, *74*, 77, 82–83, *83*, 130, *263*; Olympics, 84, 90, 106; post-Olympics, 91–92
Heiden, Eric, *vii*, 82–86, *83*, *85*, 90–92, 93, 109, 110, 130, 138, 158, 171; awards, 92; family, 82–83, 92; Olympics, 84–86, 90, 91, 106; post-Olympics, 90–92, 179
Heiden, Jack, 82, 83
Heiden, Nancy, 82
Hellickson, Russ, 231, 253
Helsinki, Finland (1952), 215, 252
Hendrickson, Jimmy, 145
Henning, Anne, 73, 75, 87, 110, 253
Henriksen, Erik, 87
Henry, Ginny, 147
Henry, Wally, 147–148, *148*
Hicks, Dan, 124, 222, 223
Hillman, Harry, 15, 16
Hird, Fred, 251
Hirsch, Corey, 99
Hitler, Adolf, 41–42, 43, 45
hockey. *See* ice hockey
Holbrook, Benjamin, 67

Holden, Mari, 255
Holum, Dianne, 83–84, 92, 106, 132
Holum, Kirsten, 88, 130
Hoopman, Beau, 67, 256
Hornqvist, Patric, 99
horse jumping: Kraut, Laura, 256; Madden, Elizabeth "Beezie," 200, 256; medals, 200, 256
Hough, Larry, 65, 252
Huck, Mark, 87
Hudson, WI, 170
Hungary, 27, 33

ice hockey, 32, 168; Bartel, Robin, 98; Berry, Ken, 98; Bye, Karyn, *ii*, 144, 156–170, *159*, *167*, 255; Chelios, Chris, 255; Decker, Brianna, 257; Duggan, Meghan, 257; Dupuis, Bob, 98; Dupuis, Guy, 99; Engstrom, Molly, 256, 257; Erat, Martin, 99; Galchenyuk, Aleksandr, 99; Guay, Paul, 98; Gunn, Chanda, 256; Hamhuis, Dan, 99; Hauer, Brett, 99; Hirsch, Corey, 99; Hornqvist, Patric, 99; Irving, Stu, 98, 253; Johannson, Jim, 99; Johansson, Andreas, 99; Johnson, Mark, viii, 85, 86, 93–98, *97*, 100–107, 253; Joseph, Fabian, 99; Josi, Roman, 99; Kessel, Amanda, 257; Kessel, Phil, 257; Knight, Hilary, 257; Lawler, Erika, 257; Lintner, Richard, 99; Mason, Bob, 98; medals, 94, 105, 107, 166, 168, 169, 253, 255, 256, 257; Miracle on Ice, 85, 86, 93, 100–106, *104*, 107, 158, 165; Moser, Simon, 99; Niskula, Janne, 99; Olvecky, Peter, 99; Pavelski, Joe, 257; Peltonen, Ville, 99; Pihlstrom, Antti, 99; Plavsic, Adrien, 99; Radulov, Aleksandr, 99; Rafalski, Brian, 255, 257; Schneider, William "Buzz," 95, 98, 25; Searle, Tom, 99; Setzinger, Oliver, 99; Shtalenkov, Mikhail, 99; Smrek, Peter, 99; Stanley Cup, 157; Suter, Bob, 85, 86, 93–98, *97*, 100–107, 253; Suter, Gary, 107, 255;

Suter, Ryan, 99, 107, 257; Timonen, Kimmo, 99; Vetter, Jessie, 257; Vokoun, Tomas, 99; Weber, Shea, 99; Weiland, Kerry, 257; Werenka, Brad, 99; women's, 106, 143–144, 156–170; Yaremchuk, Ken, 99; Zaugg-Siergiej, Jinelle, 257
Immerfall, Dan, 87, 106, 253
India: medals, 8
Innsbruck, Austria (1976), 74, 84, 94, 253
Inoue, Junichi, 117
International Baseball Association, 150
International Federation of Associated Wrestling Styles, 234
International Jewish Sports Hall of Fame, 10
International Olympic Committee, xi, 11, 24, 27, 38, 39, 42, 68, 97, 117, 118, 143, 160, 177, 204, 233
International Olympic Day, xiv
International Skating Union, 174–175, 190
International Sports Hall of Fame, 81
Ireland, 6
Ireland, Mike, 176, 181
Irving, Stu, 98, 253
Israel: terrorism, 68
Italy, 25–26, 33, 63, 79, 151, 220; medals, 31, 46; Rome, 24, 57, 252; Turin (2006), 183, 195, 256
Iverson, Melissa, 66

Jaffee, Irving, *33*
Jamaica, 49–50
James, Grant, 67
James, Ross, 67
Jansen, Dan, 33, 108–126, *109*, *123*, *125*, 129, 135, 175, 211; awards, 116, 123, 124; family, 108–110, *109*, 111, 112–114, 116, 118, 121–122, *123*, 124; Olympics, 111–123, 133–134; post-Olympics, 123–126
Jansen, Geraldine, 108, 110, 111
Jansen, Harry, 108, 109, 110–111, 113, 121, 122, 124

Jansen, Jane (daughter), 118, 122, *123*, 124
Jansen, Jane (sister), 108, *109*, 112–116, 119, 122, 124, 133
Jansen, Mike, 108, *109*, 111, 115
Japan, 36, 49, 100, 151, 164, 199; medals, 117, 179, 181, 199; Nagano (1998), ii, 141, 143–144, 160, 173–175, 190–192, 255; Russo-Japanese War, 11; Sapporo (1972), 73, 75, 110, 130, 131, 253; Tokyo (1964), 62–64, 252
Jaynes, Leigh, 234
Jefferson, Richard, 58, 256
Jews, 45, 68, 228
Jianlian, Yi, 58
Johannson, Jim, 99
Johansson, Andreas, 99
Johnson, Bob, 93–94, 95, 96, 106
Johnson, Mark, viii, 85, 86, 93–98, *97*, 100–107; awards, 94; family, 93–94; Olympics, 97–98, 100–106; post-Olympics, 106
Jonath, Arthur, 36, 40
Jones, Clint, 145
Jones, Cullen, 217–224, 227, **229**
Jones, Tom, 50, 53
Joraanstad, Nicole, *148*
Joseph, Fabian, 99
Josi, Roman, 99
Joubert, Danie, 36
judo: medals, 254; Roethke, Lynn, 254

Kakousis, Periklis, 19
Kalmoe, Megan, 67, 257
Karakulov, Nikolay, 52
Kasatonov, Alexei, 106
Keggi, Mara, 66
Kelly, John B., 27
Kemkers, Gerard, 190
Kessel, Amanda, 257
Kessel, Phil, 257
Kidd, Jason, 214
Klaiber, Jeff, 88
Kline, Michelle, 88
Knight, Hilary, 257

Koch, Bill, 69
Korean Olympic Committee, 202
Kormann, Peter, 197–198
Kostron, Kim, 87
Kraenzlein, Alvin, vii, xiv, 1–10, *2*, *4*, 15; awards, 10; family, 1, 9, 10; Olympics, 5–9; post-Olympics, 9–10
Kraenzlein, John Georg, 1
Kraut, Laura, 256
Krmpotich, Dave, 66, 254
Kuck, Jonathan, 89, 257
Kukoc, Toni, 58
Kungler, Frank, 19, 20
Kuroiwa, Toshiyuki, 117

LaBeach, Lloyd, 49–53, *51*; awards, 53; Olympics, 51–53; post-Olympics, 53
La Crosse, WI: Murphy, Edward, 32, *33*; Peplinski, Mike, 142; Poage, George, 12, *13*, *14*, 17
Lake Geneva, WI, 59, 61, 62, 70
Lake Placid, NY, vii, 32, 84–86, 93, 95, 105, 161, 176, 236–237, 252, 253
Lalovic, Nenad, 234
Lamb, Maria, 89
Lambert, George, 252
Lara, Marco, 232
Larkin, Tom, 23
Lasorda, Tommy, 151–154
Latvia, 241, 243; medals, 247
Lawler, Erika, 257
Lazo, Pedro Luis, 152
Leahy, Pat, 7
Lebanon, 49
LeBombard, Wayne, 87
Lee, Butch, 215
Lehman, Emery, 89
Leibovitz, Annie, 78
Le May Doan, Catriona, 191, 194
Leno, Jay, 182
Letterman, David, 167–168, 182
Leveille, Charles, 89
Lezak, Jason, 217–224, 226, 227, **229**
Lillehammer, Norway (1994), 118, 135, 136, 160, 173, 189, 194, 255
Lintner, Richard, 99

Lithuania, 214
London, England, 24–26, 49–55, 150, 200, 215, 232–233, 252, 257
Longo, Jeannie, 79
Los Angeles, CA, 35, 38–39, 77, 78–79, 252, 254
Louisiana Purchase Exposition, 11
Lowney, Garrett, 255
Luding-Rothenburger, Christa, 133, 134
Lunda, Kay, 87

MacDonald, Stewart, 65
Madden, Elizabeth "Beezie," 200, 256
Madison, Helene, 38–39, *39*, 252
Madison, WI, 103, 106, 171; FitzRandolph, Casey, 171; Hamilton, Suzy Favor, 186; Heiden, Beth, *74*, 77, 82; Heiden, Eric, 82; Johnson, Mark, viii, 86, 93, 106; Madison, Helene, 38; McCormick, Debbie, 147; Monk, Lori, *74*; Phinney, Connie Carpenter, 71–73, 75; Suter, Bob, 86, 93, 107. *See also* University of Wisconsin–Madison
Major League Baseball, 150
Maloney, Sandy, 197
Manning, Daniel "Danny," 58, 254
Marquette University, 21, 24–25, 35–36, 41, 47, 48, 49, 208, 214–215
Marsicano, Trevor, 89, 257
Mason, Bob, 98
Maurer, Walter, 251
May, Scott, 58, 215, 253
McCabe, Frank, 215, 252
McCarthy, Peggy, 65, 66, 253
McClanahan, Rob, 103
McCormick, Debbie, *ii*, 147–148, *148*
McCorquodale, Alastair, 52
McGinnis, Charles, 252
McLean, John, 5–6
medals, 6, 12, 23, 34, 47, 86, 121, 135, 140, 170, 199, *229*, 230, 251–257. *See also under individual athletes, countries, and sports.*
media, 6, 8, 10, 34, 42, 57, 78–79, 86, 91, 93, 96, 102, 103, 104, 105, 112, 115, 120, 124, 143, 159, 167–168, 182, 194, 216, 220, 222, 223, 225, 227, 242, 247, 248
Melbourne, Australia (1956), 252
Melges, Gloria Wenzel, 61–62, 63, *69*, 70
Melges, Harry, Jr. "Buddy," 59–64, *62*, 67–70, *69*; awards, 69–70; family, 59–61, 62, 63, *69*, 70; Olympics, 62–64, 67–69; post-Olympics, 69–70
Melges, Harry, Sr., 59–61, 63
Memmel, Chellsie, 256
Menomonee Falls, WI, 16
Mequon, WI, 200
Metcalfe, Clarence, 35
Metcalfe, Ralph, 35–48, *37*, *41*; awards, 47–48; family, 35; Olympics, 36–37, 40–47; post-Olympics, 47–48
Mexico City, Mexico (1968), 67, 252
Mey, Uwe-Jens, 117
Meyers, Mary, 130
Michaels, Al, 93, 102, 104, 105
Mickelson, Tim, 65, 253
Middleton, WI, 144, 145
Mientkiewicz, Doug, 151
Mikhailov, Boris, 100
Mills, Nathaniel, 88
Milwaukee, WI: Brosius, Carleton, 29, 34; Gehrmann, Don, 53; Hahn, Archibald, 15; Hamm, Paul, 197; Kraenzlein, Alvin, 1; Metcalfe, Ralph, 48; Osthoff, Oscar, 18, 21; Poulos, Leah, 131; Poage, George, 14, 15; Schardt, Arlie, 31. *See also* Marquette University; Milwaukee Admirals; Milwaukee Brewers; Milwaukee Bucks; Pettit National Ice Center
Milwaukee Admirals, 98–99
Milwaukee Athletic Club, 14, 15, 18, 19, 23
Milwaukee Brewers, 150, 154–155
Milwaukee Bucks, 57–58, 215

Miracle on Ice. *See under* ice hockey
Moloney, Fred, 6
Monk, Lori, *74*, 87
Montgomery, Jim, 253
Montreal, Canada (1976), 76, 253
Mortenson, Jay, 254
Moscow, USSR (1980), 90–91, 96
Moser, Simon, 99
motivation, 35, 74, 100, 103, 108, 110,
   165, 171, 177, 212–213, 216, 240
Mueller, Eric, 66, 67, 255
Mueller, Leah. *See* Poulos, Leah
Mueller, Peter, 87, 106, 117, 121, 131,
   191, 253
Munich, West Germany (1972), 68–
   69, 253; terrorism, 68
Murphy, Edward, 32, *33*, 252
Murphy, Mike, 1–3, 7, 9
Myshkin, Vladimir, 101

Nadi, Nedi, 31
Nagano, Japan (1998), ii, 141, 143–144,
   160, 173–175, 190–192, 255
Naismith, James, 57
Naismith Memorial Basketball Hall
   of Fame, 57
Nantz, Jim, 182
National Hockey League, 163, 168
National Speedskating Hall of Fame,
   92
National Track and Field Hall of
   Fame, 10
Neill, Mike, 152, 153
Nelson, Jack, 211
Nemov, Alexei, 203–204
Netherlands, xii–xiii, 46, 100, 151,
   173–175, 195; Amsterdam (1928),
   252; medals, 34, 45, 55, 191, 192
New York Athletic Club, 15, 20
New Zealand, 63
Nichols, Bob, 254
Niemann, Gunda, 191
Nilsson, Dave, 154
Niskula, Janne, 99
Norby, Dave, 145
Norway, *33*, 97, 98, 145; Lillehammer

(1994), 118, 135, 136, 160, 173, 189,
   194, 255; medals, 143
Novara-Reber, Sue, 77–78
nutrition, 2, 213, 227, 228

Obama, Barack, 138
Ochowicz, Elli, 89, 131
Ochowicz, Jim, 131
O'Connor, Peter, 6
Olson, Willis "Billy," 145
Olvecky, Peter, 99
Olympia, Greece, ix–x, 42
Olympic Development Center, 237
Olympic Training Center, 161, 232,
   240
Olympic Trials, 24, 31, 36, *37*, 53, 55,
   63, 67–68, 111, 113, 132, 139, 143,
   149, 173, *206*, 212, 216, 227, 232–233,
   233, 240, 241
Olympic Village, 35, 38, 42, 163;
   terrorism, 68; vandalism, 168
Olympics: abolished, ix; accommodations, 4, 29, 35, 38, 42, 177; and
   the arts, xi, 6, 41; athletes' creed,
   24; attendance, xi, 5, 27, 181, 220,
   248; boycotts, 7, 14–15, 38, 90–91,
   96; cancelled, 27, 42, 49; closing
   ceremonies, 123, 138, 168; college
   teams, 3, 7; demonstration sports,
   57, 141, 150, 254; drugs, 12, 122, 135,
   136, 143, 150, 184, 213, 225; excluded
   countries, 27, 49; excluded/included
   sports, ix, xi, 12, 24, 32, 57, 77, 141,
   150, 158, 160, 231, 233–234, 235;
   facilities, xi, xiii, 5, 8, 15, 24, 27, 36,
   41–42, 43, 51, 57, 117, 123, 191, 193,
   218–219, 225; flag, 29; frauds, 12, 67,
   185–186; history, ix–xiv; oath, 29;
   opening ceremonies, xi, 24, 42, 43,
   68, 106, 130, 163, 195, 217; petitions,
   xii, 29; photo finishes, 36, 37, 52,
   79, 223; protests, 7–8, 25–26, 32,
   40, 174, 202–205; records, 6, 8, 15,
   84, 179, 252, 253; rules, xi, xii, 25–
   26, 39, 53, 67, 119, 163, 177, 202, 205;
   scheduling, ix, xi, xii, 5, 6–7, 11,

Olympics (*continued*)
25, 33, 118; security, 178, 180, 241–242, 247; statistics, vii, xii, 3, 11, 27, 32, 35, 43, 90

Summer Games
—1896, xi–xii, *xi*; 1900, xii–xiv, 3–9, 11, 251; 1904, 6, 11–12, 14–16, 18, 19–21, 57, 251; 1908, 24–26, **25**, 49; 1912, 150, 251; 1916, 9–10, 27; 1920, 27–34, 65, 251, 257; 1924, 10, 32; 1928, 38, 46, 252; 1932, 35, 38–39, 44, 46, 199, 252; 1936, 8–9, 41–47, 57, 252; 1948, 49–55, 57, 252; 1952, 215, 252; 1956, 252; 1960, 57, 58, 252; 1964, 62–64, 252; 1968, 65, 67, 252; 1972, 65, 67–69, 226, 231, 253; 1976, 58, 65, 76, 231, 253; 1980, 66, 90–91, 96; 1984, 58, 66, 77, 78–79, **80**, 81, 199, 231, 254; 1988, 58, 66, 254; 1992, 58, 66, 150, 151, 185, 254; 1996, 58, 66, 139, 151, 185, 189, 231, 255; 2000, 58, 66, 151–154, 185–186, 192–193, 198, 255; 2004, 58, 66, 154, 198–205, 214, 256; 2008, 58, 66, 80, 155, 200, 207, 213, 214–215, 217–227, **224**, 256; 2012, 58, 66, 80, 150, 200, 215, 232–233, 257

suspended, 68; televised, 42, 57, 78–79, 102, 103, 220; terrorism, 68; torch, 42, 106, 218; transferred, 11, 24; transportation, 27–29, **28**, 43, **257**; vandalism, 168

Winter Games, 32–33, 118
—1924, 32, 141, 145; 1928, 32, **33**; 1932, 32, 145, 235, 252; 1936, 145, 252; 1948, 49, 145, 235, 242; 1952, 145; 1956, 145; 1960, 94, 98; 1964, 87, 145; 1968, 83, 87, 130, 145, 252; 1972, 73, 83, 87, 98, 110, 130, 131, 253; 1976, 74, **74**, 84, 87, 93–94, 98, 131, 253; 1980, vii, 74, 84–86, **85**, 87, **91**, 93, 95–98, 100–106, 131, 145, 158, 176, 182, 253; 1984, 74, 87,

88, 98, 111–112, 132–133, 145; 1988, 74, 87, 88, 98, 99, 112–116, 133–135, 137, 254; 1992, 87, 88, 99, 117–118, 135, 137, 145, 254; 1994, 33, 87, 88, 99, 118–123, 135, 136, 137, 145, 160, 173, 189, 194, 255; 1998, *ii*, 88, 89, 99, 130, 137, 141, 143–144, 147, 160, 163–168, 173–175, 190–192, 255; 2002, 88, 89, 99, 106, 107, 131, 145, 147, 160, **167**, 169, 177–183, 193–195, 235, 255; 2006, 88, 89, 99, 131, 145, 146, 183, 195, 256; 2010, 74, 89, 99, 106, 107, 147, **148**, 257; 2014, *ii*, vii, 89, 99, 107, 138, 146, 147, 238–239, 241–244, 257

Oonk, Frouke, 196
Osendarp, Tinus, 45, 46
Oslo, Norway, **33**
Osthoff, Oscar, 18–23, **19**, **22**; awards, 23; family, 18–19, 21–22, **22**, 23; Olympics, 19–21; post-Olympics, 21–23
Osthoff, Otto, 18
Osthoff, Paulina, 18
Owens, Jesse, 8–9, 41, 43–47

Panama, 50–53; medals, 52, 53
Paraskevin, Connie, 87
Pardeeville, WI, 56
Paris, France, xi, xii–xiv, *xiii*, 3–9, 11, 32, 251
Paris World's Fair, xi, xii–xiv, *xiii*, 9
Parra, Derek, 89, 255
Patton, Elizabeth. *See* Madden, Elizabeth "Beezie"
Patton, Mel, 52, 53
Pavelich, Mark, 95, 101
Pavelski, Joe, 257
Payton, Gary, 58, 255
Pearson, Nick, 89
Pelchat, Marc, 88
Peltonen, Ville, 99
Penn, William, 31
Penny, Steve, 207
Peplinski, Mike, 141–149, **142**, **146**;

family, 141, *142*, 143, 145–146; Olympics, 143–144; post-Olympics, 144–146, 149
Perrault, Joe, 145
Peterson, Benjamin, 231, 253
Peterson, John, 253
Pettit National Ice Center, xiv, 74, 136, 138, 140, 173, 177; Blair, Bonnie, 87, 138, 140; Boutiette, KC, 88; Carpenter, Cory, 88; Carpenter, Kip, 89, 177; Cheek, Joey, 89; Crowley, Margaret, 89; Cruikshank, David, 88, 136–137; D'Andrea, Moira, 88; Davis, Shani, 89; Docter, Mary, 87; Dohnal, Darcie, 88; Dudek, Alyson, 89; FitzRandolph, Casey, 89, 171; Flaim, Eric, 88; Fredricks, Tucker, 89; Goskowicz, Julie, 88; Goskowicz, Tony, 88; Greenwald, Mark, 88; Holum, Kirsten, 88; Jansen, Dan, 88; Klaiber, Jeff, 88; Kline, Michelle, 88; Kuck, Jonathan, 89; Lamb, Maria, 89; Lehman, Emery, 89; Leveille, Charles, 89; Marsicano, Trevor, 89; Mills, Nathaniel, 88; Ochowicz, Elli, 89; Parra, Derek, 89; Pearson, Nick, 89; Pelchat, Marc, 88; Pierce, Marty, 88; Raney-Norman, Catherine, 74, 89; Rodriguez, Jennifer, 89; Rookard, Jilleanne, 74, 89; Sannes, Amy, 89; Scheels, Christine, 88; Smith, Jessica, 89; Sundstrom, Becky, 88; Swider-Peltz, Nancy, Jr., 74, 89; Tamburrino, David, 88; Thometz, Nick, 87; Todd, Sugar, 89; Trevena, Jondon, 88; Wanek, Brian, 88; Whitmore, Mitchell, 89; Witty, Christine, 88; Zuckerman, Angela, 88. *See also* Wisconsin Olympic Oval
Phelps, Michael, 217–224, *224*, 226, 227, *229*
Phillips, Andre, 254
Phinney, Connie Carpenter, 71–73, 75–81, *80*; awards, 81; family, 72–73, 75, 80; Olympics, 73, 78–79, 87, 192–193; post-Olympics, 80–81
Phinney, Davis, 77–81
Phinney, Taylor, 80–81
Pierce, Marty, 88
Pietri, Dorando, 25–26
Pihlstrom, Antti, 99
Piper, Carly, 256
Plant, Michael, 87, 106
Plant, Thomas, 87, 106
Plavsic, Adrien, 99
Poage, Anna, 12, 17
Poage, George, 11–17, *13*, *14*, 51, 52; awards, 17; family, 12; Olympics, 15–16; post-Olympics, 16–17
Poage, James, 12
Poulos, Leah, 87, 106, 131, 253
Prairie du Chien, WI, 235, 241, 249–250, *249*
Prinstein, Meyer, 6–8, 10
Pritchard, Norman, 8
Provisor, Ben, 231–234, *233*; family, 234; Olympics, 232–233; post-Olympics, 234
psychologists, 116, 172–173, 177, 194, 195, 213
Puerto Rico, 49, 214, 215

Quinn, Johnny, 238–239, *239*

Radulov, Aleksandr, 99
Rafalski, Brian, 255, 257
Ramsey, Mike, 97
Raney-Norman, Catherine, 74, 89
Redd, Michael, 58, 256
Reese, Randy, 212
Reid, Herman "JR," 58, 254
Rein, Andy, 231, 254
Reoch, Miji, 75, 76
Richland Center, WI, 232
Riddoch, Greg, 154
Rio, WI, 147
River Falls, WI, 156–158, 161, 168
Robertson, Alvin, 58, 254
Robertson, Lawson, 45
Robertson, Oscar, 57, 58, 252
Rock, Andrew, 256
Rodgers, Bill, 86
Rodriguez, Jennifer, 89, 255

Roethke, Lynn, 254
Rogge, Jacques, 204
Rojeski, Shawn, *146*
Romania, 97, 98, 199
Rome, Italy, 24, 57, 252
Rookard, Jilleanne, 74, 89
Roosevelt, Teddy, 11
rowing, xii–xiii, 64–67, *65*; Ahrens, Chris, 67; Berkner, Mark, 66; Boyd, Micah, 67, 256; Cruz, Chris, 66; Eckert, Cindy, 66, 254; Espeseth, Bob, 65, 66, 254; Farooq, Yasmin, 66; Feeney, Carol, 66, 254; Folk, Torrey, 67; Garner, Sarah, 67, 255; Gengler, Sarah, 66; Graves, Carie, 65, 66, 253, 254; Halleen, Neil, 65; Hedstrom, Kristin, 67; Holbrook, Benjamin, 67; Hoopman, Beau, 67, 256; Hough, Larry, 65, 252; Iverson, Melissa, 66; James, Grant, 67; James, Ross, 67; Kalmoe, Megan, 67, 257; Keggi, Mara, 66; Kelly, John B., 27; Krmpotich, Dave, 66, 254; MacDonald, Stewart, 65; McCarthy, Peggy, 65, 66, 253; medals, 65–67, 251–257; Mickelson, Tim, 65, 253; Mueller, Eric, 66, 67, 255; Rude, Tracy, 66; Sahs, Chris, 66; Sanborn, Alden "Zeke," 65, 251; Santiago, Kim, 66; Sayner, Daniel, 66; Smith, Matt, 67; Thorsness, Kris, 66, 254; Towne, Chari, 66; Zoch, Jackie, 65, 253
Rude, Tracy, 66
Russia, 86, 99, 142, 203–205, 241; medals, 247; Russo-Japanese War, 11; Sochi (2014), ii, 138, 238–239, 241–246, 257. *See also* USSR

Sachjen, Tracy, *148*
Sahs, Chris, 66
sailing: Allen, Bill, 67–69; America's Cup, 69; Barrett, Peter, 252; Bentsen, Bill, 62–64, 67–69; medals, 64, 68, 252, 253; Melges, Harry, Jr. "Buddy," 59–64, *62*, 67–70, *69*, 252, 253

St. Louis, MO (1904), 6, 11–12, 14–16, 18, 19–21, 57, 251
St. Moritz, Switzerland, 32, 49
Salt Lake City, UT (2002), 106, 169, 175–183, 235, 255
Sanborn, Alden "Zeke," 65, 251
Sanfelippo, Becky Mane, 88
Sannes, Amy, 89
Santiago, Kim, 66
Sapporo, Japan (1972), 73, 75, 110, 130, 131, 253
Sarajevo, Yugoslavia (1984), 111–112, 132–133
Savage, Joseph K., 32
Sayner, Daniel, 66
Schardt, Arlie, 31, 251
Scheels, Christine, 88
Schenk, Franziska, 191–192
Schmidt, Maria Augusta, 1
Schneider, William "Buzz," 95, 98, 253
Schotting, Peter, 106
Schumacher, Sandra, 79
Schuster, Phillip, 251
Searle, Tom, 99
security. *See under* Olympics
Seikkula, Cindy, *74*, 87
Seiler, Paul, 151
Seoul, South Korea (1988), 254
Servais, Scott, 254
Setzinger, Oliver, 99
Severson, Dale, 145, *145*
Shea, Jimmy, 235, 240, 244
Sheets, Ben, 150–155; awards, 155; family, 155; Olympics, 151–154, *153*; post-Olympics, 154–155
Sherrill, Charles H., 42
Shimizu, Hiroyasu, 179, 181
shooting: Hird, Fred, 251; medals, 251
Shorewood Hills, WI, 92, 144
Shtalenkov, Mikhail, 99
Sieracki, Aaron, 232, *233*
Silk, Dave, 97, 102
Simpson, George, 36, *37*, 40
skating. *See* figure skating; speedskating

skeleton, 235; Antoine, Matt, 235–
238, *236*, 240–250, *246*; medals,
235, 244, 247, 257
skiing: cross-country, 32
    jumping, 32, 144–145
    —Bakke, Bill, 145; Batson,
    LaMoine, 145; Bergmann,
    Arnfin, 145; Haugen, Anders,
    145; Haugstad, Peter, 145; Hen-
    drickson, Jimmy, 145; Jones,
    Clint, 145; medals, 145; Norby,
    Dave, 145; Olson, Willis "Billy,"
    145; Perrault, Joe, 145; Severson,
    Dale, 145, *145*; Stein, Kurt, 145;
    Swenson, Lyle, 145; Zuehlke,
    Reed, 106, 145
sliding. *See* skeleton
Slijkhuis, Wim, 55
Slovakia, 99
Smith, Ben, 162, 163
Smith, Jessica, 89
Smith, Matt, 67
Smrek, Peter, 99
Smyth, Harry, 32
Sobrero-Markgraf, Kate, 255, 256
soccer. *See* football
Sochi, Russia (2014), ii, 138, 238–239,
    241–246, 257
Somerville, Raymond "Bud," 254
Somerville, Tim, 254
South Africa, 25, 36, 40, 220
South Korea, 151, 199, 202–205; med-
    als, 202; Seoul (1988), 254
Spain, 215; Barcelona (1992), 150, 151,
    185, 254
speedskating, xiv, 32, *33*; Blair, Bon-
    nie, *ii*, xiv, 33, 87, 109, 112, 116, *125*,
    127–140, *128*, *138*, 174, 189, 194,
    248, 254, 255; Carpenter, Kip, 89,
    177, 178–179, 181, 255; Cheek, Joey,
    89, 255, 256; clap skates, 173–175,
    177, 190, 194; Crowe, Peggy, *74*,
    87; Cruikshank, David, 88, 136–
    137, *138*; Davis, Shani, 89, 256, 257;
    Docter, Mary, 87, 106; Docter,
    Sarah, 77, 87, 106; Dohnal, Darcie,
    88, 254; Dudek, Alyson, 89, 257;
FitzRandolph, Casey, 89, 171–187,
    190, 255; Flaim, Eric, 88, 254, 255;
    Freisinger, Leo, 252; Gabel, Andy,
    255; Hansen, Brian, 257; Heiden,
    Beth, *74*, 77, 82–84, *83*, 87, 90, 106,
    253, *263*; Heiden, Eric, *vii*, 82–86,
    83, *85*, 90–92, 93, 106, 109, 110, 130,
    138, 158, 171, 182, 253; Henning,
    Anne, 73, 75, 87, 110, 253; Holum,
    Dianne, 73, 83–84, 87, 130, 132,
    252, 253; Immerfall, Dan, 87, 106,
    253; Jansen, Dan, 33, 88, 108–126,
    109, *123*, *125*, 129, 133, 134, 135, 175,
    211, 255; junior circuit, 110–111;
    Kuck, Jonathan, 89, 257; Marsi-
    cano, Trevor, 89, 257; medals, 32,
    83, 84, 87–89, 90, 116, 117, 121, 130,
    131, 133, 134–135, 179, 181–182, 189,
    191, 192, 194, 235, 252–257; Monk,
    Lori, *74*, 87; Mueller, Peter, 87,
    106, 117, 121, 131, 191, 253; Murphy,
    Edward, 32, *33*, 252; Ochowicz,
    Elli, 89, 131; Parra, Derek, 89, 255;
    Phinney, Connie Carpenter, 71–
    73; Plant, Michael, 87, 106; Plant,
    Thomas, 87, 106; Poulos, Leah, 87,
    106, 131, 253; protests, 32, 174; Raney-
    Norman, Catherine, 74, 89; Rodri-
    guez, Jennifer, 89, 255; Rookard,
    Jilleanne, 74, 89; Seikkula, Cindy,
    74, 87; Swider-Peltz, Nancy, Jr., 74,
    89; Swider-Peltz, Nancy, Sr., 74, *74*,
    87; Witty, Christine, 88, 188–192,
    192, 194–195, 255; Woods, Michael,
    87, 106; Young, Sheila, 75, 76, 87,
    131, 253. *See also* Pettit National Ice
    Center; Wisconsin Olympic Oval
Spitz, Mark, 226
Stadler, Joseph, 16
Stagg, Amos Alonzo, 6–7
Stanczyk, Stan, 252
Steen, Jim, 212
Steever, Jerome, 251
Stein, Kurt, 145
Stephans, Lydia, 87
Stevens Point, WI, 141; Hall, Dennis,
    231; Hamilton, Suzy Favor, 185;

Stevens Point (*continued*)
  Provisor, Ben, 231; Weber-Gale, Garrett, 209
Stockholm, Sweden (1912), 251
Stoller, Sam, 45–46
Strand, Lennart, 55
Strum, Bill, 254
Strum, Mike, 254
Sullivan, Eamon, 220
Summer Games. *See under* Olympics
Sundstrom, Becky, 88
Suter, Bob, 85, 86, 93–98, *97*, 100–107; family, 107; Olympics, 97–98, 100–106; post-Olympics, 107
Suter, Gary, 107, 255
Suter, Ryan, 99, 107, 257
Sweden, 53, 54–55, 97–98, 99, 164, 220; medals, 31, 55, 68; Stockholm (1912), 251
Swenson, Lyle, 145
Swider-Peltz, Nancy, Jr., 74, 89
Swider-Peltz, Nancy, Sr., 74, *74*, 87
swimming, xi, 24; Bleibtrey, Ethelda, 27; Boglioli, Wendy, 253; Furniss, Steve, 253; Madison, Helene, 38–39, *39*, 252; medals, 38, 223, 226, 252–256; Montgomery, Jim, 253; Mortenson, Jay, 254; Piper, Carly, 256; Walker, Neil, 255, 256; Weber-Gale, Garrett, 209–213, *210*, 216–230, *224*, *229*, 256
Switzerland, 99; medals, 143; St. Moritz, 32, 49
Sydney, Australia (2000), 151–154, 155, 192–193, 198, 255
Syria, 49

Tae-Young, Yang, 199, 202, 204–205
Tamburrino, David, 88
Tarpley, Lindsay, 256
terrorism: Olympics, 68; September 11, 2001, 106, 178, 182
Tewksbury, Walter, 8
Thometz, Kent, 87
Thometz, Nick, 87, 180
Thorsness, Kris, 66, 254
Tikhanov, Victor, 101, 106

Timmer, Marianne, 191–192
Timonen, Kimmo, 99
Todd, Sugar, 89
Tokyo, Japan (1964), 62–64, 252
Tolan, Eddie, 36–37, *37*, 40, 43
Tomita, Hiroyuki, 199
Towne, Chari, 66
track and field. *See* athletics
training, 73, 75, 78, 83–84, 86, 95, 117, 133, 137, 158, 161, 175–176, 189, 192, 193, 211–212, 227, 237, 241
Tress, Kyle, 241, 242
Tretiak, Vladislav, 100, 106
Tretyakov, Alexander, 241, 247
Trevena, Jondon, 88
Tueting, Sarah, 165
tug-of-war, *28*, *257*; Brosius, Carleton, 31, 33–34, *257*; medals, 33
Turin, Italy (2006), 183, 195, 256
Turkey, 27
Twigg, Rebecca, 79

Ukic, Roko, 58
United States: Atlanta, GA (1996), 139, 151, 185, 189, 255; Chicago, IL (1904), 11; Lake Placid, NY, vii, 32, 84–86, 93, 95, 105, 161, 176, 236–237, 252, 253; Los Angeles, CA, 35, 38–39, 77, 78–79, 252, 254; medals, xii, 6, 7, 8, 10, 12, 15, 16, 19, 21, 25–26, 31, 32, 34, 38, 40, 44, 45, 46, 47, 52, 53, 57, 58, 64, 65–67, 68, 73, 75, 79, 83, 84, 87–89, 90, 94, 105, 107, 112, 116, 121, 130, 131, 134–135, 145, 146, 151, 153, 155, 166, 169, 179, 181–182, 189, 191, 192, 194, 199, 200, 202–205, 208, 214, 215, 223, 226, 227, 231, 235, 244, 247, 251–257; St. Louis, MO (1904), 6, 11–12, 14–16, 18, 19–21, 57, 251; Salt Lake City, UT (2002), 106, 169, 175–183, 235, 255
United States Bicycling Hall of Fame, 81, 92
United States Bobsled and Skeleton Federation, 236
United States Curling Association, 141, 148

United States Olympic Committee, 11, 27, 29, 42, 46, 204–205
United States Olympic Hall of Fame, 10, 81, 92, 124, 135
United States Olympic Spirit Award, 116
United States President's Commission on Olympic Sports, 47
United States Track and Field Hall of Fame, 47
University of Pennsylvania, 1–3, 7, 9, 10
University of Wisconsin Athletic Hall of Fame, 17, 23
University of Wisconsin–Madison, 1, 13–14, 15, 18, 19, 21, 31, 49–50, 53, 54, 55, 56, 64–67, 75, 76, *91*, 93, 94, 106, 137, 144, 185
USSR, 49, 52, 90, 95, 96, 99, 100–102, 104, 105–106, 158; invasion of Afghanistan, 90; medals, 94; Moscow (1980), 90–91, 96. *See also* Russia

Vancouver, Canada (2010), 74, 106, 147, 257
van Oosten-Hage, Keetie, 77
Venezuela, 49
Verchota, Phil, 103
Verona, WI, 171
Vetter, Jessie, 257
Vilgrain, Claude, 99
Vokoun, Tomas, 99
Volker, Sabine, 194

Wade, Dwyane, 214–215, 256
Walker, Neil, 255, 256
Walker, Scott, 250
Waller, Frank, 15, 16, 251
Walters, Willie, 40
Wanek, Brian, 88
Ward, Cory, *146*
water polo: medals, 251; Steever, Jerome, 251
Waukesha, WI: FitzRandolph, Casey, 173; Hamm, Morgan, 197; Hamm, Paul, 197; Ochowicz, Jim, 131; Young, Sheila, 131

Wauwatosa, WI, 56, 209
Weber, Diane, 209–211, *210*, 213, 216, 220, 225
Weber, Shea, 99
Weber-Gale, Garrett, 209–213, *210*, 216–230; awards, 227; family, 209–211, 213, 216–217, 220, 223, 225, 228; Olympics, 213–226, *224*, *229*; post-Olympics, 227–230
weight lifting, 12; medals, 19, 21, 251, 252; Osthoff, Oscar, 18–23, *19*, *22*, 251; Stanczyk, Stan, 252
Weiland, Kerry, 257
Werenka, Brad, 99
West Allis, WI: Heiden, Beth, 83; Heiden, Eric, 83; Holum, Dianne, 83, 130; Jansen, Dan, 108, 109, 110, 129; Witty, Christine, 188–189. *See also* Pettit National Ice Center; Wisconsin Olympic Oval
West Germany, 97, 98, 100; medals, 79; Munich (1972), 68–69, 253; terrorism, 68
Westby, WI, 144
Whitmore, Mitchell, 89
Whyte, Sandra, 166
Wiesner, Kenneth, 252
Wilson, Blaine, 199
Winston, Joseph, 31
Winter Games. *See under* Olympics
Winters, Fred, 20–21
Wisconsin Athletic Hall of Fame, 17, 70, 81, 92, 124
Wisconsin connections, vii–viii, *91*, 251–257
Wisconsin Olympic Oval, 83, 108, 111, 130, 131, 132; Blair, Bonnie, 87; Crowe, Peggy, 87; Cruikshank, David, 88, 136–137; Docter, Mary, 87; Docter, Sarah, 77, 87; Flaim, Eric, 88; Goldman, Jane, 87; Greenwald, Mark, 88; Heiden, Beth, 87; Heiden, Eric, 87; Henning, Anne, 73, 75, 87; Henriksen, Erik, 87; Holum, Dianne, 73, 87, 130; Huck, Mark, 87; Immerfall, Dan, 87; Jansen, Dan, 88, 108; Klaiber, Jeff,

Wisconsin Olympic Oval (*continued*) 88; Kostron, Kim, 87; LeBombard, Wayne, 87; Lunda, Kay, 87; Monk, Lori, 87; Mueller, Peter, 87; Paraskevin, Connie, 87; Phinney, Connie Carpenter, 87; Pierce, Marty, 88; Plant, Michael, 87; Plant, Thomas, 87; Poulos, Leah, 87, 131; Sanfelippo, Becky Mane, 88; Seikkula, Cindy, 87; Stephans, Lydia, 87; Swider-Peltz, Nancy, Sr., 87; Thometz, Kent, 87; Thometz, Nick, 87; Woods, Michael, 87; Young, Sheila, 87, 131. *See also* Pettit National Ice Center
Witty, Christine, 188–196; family, 188, 189, 191, 196; Olympics, 189–194, *192*; post-Olympics, 195–196
Witty, Diane, 188
Witty, Walter, 188
women's sports, ix, 27, 35, 38–39, 71, 74, 76, 77, 78, 81, 130–131, 156–161
Woods, Michael, 87, 106
world records: athletics, 3, 6, 15, 36, 43, 46–47, 48, 50; rowing, 67, 256; speedskating, 84, 86, 110, 111, 117, 121, 134, 190, 191, 194; swimming, 38, 218, 223, 253, 256

World War I, 10, 27, 30
World War II, 42, 47, 49, 60
world's fairs, x; Paris, France, xi, xii–xiv, *xiii*; St. Louis, MO, 11
Wotherspoon, Jeremy, 176, 177, 180, 181
wrestling, ix, 12, 231, 233–234; Davis, Barry, 254; Hall, Dennis, 231–233, 255; Hellickson, Russ, 231, 253; Lowney, Garrett, 255; Maurer, Walter, 251; medals, 231, 251, 253–255; Peterson, Benjamin, 231, 253; Peterson, John, 253; Provisor, Ben, 231–234, *233*; Rein, Andy, 231, 254; Sieracki, Aaron, 232, *233*
Wykoff, Frank, 45–47

Yaremchuk, Ken, 99
Yoshioka, Takayoshi, 36
Young, Sheila, 75, 76, 87, 131, 253
Yugoslavia: Sarajevo (1984), 111–112, 132–133

Zaugg-Siergiej, Jinelle, 257
Zenda, WI, 59, 60, 61, 69, 70
Zoch, Jackie, 65, 253
Zuckerman, Angela, 88
Zuehlke, Reed, 106, 145

About the Author

BUTCH JORGENSON

Jessie Garcia is a Madison native who graduated from East High School and Boston University. An award-winning television sportscaster, she has been covering Wisconsin athletes and Olympians since 1992, first at WISC-TV in Madison and then at WTMJ-TV in Milwaukee. Garcia was one of the first women in the country to host an NFL coach's show and served as the Green Bay Packers' sideline reporter. Garcia's work has also appeared on Milwaukee Public Radio and in several newspapers and magazines, and she teaches journalism at two universities in Milwaukee. This is her third book. Her memoir *My Life with the Green and Gold: Tales from 20 Years of Sportscasting* was published by the Wisconsin Historical Society Press.